UNDERSTANDING LANGUAGE TEACHING

TEACHING

From Method to Postmethod

ESL & Applied Linguistics Professional Series
Eli Hinkel, Series Editor

Nero, Ed. • *Dialects, Englishes, Creoles, and Education*

Basturkmen • *Ideas and Options in English for Specific Purposes*

Kumaravadivelu • *Understanding Language Teaching: From Method to Postmethod*

McKay • *Researching Second Language Classrooms*

Egbert/Petrie, Eds. • *CALL Research Perspectives*

Canagarajah, Ed. • *Reclaiming the Local in Language Policy and Practice*

Adamson • *Language Minority Students in American Schools: An Education in English*

Fotos/Browne, Eds. • *New Perspectives on CALL for Second Language Classrooms*

Hinkel • *Teaching Academic ESL Writing: Practical Techniques in Vocabulary and Grammar*

Hinkel/Fotos, Eds. • *New Perspectives on Grammar Teaching in Second Language Classrooms*

Birch • *English L2 Reading: Getting to the Bottom*

Hinkel • *Second Language Writers' Text: Linguistics and Rhetorical Features*

UNDERSTANDING LANGUAGE TEACHING

From Method to Postmethod

B. Kumaravadivelu
San Jose State University

LEA LAWRENCE ERLBAUM ASSOCIATES, PUBLISHERS
2006 Mahwah, New Jersey   London

#9960570-2

Lawrence Erlbaum Associates, Inc., Publishers
10 Industrial Avenue
Mahwah, New Jersey 07430
www.erlbaum.com

Cover design by Kathryn Houghtaling Lacey

Library of Congress Cataloging-in-Publication Data

Kumaravadivelu, B., 1948–
    Understanding language teaching : from method to postmethod / B. Kumaravadivelu.
       p.   cm. — (ESL and applied linguistics professional series)
    Includes bibliographical references and index.
    ISBN 0-8058-5176-3 (acid-free paper)
    ISBN 0-8058-5676-5 (pbk. : acid-free paper)
    1. Language and languages—Study and teaching. I. Title. II. Series.

P51.K883   2005
XXXXX—dc22   2005040128
                                                          CIP

Books published by Lawrence Erlbaum Associates are printed on acid-free paper,
and their bindings are chosen for strength and durability.

Printed in the United States of America
10 9 8 7 6 5 4 3 2 1

December 15, 2006

Dedicated to
Language teachers everywhere
Who constantly wrestle with the unknown.

கற்றது கைமண்ணளவு
கல்லாதது உலகளவு

- ஔவையார்

What we've learned is a handful of sand;
What we haven't is the wide world.
—Auvaiyaar (Circa 100 BC-250 AD)

Brief Contents

Contents

Preface
The Pattern Which Connects

"*Break the pattern which connects the items of learning,*" warned the celebrated anthropologist, Gregory Bateson, "*and you necessarily destroy all quality*" (1979, p. 8, italics in original). He issued this warning in a letter to his fellow regents of the University of California, complaining about American schools that teach the students "almost nothing of the pattern which connects" (p. 8). Later, he made the phrase—*the pattern which connects*—the central thesis of his pioneering work, *Mind and Nature: A Necessary Unity*, in which he explored "the metapattern" that connects every living thing on this planet, or, as he put it, "What pattern connects the crab to the lobster and the orchid to the primrose and all the four of them to me? And me to you? And all the six of us to the amoeba in one direction and to the backward schizophrenic in another?" (p. 8).

The pattern which connects. That's what this book is all about. Not the so profound pattern that governs the evolution and ecology of all life on earth, but the more mundane pattern that connects the various elements of learning, teaching, and teacher education in the narrow field of teaching English to speakers of other languages. It may appear to be inappropriate or even anticlimactic, to link the concern for an understanding of the ecological macrocosm with the concern for an understanding of the pedagogical microcosm. But the whole point, if we follow the Batesonian argument, is that the elements constituting each are indeed interconnected in ways that may not be readily apparent.

As one who has been engaged in English language teaching and teacher education for nearly a quarter century, I have always struggled with the problem of finding the pattern which connects. And, I have seen graduate

students, practicing teachers, and professional colleagues struggling to recognize the pattern which connects. It is not easy to perceive the barely visible deep structure patterns that connect different elements of a phenomenon unless one makes a long and laborious effort. Let me hasten to add
that I am not merely talking about the need to connect the curricular objectives with class activities, teaching strategies with learning styles, evaluation
measures with learning outcomes, and so on. Of course, they are all important. But, I am more concerned about the pattern which connects higher
order philosophical, pedagogical, and ideological tenets and norms of language teaching that leads us to true understanding, not to false knowledge.

It is the task of linking and expressing the pattern which connects the
stated and the unstated higher order tenets of language teaching methods
that I have set upon myself to do. I thought the task would not be very difficult, given my personal experience of learning and teaching English as a
second language, and my professional knowledge of language learning,
teaching, and teacher education. I was wrong. It did not take much time for
me to realize that I have, after all, rushed in "where angels fear to tread."
One of the major challenges I faced was how to clear the conceptual cob-
webs and terminological bedbugs prevalent in the combinations, harmo-
nies, and discords between layers upon layers of theoretical principles, pedagogic practices, and political ideologies one comes across in the long
history of English language teaching (ELT). A related challenge was how to
separate the trivial from the profound, the fashion from the substance, and
the chafe from the grain in order to reach the heart of the matter.

At a relatively lower level, I was also faced with the challenge of determining the directions to take with regard to focus as well as audience. I convinced myself that, of all the related aspects of ELT, I know more about methods than about anything else. Besides, the concept of *method* has been a
severely contested frame of reference for thinking and writing about classroom learning and teaching. Understandably, tensions and contradictions
have arisen out of efforts aimed at its reconceptualization. Recently, the discourse on the limitations of the concept of method has become so prominent, and the desire to find alternatives to it so pronounced that they have resulted in what has been called the postmethod condition. I thought there is
certainly a need to apply current thinking, and take a fresh look at language
teaching methods, and therefore, I decided to focus sharply on them.

In order to understand language teaching, and its slow transition from
method to postmethod, I considered it necessary to take a historical perspective to the development of major language teaching methods. I decided to limit the historical orientation to about 50 years or so of innovations in language teaching, and not venture into earlier times. My rationale
is that it is only during the second half of the 20th century, with the advent
of audiolingualism, that the language teaching profession entered a decid-

edly systematic and theory-driven phase. In looking back at the past and in looking forward to the future, I have tried to create a historical significance filtered through the prism of my own personal experience and professional understanding. In that sense, this book marks the merging of the personal, the professional, and the historical.

One more remark on the focus of this book is in order. In discussing language teaching methods, I do not see much merit in making any distinction between second and foreign languages, or between teaching English as a second/foreign language and teaching other languages such as French or Spanish as a second/foreign language. I have always felt that these distinctions are based more on proprietorial rights than on pedagogical reasoning. In any case, these distinctions do not matter much to an investigation and interpretation of higher order tenets of language pedagogy. For illustrative purposes, however, I will be focusing on English language teaching; although, most of the issues and concerns treated in this book are applicable to language education in general.

As for the readership, this book is intended primarily for graduate students, practicing teachers, and teacher educators. Clearly, they all bring varying degrees of prior knowledge and precise motivation to the task of deconstructing this text. It is almost impossible to appeal to all shades of potential readers unless everything is reduced to the lowest common denomination; I have not done that. As a result, each group will find some portions of the text more pertinent than others, and some portions more engaging than others. Teacher educators may find perspectives that are, in certain cases, different from the ones with which they are already familiar. Practicing teachers may find new connections that give them ideas that they may not have thought about before. Beginning level graduate students may find that some sections of the text require a more careful reading than others. Throughout the text, I have tried to explain the concepts and terms in as simple language as possible, without, at the same time, diluting the complexity of the issues, or "dumbing down" the reader.

AN OVERVIEW OF THE BOOK

As indicated earlier, I attempt to present in this book a personal and professional perspective of English language teaching methods—a perspective that is founded at once on historical action and contemporary thought. Drawing from seminal, foundational texts and from critical commentaries made by various scholars, I narrate the profession's slow and steady march from method to postmethod, and in the process, elucidate the relationship between theory, research, and practice. I mix materials that are old and new. The book is divided into three parts: (1) Language, Learning, and

Teaching, (2) Language Teaching Methods, and (3) Postmethod Perspectives. I make it a point to highlight the underlying links within and between the parts in order to bring out the pattern which connects.

The introductory part consists of three chapters. Chapter 1 is about language, and it presents the theoretical concepts of language in its systemic, discoursal, and ideological orientations. It also outlines certain pedagogic precepts about components of competence as well as areas of knowledge and ability. Chapter 2 is about learning, and it deals with input, intake factors, and intake processes that govern adult second language learning in formal contexts. Chapter 3 is about teaching, and it describes how classroom language has to be modified in order to provide the learner with accessible and acceptable linguistic input. It also describes various types of interactional activities that promote the kind of comprehension that may lead to acquisition.

The readers will find in these initial chapters a taste of the conceptual and terminological ambiguities I alluded to earlier. I venture to simplify, with adequate justification I hope, some of the familiar usage, and, in the process, I may have committed certain transgressions. For instance, I try to explain why, from a learning/teaching point of view, it makes sense to talk about knowledge/ability instead of competence and performance, and why a simpler two-part division (linguistic knowledge/ability and pragmatic knowledge/ability) rather than the familiar four-part division (grammatical, sociolinguistic, discourse, and strategic competence) is sufficient for our purpose. The overall goal of Part One, however, is to help the reader understand how the basic elements of language, learning, and teaching relate to each other in order to make language learning and teaching possible. Thus, Part One not only identifies and interprets necessary background information but it also provides a platform on which to stand and survey what follows in Part Two and Part Three.

Part Two, which contains chapters 4 through 7, offers a brief history, description, and assessment of language teaching methods from the vantage point of the concepts and precepts identified in Part One. It presents language teaching methods within a coherent framework of theoretical principles and classroom procedures. Specifically, chapter 4 aims at guiding the reader through a maze of constituents and categories of methods, and at explaining the rationale behind grouping the major language teaching methods into three broad categories: language-centered, learner-centered, and learning-centered methods. Each of the next three chapters takes up a category, and explains with illustrative examples, its essential characteristics. The major objective of Part Two is to help the readers see, with a critical eye, the strengths and weaknesses of established methods, and more importantly, perceive the larger pattern which connects the elements within and between methods.

It is important to stress that what Part Two offers is a method analysis and not a teaching analysis. As Mackey (1965) explained, "method analysis shows how teaching is done by the book; teaching analysis shows how much is done by the teacher" (p. 139). That is, method analysis is text based, teaching analysis is classroom based. Therefore, a method analysis can be done, as I have done in this book, by analyzing and interpreting what has been written about methods, but a teaching analysis can be done only by entering the classroom arena where a method or a combination of methods is used, and by observing, analyzing, and interpreting classroom input and interaction.

There is yet another point to be made. We may be tempted to say that, because the profession is making a transition from method to postmethod (and, this is by no means a universally accepted view), prospective and practicing teachers do not need to study the historical development of methods anymore. I believe such a view is counterintuitive and counterproductive. First of all, on a broader level of human experience, as Karl Marx (or George Santayana, depending on one's political affiliation) is reported to have said, those who do not study history are condemned to repeat it. Secondly, as in many other areas of knowledge, nothing can be so revolutionary in language teaching as to make a complete break with the past. In fact, as the chapters in Part Three reveal, some of the classroom procedures associated with methods can still be reconstituted. Besides, we must also remember the conclusion Kelly (1969) reached after investigating 25 centuries of language teaching: "much that is being claimed as revolutionary in this century is merely a rethinking and renaming of early ideas and procedures" (p. ix). Much, not all. But still, it is a sobering thought to keep in mind.

The third and final part of this book provides perspectives on the emerging postmethod pedagogy, and its potential to reshape L2 teaching and teacher education. It has three chapters. The first one describes what has been called the *postmethod condition*. It recounts and relates the concepts of method, and postmethod. It shows how the concept of method contains its own seeds of subversion that invite and instigate various forms of antimethod sentiments by practicing teachers. Finally, it discusses certain parameters and indicators that constitute the essentials of postmethod pedagogy. Chapter 9 presents three different pedagogic frameworks that offer the foundational principles for teachers to build their own forms of postmethod pedagogy. Taking different approaches, the authors of the three frameworks show that postmethod pedagogy is not a monolithic entity. The final chapter highlights the postmethod predicament. It outlines some of the barriers that challenge the conception and construction of a postmethod pedagogy, and it also discusses certain facilitating factors that can help devise a meaningful response to them.

Collectively, the final three chapters seek to create an awareness about the limitations of the concept of method, to provide conceptual argumentation and practical suggestions for understanding the emerging post-method condition so that prospective and practicing teachers may devise for themselves systematic, coherent, and relevant alternatives to method that are informed by postmethod parameters. These three chapters also raise critical concerns about certain broader issues that beset any attempt to operationalize a postmethod pedagogy.

This overview summarizes the salient features of the book. I think it is also necessary to state what the book is not about. It is not about "techniques." This is not a handbook that presents teachers with a neatly compiled repertoire of classroom activities accompanied by guidelines for using them. This book is not activity-driven; it is concept-driven. Its chief objective is to help readers see the pattern which connects the higher order tenets of language teaching methods. I leave it to them to judge the extent to which I have achieved, or failed to achieve, that oft-stated objective.

ACKNOWLEDGMENTS

In writing a book that purports to bring together half a century of historical and professional perspectives, I stand on the shoulders of predecessors and contemporaries, too many to name. Also remaining unnamed are my graduate students who not merely endured the irony of me starting their Methods class with the proclamation "Method is dead," but also ensured that I effectively addressed their doubts and uncertainties about method's life after death. I owe a great deal to all of them. My thanks are also due to Eli Hinkel for persuading me to write this book, and to Naomi Silverman for providing a nurturing environment. It has been a pleasure working with them. Their trust and confidence in me made the task of writing this book easier than it might have been. I'm also indebted to LEA reviewers, William Littlewood, Hong Kong Baptist University, Sandra McKay, San Francisco State University, and Brian Morgan, York University. Their critical comments and valuable suggestions made this book much more readable. As usual, my gratitude goes to my wife, Revathi who, amidst her own professional preoccupation, found time to graciously shield me from the onslaught of daily chores. Finally, my affectionate thanks to our kids, Chandrika and Anand, who injected a sobering dose of wisdom by repeatedly asking me why I'm writing yet another book when there are already so many books in the world!

Part One

LANGUAGE, LEARNING, AND TEACHING

Chapter 1

Language: Concepts and Precepts

1. INTRODUCTION

"A definition of language," observed the British cultural critic, Raymond Williams, "is always, implicitly or explicitly, a definition of human beings in the world" (1977, p. 21). That is because language permeates every aspect of human experience, and creates as well as reflects images of that experience. It is almost impossible to imagine human life without it. And yet, we seldom think about it. We are oblivious of its ubiquitous presence in and around us, just as the fish is (or, is it?) unmindful of the water it is submerged in. Even those who systematically study language have not fully figured out what it is. A case in point: After brilliantly synthesizing both Western and non-Western visions of language developed through the ages, the leading French linguist and psychoanalyst, Julia Kristeva (1989, p. 329) ends her erudite book on language with the humbling phrase: "that still unknown object—language."

Without delving deep into that still unknown object, I briefly outline in this chapter my understanding of how theoretical linguists have attempted to decipher the fundamental concepts of language and how applied linguists have tried to turn some of those theoretical concepts into applicable pedagogic precepts.

1.1. THEORETICAL CONCEPTS

Although there are timeless and endless debates on what constitutes language, for the limited purpose of understanding its relevance for language

3

learning and teaching, I look at it from three broad conceptual vantage points: language as system, language as discourse, and language as ideology.

1.1.1. Language as System

We all know that a human language is a well-organized and well-crafted instrument. That is to say, all the basic components of a language work in tandem in a coherent and systematic manner. They are certainly not a random collection of disparate units. From one perspective, a study of language is basically a study of its systems and subsystems. By treating language as system, we are merely acknowledging that each unit of language, from a single sound to a complex word to a large text—spoken or written—has a character of its own, and each is, in some principled way, delimited by and dependent upon its co-occurring units.

As we learn from any introductory textbook in linguistics, the central core of language as system consists of the phonological system that deals with the patterns of sound, the semantic system that deals with the meaning of words, and the syntactic system that deals with the rules of grammar. For instance, at the phonological level, with regard to the pattern of English, stop consonants are distinguished from one another according their place of articulation (bilabial, alveolar, velar) and their manner of articulation (voiceless, voiced) as shown:

	Bilabial	Alveolar	Velar
Voiceless	/p/	/t/	/k/
Voiced	/b/	/d/	/g/

These minimal sounds, or phonemes as they are called, have contrastive value in the sense that replacing one with another will make a different word as in pit–bit, or ten–den, and so forth.

Understanding the sound system of a language entails an understanding of which sounds can appear word-initially or word-finally, or which can follow which. It also entails an understanding of how certain sound sequences signify certain meanings. In the aforementioned example, the user of English knows that *ten* and *den* are two different words with two different meanings. We learn from semantics that every *morpheme*, which is a collection of phonemes arranged in a particular way, expresses a distinct meaning, and that there are free morphemes that can occur independently (as in den, dance) or bound morphemes like plural -*s*, or past tense -*ed*, which are attached to a free morpheme (as in den*s*, danc*ed*).

Different words are put together to form a sentence, again within the confines of a rule-governed grammatical system. The sentence, *The baby is sleeping peacefully*, is grammatical only because of the way the words have been strung together. A change in the sequence such as *Sleeping is the peacefully baby* will make the sentence ungrammatical. Conversely, sentences that may have a grammatically well-formed sequence as in the well known example, *Colorless green ideas sleep furiously*, may not make any sense at all. These examples show, in part, that "the nouns and verbs and adjectives are not just hitched end to end in one long chain, there is some overarching blueprint or plan for the sentence that puts each word in a specific slot" (Pinker, 1994, p. 94).

Language as system enables the language user to combine phonemes to form words, words to form phrases, phrases to form sentences, and sentences to form spoken or written texts—each unit following its own rules as well as the rules for combination. Crucial to understanding language, then, is the idea of *systematicity*. Language as system, however, is much more complex than the description so far may lead us to believe. A true understanding of the complexity of language requires a robust method of analysis. More than anybody else in the modern era, it is Chomsky who has persuasively demonstrated that language as system is amenable to scientific analysis and, in doing so, he has elevated our ability to deal with language as system to a higher level of sophistication.

Chomsky (1959, 1965, and elsewhere) began by pointing out certain fundamental facts about language as system. First and foremost, all adult native speakers of a language are able to produce and understand myriad sentences that they have never said or heard before. In other words, an infinite number of sentences can be produced using a finite number of grammatical rules. Second, with regard to the child's first language acquisition, there is what Chomsky calls "the poverty of stimulus," that is, the language input exposed to the child is both quantitatively and qualitatively poor but still the child is able to produce, in a short period of time, language output that is immensely rich. The stimulus (that is the language data) available to the child is impoverished in the sense that it has only a limited set of sentences among all possible sentences in a language, and a large number of grammatical types remain unrepresented in the data as well. Besides, the parents' or the caretakers' language addressed to the child may not be the best possible sample because it is full of hesitations, false starts, sentence fragments, and even grammatical deviations. But still, all children, except those who may have neurological or biological defects, acquire the complex language rapidly, and, more importantly, without any formal instruction.

The Chomskyan thought about these and other "logical problems of language acquisition" is essentially premised upon mentalism, which states that much of human behavior is biologically determined. And, language behavior is no exception. Positing the notion of "innateness," Chomsky argues that human beings, by virtue of their characteristic genetic structure, are born with an "innate ability," that is, with an "initial state" of "language faculty" in which general properties of language as system are prewired. Using this "prewired" system, children are able to distill and develop the complex grammatical system out of the speech of their parents and caretakers. The system that the child is born with is common to the grammars of all human languages, and hence Chomsky calls it "Universal Grammar."

The *Universal Grammar* is a set of abstract concepts governing the grammatical structure of all languages that are genetically encoded in the human brain. It comprises principles and parameters. The way it is considered to work is that children, using the unconscious knowledge of Universal Grammar, would know the underlying universal principles of language; for instance, languages usually have nouns, pronouns, and verbs. They would also know their parameters; for instance, in some languages verbs can be placed at the end of the sentence, or in some languages pronouns can be dropped when in the subject position, and so forth. Thus, based on the specific language they are exposed to, children determine, of course unconsciously, whether their native language (L1) allows the deletion of pronouns (as in the case of Spanish), or not (as in the case of English). Such unconscious knowledge helps children eventually to "generate" or create all and only grammatical sentences in their L1.

The abstract generative system of grammar that Chomsky has proposed (which he has frequently updated) is actually a theory of linguistic competence. He makes "a fundamental distinction between *competence* (the speaker-hearer's knowledge of his language) and *performance* (the actual use of language in concrete situations)" (1965, p. 4) and he is concerned only with discovering the mental reality (i.e., competence) underlying the actual behavior (i.e., performance) of a speaker–hearer. He is very clear in emphasizing that his linguistic theory

> is primarily concerned with an ideal speaker–listener, in a completely homogeneous speech community who knows its language perfectly and is unaffected by such grammatically irrelevant conditions as memory limitations, distractions, shifts of attention and interest, and errors (random or characteristic) in applying his knowledge of language in actual performance. (Chomsky, 1965, p. 3)

Clearly, the speaker-hearer Chomsky is talking about is an artificially constructed idealized person; not an actual language user. In addition, as Lyons (1996, p. 30) pointed out, for Chomsky, "linguistic competence is the speaker–hearer's tacit, rather than conscious or even cognitively accessible, knowledge of the language-system."

Chomsky's theory of linguistic competence is actually a theory of grammatical competence. It should, however, be remembered that his term, *lin-*

guistic competence, subsumes phonological, syntactic, and semantic subsystems. That is why the unconscious possession of this abstract linguistic competence helps native speakers of a language to discriminate well-formed sentences from ill-formed word-sequences as well as well-formed sentences that make sense from those that do not (see the previously given examples). In the same way, native speakers of English can also identify the ambiguity in sentences like

Visiting mother-in-law can be boring.

or tell who the agent is in structurally identical pairs like

John is easy to please.
John is eager to please.

In other words, linguistic competence entails a semantic component that indicates the intrinsic meaning of sentences. This intrinsic meaning is semantic meaning and should not be confused with pragmatic meaning, which takes into consideration actual language use, that is, the speaker–hearer's ability to use utterances that are deemed appropriate in a particular communicative situation. As Chomsky clarifies, the notion of competence does not include actual language use: "The term 'competence' entered the technical literature in an effort to avoid the slew of problems relating to 'knowledge,' but it is misleading in that it suggests 'ability'—an association I would like to sever" (Chomsky, 1980, p. 59).

By not considering the pragmatic aspect of language use in formulating his theory of linguistic competence, Chomsky is in no way dismissing its importance. For purposes of "enquiry and exposition," he considers it fit "to distinguish 'grammatical competence' from 'pragmatic competence,' restricting the first to the knowledge of form and meaning and the second to knowledge of conditions and manner of appropriate use . . ." (Chomsky, 1980, p. 224). In other words, he is interested in looking at human language as a cognitive psychological mechanism and not as a communicative tool for social interaction. Those who do treat language as a vehicle for communication find it absolutely necessary to go beyond language as system and seriously consider the nature of language as discourse.

1.1.2. Language as Discourse

In the field of linguistics, the term *discourse* is used to refer generally to "an instance of spoken or written language that has describable internal relationships of form and meaning (e.g., words, structures, cohesion) that relate coherently to an external communicative function or purpose and a given audience/interlocutor" (Celce-Murcia & Olshtain, 2000, p. 4). The focus here is a connected and contextualized unit of language use. During the 1970s, discourse analysis began to gain grounds partly as a response to the dominance of the Chomskyan view of language as system that focused mainly on disconnected and decontextualized units of phonology, syntax, and semantics. Although there are many who have made contributions to our understanding of language as discourse, I briefly consider here the seminal works of Halliday, Hymes, and Austin.

Rejecting the Chomskyan emphasis on grammar, Halliday (1973) defined language as *meaning potential,* that is, as sets of options in meaning that are available to the speaker–hearer in social contexts. Instead of viewing language as something exclusively internal to the learner, as Chomsky does, Halliday views it as a means of functioning in society. From a functional perspective, he sees three metafunctions or macrofunctions of language: the ideational, the interpersonal, and the textual. The *ideational function* represents the individual's meaning potential and relates to the expression and experience of the concepts, processes, and objects governing the physical and natural phenomena of the world around. The *interpersonal function* deals with the individual's personal relationships with people. The *textual function* refers to the linguistic realizations of the ideational and interpersonal functions enabling the individual to construct coherent texts, spoken or written.

For Halliday, language communication is the product or the result of the process of interplay between the ideational, interpersonal, and textual functions of language. Through this interplay, the meaning potential of language is realized. Learning a language, then, entails "learning to mean." As the child interacts with language and language users, he or she begins to understand the meaning potential within the language, and develops a capacity to use it. It is only through meaningful interactive activities in communicative contexts that a learner broadens and deepens the capacity for language use. And, language use is always embedded in a sociocultural milieu. That is why Halliday (1973) preferred to define meaning potential "not in terms of the mind but in terms of the culture" (p. 52).

Unlike Halliday who questions the Chomskyan notion of competence and seeks to replace it, Hymes seeks to expand it. For Chomsky, competence is a mental structure of tacit knowledge possessed by the idealized speaker–hearer, but for Hymes, it is that plus the communicative ability to use a language in concrete situations.

> We have to account for the fact that a normal child acquires knowledge of sentences not only as grammatical but also as appropriate. He or she acquires competence as to when to speak, when not, and as to what to talk about with whom, when, where, and in what manner. In short, a child becomes able to

accomplish a repertoire of speech acts, to take part in speech events, and to evaluate their accomplishment by others. (Hymes, 1972, pp. 277–278)

And the way Hymes seeks to account for that fact is by positing the concept of *communicative competence,* which "is dependent upon both (tacit) knowledge and (ability for) use" (1972, p. 282).

Communicative competence consists of grammatical competence as well as sociolinguistic competence, that is, factors governing successful communication. Hymes (1972) identified these factors, and has used an acronym SPEAKING to describe them:

Setting refers to the place and time in which the communicative event takes place.

Participants refers to speakers and hearers and their role relationships.

Ends refers to the stated or unstated objectives the participants wish to accomplish.

Act sequence refers to the form, content, and sequence of utterances.

Key refers to the manner and tone (serious, sarcastic, etc.) of the utterances.

Instrumentalities refers to the channel (oral or written) and the code (formal or informal).

Norms refers to conventions of interaction and interpretation based on shared knowledge.

Genre refers to categories of communication such as lecture, report, essay, poem, and so forth.

These flexible, overlapping factors, which vary from culture to culture, provide the bases for determining the rules of language use in a given context. For Hymes, knowing a language is knowing not only the rules of grammatical usage but also the rules of communicative use. He makes that amply clear in his oft-quoted statement: "There are rules of use without which the rules of usage are useless."

Because both Chomsky and Hymes accept and use the notion of competence, it is instructive to compare it in its broadest terms. Chomsky's notion is limited to the tacit knowledge of formal linguistic properties possessed by the idealized speaker–hearer. Hymes' notion goes well beyond that to include actual knowledge and ability possessed by the language user. Furthermore, Chomsky's notion is biologically based, whereas Hymes' is more socially based. "The former is purely individual, the latter is mainly social. The former concerns form; the latter concerns function. The former characterizes a state; the latter involves processes" (Taylor, 1988, p. 156). It is rather apparent, then, that Hymes brings a much wider perspective to the notion of competence, one that has more relevance for treating and understanding language as a vehicle for communication.

Yet another aspect of language communication that is relevant for our discussion here is the notion of speech acts. In his classic book, *How to Do Things With Words*, published in 1962, Austin, a language philosopher, raised the question *What do we do with language?* and answered, simply: We perform speech acts. By *speech acts*, he refers to the everyday activity of informing, instructing, ordering, threatening, complaining, describing, and scores of other such activities for which we use our language. In other words, language is an activity that we *do* in myriad situations and circumstances. Of all the numerous phenomena of language, Austin asserts: "The total speech act in the total speech situation is the *only actual* phenomenon which, in the last resort, we are engaged in elucidating" (1962, p. 148, emphasis in original).

To elucidate Austin's speech act theory in simple terms: Every speech act that we perform has three components, which he calls *locution, illocution,* and *perlocution*. The first refers to a propositional statement, the second to its intended meaning, and the third to its expected response. The act of saying something, in and of itself, is a locutionary act. It is no more than a string of words containing phonological (sounds), syntactic (grammar), and semantic (word meaning) elements put together in a systemically acceptable sequence. In performing a locutionary act, one often performs such an act as "asking or answering a question, giving some information or an assurance or a warning, announcing a verdict or an intention, pronouncing sentence, making an appointment or an appeal or a criticism, making an identification or giving a description, and the numerous like" (Austin, 1962, pp. 98–99). The perlocutionary act is the effect or the consequence of an utterance in a given situation.

To illustrate a speech act, take a simple and short utterance, *Move it.* Here the locutionary act is the act of saying *move it* meaning by *move* move, and referring by *it* to the object in question. If we assume an appropriate context, the illocutionary act in this case is an act of ordering (or, urging or advising, or suggesting, etc., in different contexts) somebody to move it. The perlocutionary act, again assuming an appropriate context here, is the act of actually moving it.

The most important component of a speech act is the illocutionary act. For it to have what Austin calls *illocutionary force*, a speech act has to meet certain socially agreed upon demands or conventions. For instance, a statement like *I now pronounce you man and wife* has its intended illocutionary force only if it is uttered in a proper context (e.g., a church) and by a proper person (e.g., a priest). The same statement uttered by a clerk in a department store will not render two customers a married couple! The statement gains its illocutionary force only because of the situational context in which it is uttered and not because of its linguistic properties. Or, to quote Joseph, Love, and Taylor (2001):

the illocutionary force of an utterance is not part of meaning the words have simply in virtue of being those words. On the other hand, the illocutionary act is performed *by* or *in* rather than merely *through* using those words. The illocutionary force of an utterance is simultaneously both context-dependent and, in context, inherent in the uttering of the words themselves. (p. 103, italics in original)

The key word in the above quote is *context*. It is also key to language as discourse in general. In linguistics, discourse was initially defined as a unit of coherent language consisting of more than one sentence, to which was added a reference to language use in context. Combining these two perspectives, Celce-Murcia and Olshtain (2000) gave the definition quoted at the beginning of this section and repeated here for convenience: Discourse "is an instance of spoken or written language that has describable internal relationships of form and meaning (e.g., words, structures, cohesion) that relate coherently to an external communicative function or purpose and a given audience/interlocutor" (p. 4). Some discourse analysts (e.g., McCarthy & Carter, 1994) go beyond internal relationships of form and meaning to include "the interpersonal, variational and negotiable aspects of language" (p. xii), and some others (e.g., G. Cook, 1994) include "a form of knowledge of the world" (p. 24) as well.

The added focus on context has certainly facilitated a useful connection between language structure and the immediate social context in which it is used. It has also aided, from a classroom discourse point of view, the study of the routines of turn-taking, turn sequencing, activity types, and elicitation techniques in the language classroom. However, a truly discourse-based view of language should have also considered "the higher order operations of language at the interface of cultural and ideological meanings and returning to the lower-order forms of language which are often crucial to the patterning of such meanings" (McCarthy & Carter, 1994, p. 38). And yet, most "mainstream" discourse analysts have found contentment in analyzing "the lower order forms of language" and leaving "the higher order operations of language" largely untouched. That challenging task has been recently taken up by *critical* discourse analysts who explore language as ideology.

1.1.3. Language as Ideology

Ideology is "a systematic body of ideas, organized from a particular point of view" (Kress & Hodge, 1979, p. 6). Stated as such, it sounds rather simple and straightforward. As a matter of fact, ideology is a contested concept. Its reference and relevance cut across disciplines such as anthropology, sociology, political science, history, and cultural studies. Linguistics is a much belated and bewildered entrant, in spite of the fact that language and ideology are closely connected. Among the many interpretations of the concept of ideology, there is one common thread that unfailingly runs through all of them: its ties to power and domination.

In an authoritative book on *Ideology and Modern Culture*, Thompson (1990) defined ideology rather briskly as "*meaning in the service of power*" (p. 7, emphasis in original). Therefore, "*to study ideology is to study the ways in which meaning serves to establish and sustain relations of domination*" (p. 56, emphasis in original). The best way to investigate ideology, according to Thompson, is

> to investigate the ways in which meaning is constructed and conveyed by symbolic forms of various kinds, from everyday linguistic utterances to complex images and texts; it requires us to investigate the social contexts within which symbolic forms are employed and deployed; and it calls upon us to ask whether, and if so how, the meaning mobilized by symbolic forms serves, in specific contexts, to establish and sustain relations of domination. (1990, p. 7)

In a very succinct manner, Thompson has made the connection between language and ideology very clear.

Expanding that connection, anthropologist Kroskrity (2000, all italics in original) suggested that it is profitable to think of language ideologies as a cluster of concepts consisting of four converging dimensions:

- First, "*language ideologies represent the perception of language and discourse that is constructed in the interests of a specific social or cultural group*" (p. 8). That is, notions of language and discourse are grounded in social experience and often demonstrably tied to the promotion and protection of political-economic interests.
- Second, "*language ideologies are profitably conceived as multiple because of the multiplicity of meaningful social divisions (class, gender, clan, elites, generations, and so on) within sociocultural groups that have the potential to produce divergent perspectives expressed as indices of group membership*" (p. 12). That is, language ideologies are grounded in social experiences that are never uniformly distributed across diverse communities.
- Third, "*members may display varying degrees of awareness of local language ideologies*" (p. 18). That is, depending on the role they play, people develop different degrees of consciousness about ideologically grounded discourse.
- Finally, "*members' language ideologies mediate between social structures and forms of talk*" (p. 21). That is, people's sociocultural experience and interactive patterns contribute to their construction and understanding of language ideologies.

These four dimensions, according to Kroskrity, must be considered seriously if we are to understand the connection between language and ideology.

These four dimensions of language ideology are a clear echo of the broad-based concept of discourse that poststructural thinkers such as Foucault have enunciated. Foucault's concept of *discourse* is significantly different from that of mainstream linguists. For him discourse is not just the suprasentential aspect of language; rather, language itself is one aspect of discourse. In accordance with that view, he offers a three-dimensional definition of discourse "treating it sometimes as the general domain of all statements, sometimes as an individualizable group of statements, and sometimes as a regulated practice that accounts for a number of statements" (Foucault, 1972, p. 80). The first definition relates to all actual utterances or texts. The second relates to specific formations or fields, as in "the discourse of racism" or "the discourse of feminism." The third relates to sociopolitical structures that create the conditions governing particular utterances or texts. Discourse thus designates the entire conceptual territory on which knowledge is produced and reproduced. It includes not only what is actually thought and articulated but also determines what can be said or heard and what silenced, what is acceptable and what is tabooed. Discourse in this sense is a whole field or domain within which language is used in particular ways. This field or domain is produced in and through social practices, institutions, and actions.

In characterizing language as one, and only one, of the multitude of organisms that constitute discourse, Foucault (1970, and elsewhere) significantly extended the notion of linguistic text. A *text* means what it means not because of any inherent objective linguistic features but because it is generated by discursive formations, each with its particular ideologies and particular ways of controlling power. No text is innocent and every text reflects a fragment of the world we live in. In other words, texts are political because all discursive formations are political. Analyzing text or discourse therefore means analyzing discursive formations, which are essentially political in character and ideological in content.

Such a concept of *language ideology* is usually reflected in the ideologically grounded perceptions and practices of language use that are shaped and reshaped by dominant institutional forces, historical processes, and vested interests. For instance, the preeminent cultural critic, Said (1978), in his book, *Orientalism*, presented compelling textual evidence from literary, historical, sociological, and anthropological texts produced by the colonial West to represent the colonized people. He uses the term *Orientalism* to refer to a systematically constructed discourse by which the powerful West "was able to manage—and even produce—the Orient politically, sociologically, militarily, ideologically, scientifically, and imaginatively . . ." (Said, 1978, p. 3). It forms an interrelated web of ideas, images, and texts from the scholarly to the popular, produced by artists, writers, missionaries, travelers, politicians, militarists, and administrators, that shape and structure Western representations of colonized peoples and their cultures.

In yet another manifestation of the nexus between power and language, the French sociologist, Bourdieu (1991), in his book, *Language and Symbolic Power,* described symbolic power "as a power of constituting the given through utterances, of making people see and believe, of confirming or transforming the vision of the world and thereby, action on the world and thus the world itself . . ." (p. 170). He also showed the innumerable and subtle strategies by which language can be used as an instrument of communication as well as control, coercion as well as constraint, and condescension as well as contempt. He pointed out how variations in accent, intonation, and vocabulary reflect differential power positions in the social hierarchy. According to him, "what creates the power of words and slogans, a power capable of maintaining or subverting the social order, is the belief in the legitimacy of words and of those who utter them" (p. 170). In another work, Bourdieu (1977) invoked the notion of "legitimate discourse" and elaborated it by saying that "a language is worth what those who speak it are worth, so too, at the level of interactions between individuals, speech always owes a major part of its value to t ıe value of the person who utters it" (p. 652).

On a personal note, I was recently reminded of the significance of Bourdieu's statement when I read the remarks of a prominent applied linguist, Larsen-Freeman, about her inventing a new word, *grammaring.* In explaining how she, as a native speaker of English, is empowered to invent new words, she says:

> The point is that as language teachers, we should never forget that issues of power and language are intimately connected. For example, it is unfair, but nevertheless true, that native speakers of a language are permitted to create neologisms, as I have done with *grammaring.* Such a coinage, however, might have been corrected if a nonnative speaker of English had been its author. (Larsen-Freeman, 2003, p. 64)

I take this as a gentle reminder that I, as a nonnative speaker of English, do not have "permission" to coin a new word, and if I had coined one, it might have been corrected. It is unfair, but nevertheless true!

It is the unfair and true nature of language ideology that a group of linguists, who call themselves *critical discourse analysts,* attempt to unravel. By critically analyzing the systematic distortion of language use, they focus on the exploitation of "*meaning in the service of power.*" More specifically, as Fairclough (1995), in his introductory book, *Critical Discourse Analysis,* explained, critical discourse analysts aim to systematically explore often opaque relationships of causality and determination between (a) discursive practices, events and texts, and (b) wider social and cultural structures, relations and processes; to investigate how such practices, events and texts arise out of and are ideologically shaped by relations of power and struggles over power. (p. 132)

In the context of language ideology, they see power in terms of "asymmetries between participants in discourse events, and in terms of unequal capacity to control how texts are produced, distributed and consumed (and hence the shapes of texts) in particular sociocultural contexts" (Fairclough, 1995, p. 1). Their working assumption is that any level of language structure and use is a relevant site for critical and ideological analysis. Their method of analysis includes *description* of the language text, *interpretation* of the relationship between the text and the discursive processes, and *explanation* of the relationship between the discursive processes and the social practices.

Recognizing the importance of critical discourse analysis, Pennycook (2001), in his book, *Critical Applied Linguistics*, has introduced a newly defined area of applied linguistic work that seeks to take a critical look at the politics of knowledge, the politics of language, the politics of text, and the politics of pedagogy within a coherent conceptual framework. He has called for a strengthening of critical discourse analysis by going beyond any prior sociological analysis of power and its connection to language, and by conducting linguistic analyses of texts to show how power may operate through language. His aim is to make the task of applied linguistics "to be one of exploration rather than of mere revelation" (p. 93).

From an educational point of view, critical discourse analysts see language teaching as a prime source for sensitizing learners to social inequalities that confront them, and for developing necessary capabilities for addressing those inequalities. Therefore, they advocate the creation of critical language awareness in our learners. Such a task should be fully integrated, not only with the development of language practices across the curriculum, but also with the development of the individual learner's intellectual capabilities that are required for long-term, multifaceted struggles in various sociopolitical arenas. They, however, caution that instruction in critical language awareness "should not push learners into oppositional practices which condemn them to disadvantage and marginalization; it should equip them with the capacities and understanding which are preconditions for meaningful choice and effective citizenship in the domain of language" (Fairclough, 1995, p. 252).

Applying the principles of critical discourse analysis to explore the nature of input and interaction in the language classroom, I have questioned the present practice of conducting classroom discourse analysis that focuses narrowly on turn-taking, turn sequencing, activity types, and elicitation techniques. I have argued that a true and meaningful understanding of sociocultural aspects of classroom discourse can be achieved not by realizing the surface level features of communicative performance or conversational style but only by recognizing the complex and competing world of discourses that exist in the classroom. (Kumaravadivelu, 1999a, p. 470)

Accordingly, I have suggested a conceptual framework for conducting critical classroom discourse analysis (CCDA) that will cross the borders of the classroom to investigate broader social, cultural, political, and historical structures that have a bearing on classroom input and interaction.

To sum up our discussion of the theoretical concepts of language, we learned that language as system deals with the phonological, syntactic, and semantic features of language, and with the notion of linguistic competence that is mostly confined to semantico-grammatical knowledge of the language. Language as discourse, on the other hand, focuses on the nature of language communication, with its emphasis on the rules of language use that are appropriate to a particular communicative context. Language as ideology, however, goes way beyond the confines of systemic and discoursal features of language, and locates it as a site for power and domination by treating it both as a transporter and a translator of ideology that serves vested interests. These three theoretical concepts of language demonstrate the complexity of "that still unknown object—language."

1.2. PEDAGOGIC PRECEPTS

The theoretical concepts already discussed have helped applied linguists to derive useful and usable conceptual guidelines about language for purposes of classroom teaching. I use the term *pedagogic precepts* to refer to these conceptual guidelines. They are aimed at addressing questions such as what is language, and what does it mean to know and use a language. They form the bases for effective language teaching. I discuss them in terms of components of language competence, and areas of language knowledge/ability.

1.2.1. Components of Competence

In an influential paper published in 1980, Canadian applied linguists Canale and Swain presented a comprehensive framework establishing "a clear statement of the content and boundaries of communicative competence—one that will lead to more useful and effective second language teaching and allow more valid and reliable measurement of second language communication skills" (1980, p. 1). Their framework initially consisted of three components of competence, and was later revised to include a fourth one (Canale, 1983). The components they have identified are: grammatical competence, sociolinguistic competence, discourse competence, and strategic competence. The framework is derived from the prevailing perspectives on language as system and language as discourse previously discussed, as well as from the authors' own insights and interpretations.

For Canale and Swain, grammatical competence includes "knowledge of lexical items and the rules of morphology, syntax, sentence-grammar semantics, and phonology" (p. 29). Recall from the earlier discussion that this cluster of items constitutes what Chomsky has also called *grammatical competence*, although this may include the ability to use grammar (Chomsky's performance) as well. However, Canale and Swain make it clear that they are not linking it to any single theory of grammar. This component addresses language as system.

Sociolinguistic competence that constituted a single component in the original version was later split into two: sociolinguistic competence and discourse competence. These two components deal with different aspects of language as discourse. By *sociolinguistic competence* is meant the knowledge of "the extent to which utterances are produced and understood appropriately in different sociolinguistic contexts depending on contextual factors such as status of participants, purposes of the interaction, and norms or conventions of interaction" (Canale, 1983, p. 7). This component emphasizes, following Hymes, sociocultural appropriateness of an utterance.

Discourse competence takes care of some other aspects of language as discourse such as how a series of sentences or utterances are connected into a whole text, spoken or written. In the opinion of Celce-Murcia and Olshtain (2000), discourse competence forms "the core" of the Canale and Swain framework because it "is where everything else comes together: It is in discourse and through discourse that all of the other competencies are realized. And it is in discourse and through discourse that the manifestation of the other competencies can best be observed, researched, and assessed" (p. 16).

The last of the components, *strategic competence*, is made up of "verbal and non-verbal communication strategies that may be called into action to compensate for breakdowns in communication due to performance variables or to insufficient competence" (Canale & Swain, 1980, p. 30). As Savignon (1983) pointed out, this component consists of coping or survival strategies such as paraphrase, circumlocution, repetition, hesitation, avoidance, and guessing, as well as shifts in register and style.

The Canale/Swain framework is perhaps the first one to make use of the prevailing understanding of language as system and language as discourse in order to derive a comprehensive theoretical framework of language competence with pedagogic application in mind. It is specifically designed for language teaching and testing. However, language teaching experts such as Skehan (1998) and Widdowson (2003) have questioned Canale and Swain's (1980) claim that the framework establishes a clear statement of the content and boundaries of communicative competence just as testing experts such as Bachman (1990) and Shohamy (1996) have doubted their claim that it allows more valid and reliable measurement of second language communication skills.

To consolidate the concerns expressed by critics: the major drawback of the framework is that the four competencies conceptually overlap and that the interdependencies among them are not at all apparent. For instance, as Widdowson (2003) pointed out, although grammatical competence incorporates lexical knowledge, it is not clear how sociolinguistic competence acts upon it in the speaker's choice of grammatical or lexical forms. Similarly, "discourse competence, isolated in the Canale scheme as a separate component of communicative competence, only exists as a function of the relationship between the grammatical and the sociolinguistic; without this relationship it has no communicative status whatever" (p. 167). According to Skehan (1998), the framework does not advance in any substantial way the prediction and generalization necessary for measurement of language learning because there is "no direct way of relating underlying abilities to performance and processing conditions, nor is there any systematic basis for examining the language demands, of a range of different contexts" (p. 158). As a result, he concludes that the framework cannot be considered either "working" or "comprehensive," although it is "full of insights" (p. 159).

The necessity for the distinctness of strategic competence has also been questioned. For instance, Taylor (1988) points out that strategic competence fails "to distinguish between knowledge and ability, or rather they incorporate both, and on the other hand they do not distinguish between those strategies which all speakers have, both native and non-native, and those which are peculiar to non-native speakers" (p. 158). In other words, by virtue of their mastery in their first language, L2 speakers may already possess some of the coping or compensation strategies necessary to get over communicative breakdowns; and, the Canale/Swain framework does not take that into consideration. Even if it is a competence that has to be learned anew, it does not, as Widdowson (2003) argues,

> seem to be a separate component of competence, but rather a tactical process whereby the other components are related and brought into pragmatic plays required for a particular communicative occasion. As such it is hard to see how it can be specified. It seems reasonable enough to talk about a knowledge of grammatical rules or sociocultural conventions, but knowing how to compensate for relative incompetence will surely often, if not usually, be a matter of expedient tactical maneuver. (p. 166)

As a result of these and other shortcomings of the Canale/Swain framework, other formulations of language competence have been proposed. Bachman (1990), for instance, has proposed a Communicative Language Ability model. It divides overall language competence into two broad categories: organizational competence and pragmatic competence. Organizational competence is further divided into grammatical competence and textual competence. Similarly, pragmatic competence is divided into illocutionary competence and sociolinguistic competence. In yet another model, Celce-Murcia, Dornyei, and Thurrell (1995) divided communicative competence into linguistic, sociolinguistic, discourse, strategic, and actional competencies where *actional competence* refers to more formulaic aspects of language such as the oral speech acts or the written rhetorical moves that function as part of communicative competence.

It is apparent that the newer approaches to components of competence take the Canale/Swain model as a point of departure and provide an extension or a reformulation of the same, and as such they all share the same conceptual problems that the original model has been criticized for. As Widdowson (2003) rightly points out, "the essential problem with these different models of communicative competence is that they analyse a complex process into a static set of components, and as such cannot account for the dynamic interrelationships which are engaged in communication itself" (pp. 169–170).

There is yet another crucial construct of competence that has long been neglected by many. The concept of *competence* proposed by Chomsky and reinterpreted and reinforced by others deals with the language competence residing in the monolingual mind. This cannot but offer only a limited and limiting perspective on competence because

> the description of linguistic competence has been misleadingly based on monolinguals, like a description of juggling based on a person who can throw one ball in the air and catch it, rather than on a description of a person who can handle two or more balls at the same time. Calling the knowledge of a person who knows one language linguistic competence may be as misleading as calling throwing one ball in the air juggling. (V. Cook, 1996, p. 67)

In order, therefore, to mend the misleading concept and to cover the overall system of competence of more than one language in the mind of a bilingual speaker or an L2 learner, the British applied linguist, Cook, introduced the term *multicompetence*. In a series of writings, Cook has vigorously defended the concept (see V. Cook, 1991, 1992, 1996, 2002). He defines multicompetence as "the compound state of a mind with two grammars" (1991, p. 112) to contrast with *monocompetence*, the state of mind with only one grammar. He maintains that language knowledge of the L2 user is different from that of the monolingual. He has consolidated research in first- and second-language acquisition to show that "the multicompetent individual approaches language differently in terms of metalinguistic awareness; multicompetence has an effect on other parts of cognition" (1992, p. 564) resulting in a greater metalinguistic awareness and a better cognitive processing; and that "multicompetent speakers think differently from monolinguals, at least in some areas of linguistic awareness" (1992, p. 565). *Multicompetence*, in short, is a different state of mind.

Citing the naturalness, smoothness, and comprehensibility of code switching among bilingual speakers, and the ease with which they borrow lexical items from the known languages as clear evidence in favor of holistic multicompetence, Cook suggests that the applied linguistics profession cannot ignore the compound state of mind of the L2 learner. As Brown, Malmkjaer, and Williams (1996) suggest, there are at least two senses—one theoretical and another practical—in which the notion of multicompetence is of relevance. First, "it is independent of the debate over the role of universal grammar in adult second language acquisition. The issue is whether the polyglot's language systems are completely independent" (p. 56). Second, from a teaching point of view, the notion "advocates a change in philosophy concerning such issues as the 'target' for second language acquisition (which cannot by definition be monolingual competence). It challenges the idea that the learners' L1 should be kept out of the classroom . . ." (p. 56). A further implication, according to them, is that "if an atmosphere is created in which the first language competence of an individual is recognized and valued then this might potentially have an important affective and motivational impact on their approach to learning a second language" (p. 56). Clearly, much work needs to be done in this area of competence.

The fact of the matter is that for all the impressive strides made in the last half century, the concept of *language competence* (mono- or multi-) still remains "a puzzle wrapped in mystery inside an enigma." First of all, we are trying to decipher an internal psychological mechanism to which we do not have direct access, and to analyze it only through its external manifestation in terms of language behavior. Besides, the concept itself is too divergent to capture neatly, too elusive to define elegantly, and too complicated to apply effectively. Added to that is the tendency to conflate distinctions and to confuse terms, with the result that the term *competence* "has been used so widely and so divergently in so many different contexts that it has ceased to have any precise meaning" (Taylor, 1988, p. 159). Take for instance, the following short passage from Bachman and Palmer's 1996 book on language testing, and notice how words like competence, knowledge, ability, strategies are used:

The model of language ability that we adopt in this book is essentially that proposed by Bachman (1990), who defines language ability as involving two components: language competence, or what we will call *language knowledge*, and *strategic competence*, which we will describe as a set of metacognitive strategies. It is this combination of language knowledge and metacognitive strategies that provides language users with the ability, or capacity, to create and interpret discourse, either in responding to tasks on language tests, or in nontest language use. (p. 67, italics in original)

Such conceptual and terminological ambiguities abound in the literature.

1.2.2. Areas of Knowledge/Ability

As the field of applied linguistics waits for the conceptual complexity of competence to be sorted out, I think it is prudent to use less problematic and less loaded terms in order to make sense of the theoretical concepts and pedagogic precepts that have a bearing on classroom learning and teaching. To that end, I try as far as possible to use the terms that are already in circulation, modifying and extending the usage of some of them if necessary. Let me begin with language knowledge and language ability.

Several scholars have written about knowledge and ability from theoretical as well as pedagogic perspectives (e.g., Anderson, 1983; Bachman, 1990; Bialystok, 1982; Widdowson, 1989). Without going into details about their arguments or their differences, it may be simply stated that *language knowledge* is what is in the mind of the language users, and when they use it appropriately to achieve their communicative purpose in a given context, they exhibit their *language ability*. As Widdowson (1989) has observed, "knowledge can be characterized in terms of degrees of analyzability, ability can be characterized in terms of degrees of accessibility" (p. 132). In other words, language ability involves "knowledge systems on the one hand and control of these systems on the other" (Bialystok & Sharwood-Smith, 1985, p. 106). It is, of course, possible to posit different types of knowledge. At a broader level, Anderson (1983), for instance, distinguishes between *declarative knowledge* which relates to knowledge about the language system, and *procedural knowledge* which relates to knowledge of how to use the language system. What this observation indicates is that a language learner develops a knowledge of knowledge, and a knowledge of ability, and that the two are closely linked.

At a more specific, and decidedly pedagogic, level, Bachman and Palmer (1996), based on Bachman (1990), provide the following list of areas of language knowledge. They do so with particular reference to language testing, but, their framework can easily be extended to language learning and teaching as well.

Organizational Knowledge
(how utterances or sentences and texts are organized)

Grammatical Knowledge
(how individual utterances or sentences are organized)
Knowledge of vocabulary
Knowledge of syntax
Knowledge of phonology/graphology

Textual Knowledge
(how utterances or sentences are organized to form texts)
Knowledge of cohesion
Knowledge of rhetorical or conversational organization

Pragmatic Knowledge
(how utterances or sentences and texts are related to the communicative goals of the
   language user and to the features of the language use setting)

Functional Knowledge
(how utterances or sentences and texts are related to the communicative goals of the
   language users)
Knowledge of ideational functions
Knowledge of manipulative functions
Knowledge of heuristic functions
Knowledge of imaginative functions

Sociolinguistic Knowledge
(how utterances or sentences and texts are related to features of the language use set-
   ting)
Knowledge of dialects/varieties
Knowledge of registers
Knowledge of natural or idiomatic expressions
Knowledge of cultural references and figures of speech

(Bachman & Palmer, 1996, p. 68)

To this list of knowledge areas, Bachman and Palmer (1996) add strategic competence, which includes metacognitive strategies of (a) goal setting, that is, deciding what one is going to do; (b) assessment, that is, taking stock of what is needed, what one has to work with, and how well one has done; and (c) planning, that is, deciding how to use what one has. For them, the areas of knowledge and strategic competence together constitute language ability.

In spite of all the conceptual and terminological ambiguities one finds in the literature, language competence is generally seen as a combination of language knowledge and language ability. There is, however, a tendency to treat knowledge and ability as dichotomies. It would be wrong to do so because of their complex connectivity. Trying to separate them is, in a sense, trying to separate the dance from the dancer, the art from the artist. Halliday (1978) is one of the very few who has consistently rejected the dichotomy between competence and performance or between knowing and doing. He states unequivocally: "There is no difference between knowing a language and knowing how to use it" (p. 229). For purposes of learning and teaching, in particular, it is better to treat them as two sides of the same coin. Therefore, in this book, I use the terms *knowledge* and *ability* as one integrated component and indicate that integration by joining them with a slash: *knowledge/ability*. By doing so, I avoid using the problematic term, *competence*.

Furthermore, recall that serious concerns have been expressed about various components of competence mainly because of a lack of their interdependencies and distinctiveness. I would, therefore, argue that it is beneficial to collapse different types of competence already outlined into two major classifications identified long ago by Chomsky, namely, *grammatical* competence and *pragmatic* competence. However, in light of all the advancement we have made in our understanding of language as system, language as discourse and language as ideology, we have to attribute certain additional characteristics to these two umbrella terms. Instead of the term, *grammatical*, which is not commonly seen to include phonological and semantic elements of the language although Chomsky does include them, I prefer to use the word, *linguistic*, and retain the term, *pragmatic* as is (see Celce-Murcia & Olshtain, 2000, for a similar use). And, as I mentioned in the previous paragraph, I use the term *knowledge/ability* instead of *competence*.

So, to clear at least part of the terminological confusion, let me provide an operational definition of some of the terms I employ. In this book, the term *language knowledge/ability* is used to refer to the level of overall language know-how that a competent language user has, or a language learner seeks to have. The overall language knowledge/ability is considered to have two interrelated dimensions: *linguistic knowledge/ability* and *pragmatic knowledge/ability*. In this scenario, *language development* involves the development of linguistic knowledge/ability and pragmatic knowledge/ability. In order to develop the desired level of linguistic and pragmatic knowledge/ability, the learner, of course, has to make use of all possible learning strategies as well as communication strategies.

To elaborate further, linguistic knowledge/ability includes the knowledge/ability of phonological, morphological, semantic, and syntactic features of a language. It treats language as system. It entails both implicit and explicit knowledge *and* control of semantico-grammatical categories of language. Pragmatic knowledge/ability includes the knowledge/ability of language use in a textually coherent and contextually appropriate manner. To that extent, it treats language as discourse. But, as I use it here, this dimension also includes the knowledge/ability to intelligently link the word with the world, that is, to be critically conscious of the way language is manipulated by the forces of power and domination. In that sense, it also includes aspects of language as ideology.

In collapsing various types of competence, and in opting for the two-dimensional linguistic and pragmatic knowledge/ability, I am not minimizing the importance of all the insightful contributions that have been made by various scholars. Undoubtedly, such knowledge production is essential for any academic discipline to make progress. My intention here is to offer a simple frame of reference that can be used to clear certain conceptual and terminological clouds in order to shed some light on the process of language learning and the practice of language teaching.

1.3. CONCLUSION

The purpose of this chapter has been to explore the fundamental concepts of language and the pedagogic precepts that could be possibly derived from them. I discussed the concepts of (a) language as system that focuses on the phonological, semantic, and syntactic elements of language; (b) language as discourse, which pertains mainly to the coherent and cohesive features that unite the disparate systemic elements of language, as well as features of language use in communicative contexts; and (c) language as ideology, which deals mainly with issues of how the social and political forces of power and domination impact on language structures and language use. The field of applied linguistics has invested much of its effort to explore language as system and, to some extent, language as discourse, but has virtually ignored language as ideology until very recently.

I also outlined certain pedagogic precepts about components of competence as well as areas of knowledge/ability. We learned that the introduction of various types of competence has actually advanced our understanding of the systemic and discoursal functions of language. It was, however, suggested that for the specific purpose of discussing issues related to language learning and teaching, it is better to collapse various components of competence into two broad categories: linguistic knowledge/ability and pragmatic knowledge/ability.

In the next chapter, we take a close look at how and to what extent the theoretical concepts and pedagogic precepts have influenced the formulation of language-learning theories and practices. Following that, in chapter 3, we see how the concepts of language and the theories of learning have contributed to shape the instructional processes and strategies in the language classroom.

Chapter 2

Learning: Factors and Processes

2. INTRODUCTION

In the previous chapter, I stated that knowing an L2 may be considered as having linguistic knowledge/ability and pragmatic knowledge/ability required to use the language with grammatical accuracy and communicative appropriacy. In the context of classroom-based L2 learning and teaching, it is the task of the teacher to help learners reach a desired level of linguistic and pragmatic knowledge/ability that addresses their needs, wants, and situations. In order to carry out such a task, the teacher should be aware of the factors and processes that are considered to facilitate L2 development. An important aspect of L2 development is the conversion of language input into learner output.

It is widely recognized that there is both a qualitative and a quantitative mismatch between the language output produced by L2 learners and the language input they are exposed to. In a seminal paper written nearly four decades ago, Corder (1967) highlighted this mismatch and made an important distinction between input and what he called *intake*. Since then, several attempts have been made (see Gass, 1997, for a review) to explore the connection between input, intake, and L2 development. Despite nearly a quarter century of exploration of that connection, we have hardly reached a clear consensus on the fundamental characteristics of intake, let alone a cogent understanding of the psycholinguistic processes governing it—a state of affairs that attests to the complexity of the construct with which we are wrestling.

In this chapter, I discuss five major constructs that constitute the input–output chain: input, intake, intake factors, intake processes, and output as they relate to adult L2 development in formal contexts, and then present a revised version of what I have called an *interactive framework of intake processes* (Kumaravadivelu, 1994a). I do so by synthesizing theoretical and empirical insights derived from areas such as second language acquisition, cognitive psychology, and information processing.

2.1. INPUT

Input may be operationally defined as oral and/or written corpus of the target language (TL) to which L2 learners are exposed through various sources, and recognized by them as language input. This definition posits two conditions: availability and accessibility.

The first condition is rather obvious: either input has to be made available to learners or they have to seek it themselves. One can easily identify three types of input attributable to three different, but not mutually exclusive, sources from which learners are likely to get/seek input:

- *Interlanguage input:* the still-developing language of the learners and of their peers with all its linguistically well-formed as well as deviant utterances;
- *simplified input:* the grammatically and lexically simplified language that teachers, textbook writers, and other competent speakers use in and outside the classroom while addressing language learners; and
- *nonsimplified input:* the language of competent speakers without any characteristic features of simplification, that is, the language generally used in the media (TV, radio, and newspapers), and also the language used by competent speakers to speak and write to one another.

Each of these three sources of input can manifest itself in various forms: spoken and written, formal and informal, and so on. Learners are exposed to input from these sources at different points in their learning experience and in varying degrees.

The second condition—accessibility—is less obvious than the first but is equally important: input has to be recognized by learners as language input, and accepted by them as something with which they can cope. In other words, input should be linguistically and cognitively accessible to them. The language input that is available, but not accessible, is no more than noise. Some segments of the language input available to learners has the potential to become accessible, in part, through the process of what Gass (1997) called *apperception.* Apperception is an internal cognitive act in which a linguistic form is related to some bit of existing knowledge (or gap in knowledge). We can think of apperception as a priming device that prepares the input for further analysis. Thus, apperceived input is that bit of language that is noticed in some way by the learner because of some particular recognizable features. (p. 4)

What actually makes the learners notice and accept a subset of language exposed to them as potential input is not clear. Schmidt (1990, 1993) suggested factors such as frequency of occurrence, perceptual salience, linguistic complexity, skill level, and task demands. One might also add other factors, such as learners' needs and wants, as well as their interests and motivation.

2.2. INTAKE

Unlike input, the concept of intake is not easy to pin down. The literature on second language acquisition (SLA) presents several conflicting definitions and explanations for the term intake. Amid all the conceptual and terminological ambiguity, two strands of thought emerge: one that treats intake primarily as product, and the other that treats it primarily as process. Taking a product view, Kimball and Palmer (1978) defined intake as "input which requires students to listen for and interpret implicit meanings in ways similar to the ways they do so in informal communication" (pp. 17–18). This has been echoed by Krashen (1981) for whom "intake is simply where language acquisition comes from, that subset of linguistic input that helps the acquirer acquire language" (pp. 101–102). A common thread running through these definitions is that all of them treat intake primarily as a product, a subset of linguistic input exposed to the learner.

Perhaps the first one to emphasize the role of "language acquisition mechanism" in converting input into intake is Corder who defined intake as "what goes in and not what is *available* to go in" (1967, p. 165, emphasis in original). Similarly, Faerch and Kasper (1980) defined intake as "the subset of the input which is assimilated by the IL (interlanguage) system and which the IL system accommodates to" (p. 64). Hatch (1983) is in agreement when she defines intake as a subset of input that "the learner actually successfully and completely processed" (p. 81). Likewise, Chaudron (1985) referred to intake as "the mediating process between the target language available to the learners as input and the learner's internalized set of L2 rules and strategies for second language development" (p. 1). Liceras (1985) also opted for a process-oriented definition when she talks of cognitive capacities that intervene at the level of intake. A more recent definition by Gass (1997) also conceptualized intake "as apperceived input that has been further processed" (p. 23).

Notice that the product view identifies intake as a subset of input *before* the input is processed by learners. In other words, intake *is* input, even though it is only a part of it. The process view, however, identifies intake as what comes *after* psycholinguistic processing. That is, intake is already part of the learner's IL system. According to the product view, intake then is *unprocessed* language input; according to the process view, it is *processed* language input. The two views can be diagrammatically represented as follows (Fig. 2.1 and Fig. 2.2):

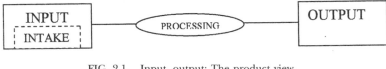

FIG. 2.1.   Input, output: The product view.

FIG. 2.2.   Input, intake, output: The process view.

The product view of intake appears to be severely flawed. It implies that there is no need to differentiate input from intake because intake, after all, is no more than a part of input and is independent of language-learning processes. In such a scenario, the distinction between input and intake, crucial to the nature of L2 development, becomes insignificant if not irrelevant. Furthermore, without such a distinction, we will not be able to account for the fact that "input is not perceived and processed by different learners in an identical manner" (Stern, 1983, p. 393).

Intake, then, is an abstract entity of learner language that has been fully or partially processed by learners, and fully or partially assimilated into their developing IL system. It is the result of as yet undetermined interaction between input and intake factors mediated by intake processes (see below). It is not directly observable, quantifiable, or analyzable; it is a complex cluster of mental representations. What is available for empirical verification is the product of these mental representations, generally called *output*. Intake is treated as a subset of input only to the extent that it originates from a larger body of input data. Features of learners' output can be traced, not only to the input they are exposed to, but to the dynamics of intake processes as well. The relationship between input, intake, and output can be diagrammatically represented as shown in Fig. 2.3.

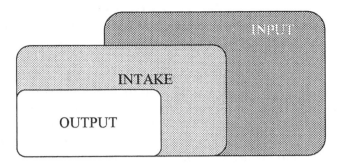

FIG. 2.3.   Input, intake, output: A quantitative view.

This figure shows that, quantitatively speaking, output is a subset of what has been internalized, which in turn is a subset of input. However, there is no simple part–whole relationship between intake and input, and between intake and output. Furthermore, parts of learner intake and learner output can go beyond the boundaries of language input because the learners' developing system provides instances of grammatically deviant utterances that are not part of input. This happens when, as Gass (1988) pointed out, "a learner imposes regularities on the data or uses native language markedness values" (p. 199). It may also happen when learners use various communication strategies (see text to come) that result in linguistically deviant forms of expression. What part of input gets converted into intake is determined by certain intake factors and intake processes.

2.3. INTAKE FACTORS

Intake factors refer to learner internal and learner external factors that are brought to bear on the psycholinguistic processes of language learning. Just as scholars differ on the concept of intake, they differ widely on their choice of intake factors as well. Corder (1967) suggested that "it is the learner who controls the input or more properly his intake" (p. 165). To the learner control, he added "the characteristics of his language acquisition mechanism" as another factor. He explained further, "what elements are, in fact, processed from the data that is available is determined by what the current state of the learner's interlanguage grammar permits him to take in at that moment" (Corder, 1978, pp. 81–82). Hatch (1983) believed that if input "is held in memory long enough to be processed (or if processing breaks down and the learner asks for a new clarification), it has been taken in" (p. 80). Seliger (1984) echoed the same idea: "long term memory and its effect on the selection of tactics is what determines when input will become intake" (p. 45).

Krashen (1981, and elsewhere) asserted that comprehensible input and low affective filter are the only two factors that determine intake. He is convinced that "every other factor hypothesized to relate to SLA reduces to input plus low filter" (1983, p. 141). Larsen-Freeman (1983) too suggested that "the key to input's becoming intake is its comprehensibility" (p. 14). Sharwood Smith (1985) took exception to these views and stated that it is "particularly unreasonable to give L2 input the unique role in explanation of intake" (p. 402). Instead, he emphasized the role played by cross-linguistic (i.e. language transfer) features in intake processing. According to Swain (1985) comprehensible output is crucial for converting input into intake. Although these scholars highlight the importance of one or two intake factors that are understandably the focus of their immediate research, Spolsky (1989), in a comprehensive review of the SLA literature, isolated, defined, and explained no less than 74 factors (he called them "conditions") of varying importance that, separately or in combination, contribute to L2 development.

The multiplicity of definitions and interpretations one finds in the SLA literature is evidently a result of varied perspectives with which researchers have approached the concept of intake and intake factors. Although the diversity of perspectives has undoubtedly broadened our understanding of intake, the sheer range of intake factors hypothesized to influence L2 development—two according to Krashen and 74 according to Spolsky—might militate against a proper understanding. It seems to me that we need an integrated view of the major intake factors in order to help us make informed judgments about L2 development and consequently about L2 teaching.

The task of isolating major intake factors then rests largely on individual perception rather than on indisputable evidence. My attempt to isolate factors that facilitate L2 development has yielded a cluster of six major factors, and two variables within each. Notice that I call these intake factors *facilitating*, not *causal*, factors. I do so because, to my knowledge, no direct causal relationship between any of the intake factors and adult L2 development has been established beyond doubt. It is, however, fairly reasonable to assume that each of these factors plays a facilitating role of varying importance. The major intake factors I highlight can be represented by an acronym, INTAKE:

Individual factors: age and anxiety;
Negotiation factors: interaction and interpretation;
Tactical factors: learning strategies and communication strategies;
Affective factors: attitudes and motivation;
Knowledge factors: language knowledge and metalanguage knowledge;
Environmental factors: social context and educational context.

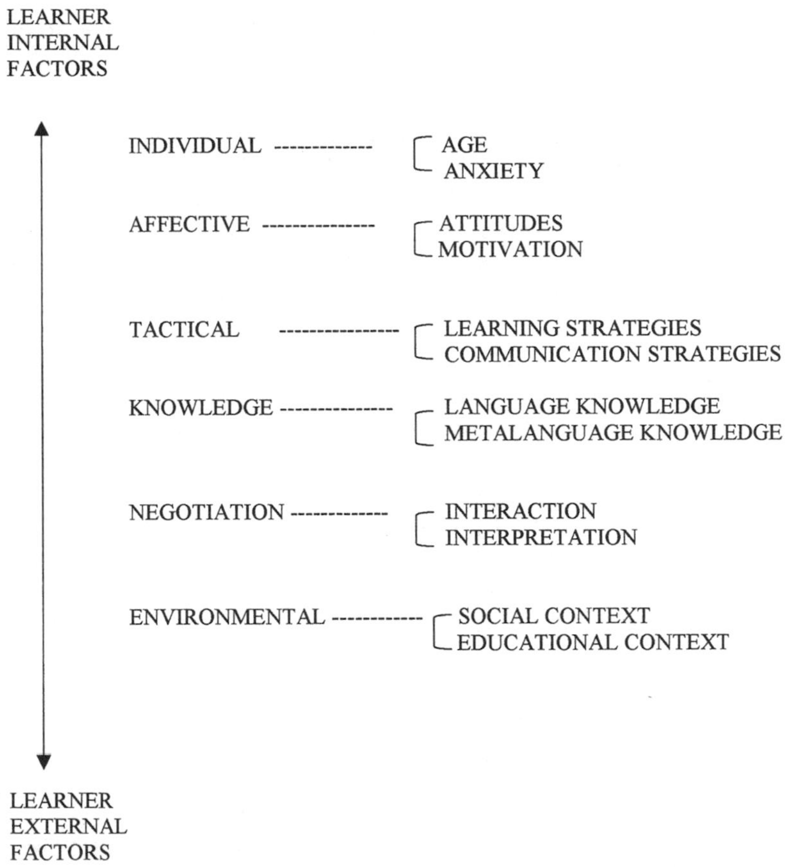

LEARNER
INTERNAL
FACTORS

INDIVIDUAL ------------- ⌈ AGE
                                             ⌊ ANXIETY

AFFECTIVE ---------------- ⌈ ATTITUDES
                                             ⌊ MOTIVATION

TACTICAL ---------------- ⌈ LEARNING STRATEGIES
                                             ⌊ COMMUNICATION STRATEGIES

KNOWLEDGE --------------- ⌈ LANGUAGE KNOWLEDGE
                                             ⌊ METALANGUAGE KNOWLEDGE

NEGOTIATION ------------- ⌈ INTERACTION
                                             ⌊ INTERPRETATION

ENVIRONMENTAL ------------ ⌈ SOCIAL CONTEXT
                                             ⌊ EDUCATIONAL CONTEXT

LEARNER
EXTERNAL
FACTORS

FIG. 2.4. Intake factors continuum.

These factors can be classified into two broad categories: *learner internal* and *learner external* factors. By this categorization, I do not suggest a dichotomous relationship between the two categories; rather, I look at them as a continuum as represented in Fig. 2.4. In the rest of this section, I briefly sketch the facilitating role played by each of these intake factors in developing the learner's L2 knowledge/ability. I do so by drawing upon currently available theoretical as well as empirical knowledge. Because of the vast body of information available in the literature, what follows cannot be more than a brief summary.

2.3.1. Individual Factors

Several individual factors have been studied in order to assess their role in L2 development. They include age, anxiety, empathy, extroversion, introversion, and risk-taking. Of these variables, age and anxiety appear to play a relatively greater role than the others.

2.3.1.1. Age. It is generally believed that the age at which learners begin to learn a second language influences their ultimate attainment in language knowledge/ability. In 1967, Lenneberg proposed a critical period hypothesis (CPH), arguing that languages are best learned before puberty, after which everyone faces certain constraints in language development. In a comprehensive review of the SLA research based on this hypothesis, Scovel (2001) found three different strands of thought. The first strand holds that there is a critical period but it is confined only to foreign accents. Citing evidence that demonstrates a massive mismatch between the L2 learners' excellent lexicogrammatical and their deficient phonological abilities, researchers claim that, if L2 learners begin their language learning after about the age of 12, they will end up with some degree of foreign accent. The reason is that L2 phonological production is presumably the only aspect of language performance that has a neuromuscular basis. The second strand is that there is a critical period, not only for accents, but also for grammar. Scovel finds very little evidence to support this claim. The third strand is that there is no critical period, not even for pronunciation. There are studies that suggest that, given adequate phonetic training and proper conditions for learning, L2 learners can actually acquire sufficient phonological competence to pass for native speakers. But such cases are rare.

Those in favor of the "younger is better" case (e.g., Krashen, 1981) argued that L2 development by children and adults might actually involve different processes; the former utilizing innate properties of language acquisition as in L1 acquisition, the latter employing general problem-solving abilities, and thus accounting for the differential effect of age. But, there are others who suggest that "older is better" because older learners have cognitive and literacy skills that tend to enhance their L2 development (McLaughlin 1987; Snow 1983). They suggest that there are contexts in which teenagers and adults not only reach nativelike proficiency, but they also progress more rapidly and perform with greater accuracy in the early stages of learning than do their younger counterparts.

A balanced approach suggests a *sensitive* rather than a *critical* period for L2 development (Lamendella, 1977; Singleton, 1989). As Hyltenstam and Abrahamsson (2003) pointed out in a recent review, in the *critical* period formulation, "maturation is thought to take place and come to an end within an early phase of the life span, abruptly set off from the rest at a specific age (puberty or earlier)" (p. 556). But, in the *sensitive* period formulation, "the sensitivity does not disappear at a fixed point; instead it is thought to fade away over a longer period of time, perhaps covering later childhood, puberty and adolescence" (p. 556). In other words, the *critical* period represents a well-defined "window of opportunity," whereas the *sensitive* period represents "a progressive inefficiency of the organism." Such a suggestion acknowledges that certain language skills are acquired more easily at particular times in development than at other times, and some language skills can be learned even after the critical period, although less easily. It seems reasonable to deduce from research that age does have an influence on L2 development, but the nature of influence will depend on which intake factors, when, and in what combination, are brought to bear on the learning experience of an individual learner.

2.3.1.2. Anxiety. *Anxiety* refers to an emotional state of apprehension, tension, nervousness, and worry mediated by the arousal of the automatic nervous system. In the context of L2 learning, anxiety is characterized by feelings of self-consciousness, fear of negative evaluation from peers and teachers, and fear of failure to live up to one's own personal standards and goals (e.g., E. K. Horwitz, M. B. Horwitz, & Cope, 1986). Adult L2 learners typically develop a sense of incompetence about internalizing the properties of their L2, and about the inability to present themselves in a way consistent with their self-image and self-esteem.

Although psychologists postulate a positive, facilitating anxiety, and a negative, debilitating anxiety, each working in tandem (Alpert & Haber, 1960), L2 researchers have by and large focused on the effect of the latter. In a series of experiments, Gardner and his colleagues (Gardner, 1985; Gardner, Day, & MacIntyre, 1992; MacIntyre & Gardner, 1989; 1991, 1994) found that anxiety has a significant deleterious effect on L2 development. Language anxiety has also been found to correlate negatively with global measures of achievement such as objective tests and course grades as well as measures involving specific processes, such as vocabulary recall. Similarly, studies conducted by E. K. Horwitz et al. (1986), and Madsen, Brown and Jones (1991) showed that a significant level of anxiety is experienced by a majority of their subjects in response to at least some aspects of L2 development.

Gardner and his colleagues explain the effects of language anxiety by surmising that it consumes attention and cognitive resources that could otherwise be allocated to developing L2 knowledge/ability. Thus, anxiety may occur at any of the three levels of language development: input, intake processing, or output (Tobias, 1986). At input, it may cause attention deficits, thus impacting on the initial representation of items in memory; intake processing may be affected because time is divided between the processing of emotion-related and task-related cognition; and, it may also interfere with storage and retrieval of previously learned information, thereby affecting output. The combined effects of language anxiety at all three stages,

MacIntyre and Gardner (1994) argued, "may be that, compared with re-laxed students, anxious students have a small base of second language knowledge and have more difficulty demonstrating the knowledge that they do possess" (p. 301).

The experimental studies just cited uphold a persistent argument by Krashen (1983) that high anxiety can impede language acquisition, where-as low anxiety is "conducive to second language acquisition, whether meas-ured as personal or classroom anxiety" (p. 31). Although a clear picture of how anxiety actually affects L2 processes is yet to emerge, it appears that anxiety may have different effects at different stages of L2 development de-pending on its interplay with other intake factors and intake processes.

2.3.2. Negotiation Factors

The term *negotiation* has been widely used in conversation analysis to refer to the ways in which participants in a communicative event structure their social relationships through interaction. Negotiation is important for L2 development because it implies the use and constant refinement of both linguistic and pragmatic knowledge/ability. There are at least three dimen-sions to negotiation: introspection, interaction, and interpretation. *Intro-spection* is intra-personal, involving a language learner's lonely mental jour-ney through and about meanings and contexts. It can sometimes lead to hypothesis formation and testing (see following). But, it is rarely available for direct observation and analysis. The other two dimensions of negotia-tion—*interaction* and *interpretation*—are largely interpersonal involving joint exploration of meaning between participants in a communicative event, and are directly available for investigation.

2.3.2.1. Interaction. *Negotiated interaction* in the L2 context entails the learner's active involvement in such communicative activities as clarifica-tion, confirmation, comprehension checks, requests, repairing, reacting, and turn-taking. Several experimental studies have revealed that negotiated interaction plays a facilitative, not a causal, role in helping L2 learners de-velop necessary language knowledge/ability. In a series of studies on the re-lationship between input, interaction, and L2 development spanning over a period of 15 years, Long (1981) proposed and updated (Long, 1996) what has come to be known as the *interaction hypothesis*. To put it simply, the hy-pothesis claims that interaction in which communication problems are ne-gotiated between participants promotes comprehension and production, ultimately facilitating L2 development.

Subsequent studies have shown that learners who maintained high levels of interaction in the L2 progressed at a faster rate than learners who inter-acted little in the classroom (Seliger, 1983) and that learners gain opportunities to develop their productive capacity in the L2 if demands are placed on them to manipulate their current IL system so that they can make their initially unclear messages become more meaningful (Swain, 1985). These results have been reinforced by Pica and her colleagues (e.g., Pica, 1992) and by Gass and her colleagues (see Gass, 1997, for a review) who report that what enables learners to move beyond their current interlanguage receptive and expressive capacities are opportunities to modify and restructure their interaction with their participants until mutual comprehension is reached. Furthermore, interaction helps the learners notice the gap between target language forms and learner-language forms, as it "connects input, internal learner capacities, particularly selective attention, and output in productive ways" (Long, 1996, p. 452). These studies lend credence to an earlier claim by Allwright (1984) that "the importance of interaction is not simply that it creates learning opportunities, it is that it constitutes learning itself" (p. 9).

2.3.2.2. Interpretation.   Closely associated with the opportunity to interact is the capacity to interpret target language utterances as intended. Interpretative procedures help learners differentiate what is said from what is meant. Inability to do so results in pragmatic failure (Thomas, 1983). The L2 learner's interpretive ability entails an understanding of pragmatic rules such as those enunciated in the Hymesian concept of communicative competence (see chap. 1, this volume, for details).

Interpretive procedures have implications for L2 development for, as Widdowson (1983) pointed out, they are "required to draw systemic knowledge into the immediate executive level of schemata and to relate these schemata to actual instances" (p. 106). Thus, the L2 learner encountering TL instances has to learn to deal with several possibilities, such as: (a) utterances may convey more than their literal meaning. *It's cold in here,* when, spoken in certain contexts, may convey the meaning of *Would you mind closing the Window?*; (b) utterances may not convey their literal meaning. In a day-to-day conversation, *How are you?* is no more than a polite question, one for which the speaker does not expect to hear a litany of the hearer's ailments; (c) utterances may convey meaning only if they are accompanied by certain specifications. In American English, as several foreign students are likely to find out to their chagrin, *Drop in any time* is not a genuine invitation unless clearly followed by the mention of time and place.

In addition, learners need to be aware that norms of interpretation are likely to diverge at cultural (Gumperz, 1982) as well as at subcultural levels of ethnic heritage, class, age, or gender (Tannen, 1992). Acquiring pragmatic knowledge/ability of how extralinguistic factors contribute to the process of meaning making implies acquiring knowledge of how language features interface with cultural and subcultural expectations. Emphasizing that the mastery of cultural norms of interpretation poses a severe challenge to L2 learners and users, Kasper (2001) advocated creation of learning opportunities both inside and outside the classroom: "*inside* the classroom by raising learners' awareness about implicature and improving their comprehension of it, and *outside* the classroom by focusing their attention to implicatures and encouraging them to seek out practice opportunities" (p. 56).

For a realization of the full potential of negotiation factors, a positive correlation with other intake factors, particularly, the individual factor of anxiety and the affective factors of attitude and motivation (see text to come) may be required. Aston (1986), for instance, found that interactive classroom tasks designed to promote negotiation may indeed fail to do so if they produce tension and anxiety in the learner. Thus, in conjunction with other relevant intake factors, negotiation factors provide ample opportunities for L2 learners to pay particular attention to new features of the linguistic input that are being currently learned thereby contributing to activate psycholinguistic processes.

2.3.3. Tactical Factors

Tactical factors refer to an important aspect of L2 development: the learners' awareness of, and their ability to use, appropriate tactics or techniques for effective learning of the L2 and efficient use of the limited repertoire developed so far. In the L2 literature, such tactics are discussed under the general rubric of learning strategies and communication strategies.

2.3.3.1. Learning Strategies. *Learning strategies* are operations and routines used by the learner to facilitate the obtaining, storage, retrieval, and use of information (Rubin, 1975). They are also "specific actions taken by the learner to make learning easier, faster, more enjoyable, more self-directed, more effective, and more transferable to new situations" (Oxford, 1990, p. 8). The term learning strategies then refers to what learners know and do to regulate their learning.

It is only during the 1970s that researchers began to study systematically the explicit and implicit efforts learners make in order to learn their L2 (Naiman, Frohlich, Stern, & Todesco, 1978; Rubin, 1975). Major typologies of learning strategies were proposed by Rubin (1975), O'Malley and Chamot (1990), Oxford (1990) and Wenden (1991). Although there are subtle differences between them, they generally classify learning strategies into three broad categories: metacognitive, cognitive, and social/affective strategies. *Metacognitive strategies* refer to higher order executive strategies such as thinking about the learning process, planning for and monitoring learning as it takes place, and self-evaluation of learning after the learning activity. *Cognitive strategies* refer to conscious ways of tackling learning materials and linguistic input. They include specific steps such as note-taking, summarizing, deducing, transferring, and elaborating. *Social/affective strategies* refer to interpersonal strategies that are consistent with the learners' psychological and emotional conditions and experiences. They include co-operative learning, peer group discussion, and interacting with competent speakers. As Dornyei and Skehan (2003) concluded, "the students' own active and creative participation in the learning process through the application of individualized learning techniques" (p. 608) cause them to excel in their L2 development.

Research conducted by some of the aforementioned scholars shows that there are different ways of learning a language successfully and that different learners will approach language learning differently. This is because individual learners not only have to consider the strategies that contribute to effective learning but, more importantly, they have to discover those that suit best their learning objectives as well as their personality traits. Research also reveals that more effective learners use a greater variety of strategies and use them in ways appropriate to the language-learning task and that less effective learners not only have fewer strategy types in their repertoire but also frequently use strategies that are inappropriate to the task (O'Malley & Chamot, 1990). Therefore, one of the primary objectives of research on learning strategies has been to make the intuitive knowledge possessed by good language learners more explicit and systematic so that such knowledge can be used for strategy training to improve the language learning abilities of other learners. Strategy training manuals (e.g., Chamot, Bernhardt, El-Dinery, & Robbins, 1999; Ellis & Sinclair, 1989; Scharle & Szabo, 2000) offer practical suggestions to make learners more active participants in their language learning, and to make teachers more sensitive to learner diversity and learning difficulties.

2.3.3.2. Communication Strategies.   In addition to learning strategies, L2 learners also use what are called communication strategies, which are "potentially conscious plans for solving what to an individual presents itself as a problem in reaching a particular communicative goal" (Faerch & Kasper, 1980, p. 81). These are compensatory or coping strategies that learners employ in order to make do with their still-developing linguistic and pragmatic knowledge/ability. One of the earliest taxonomies of communication strategies is the one proposed by Tarone (1977). It has three broad categories: *paraphrase*, involving the use of an elaborate descriptive phrase instead of a core lexical item; *borrowing*, involving a word-for-word literal translation from native language; or *avoidance*, involving the attempt to avoid using a required expression or just to give up the effort to communicate. Other taxonomies (e.g., Paribakht, 1985; Dornyei & Scott, 1997) provide more elaborate and more nuanced lists of communication strategies used by L2 learners.

Although earlier taxonomies of communication strategies focused on product-oriented, surface-level features, subsequent research (e.g., Bialystok, 1990; Bialystok & Kellerman, 1987; Dornyei & Scott, 1997; Kumaravadivelu, 1988) attempted to differentiate surface-level communication strategies from deep-level psychological processes. Bialystok & Kellerman, for instance, suggest that the strategic behavior of learners can be classified into linguistic and conceptual strategies. The *linguistic strategy* refers to the use of features and structures from another language (usually L1), and the *conceptual strategy* refers to the manipulation of the intended concept. They further divide conceptual strategy into two possible approaches: holistic and analytic. *Holistic* approach involves using a similar referent, as in *stove* for *microwave*. *Analytic* approach involves selecting criterial properties of the referent, as in *a machine that cooks and defrosts very fast by means of waves* for *microwave*.

Although scholars differ on the relative explanatory power of various taxonomies, and the complex nature of implicit and explicit mental processes that are involved in the use of communication strategies, they generally agree that they are "responsible for plans, whether implicit or explicit, by which communication is shaped" (*Routledge Encyclopedia*, 2000, p. 577). There is, thus, a general consensus on the facilitating role played by tactical factors in L2 development. Tactical factors can help learners pay attention to potentially useful linguistic input and also promote opportunities for negotiation thereby activating necessary cognitive processes.

2.3.4. Affective Factors

The individual learner's disposition to learn has always been recognized as crucial for L2 development. The term *affective factors* stands for several variables that characterize learner disposition, the most important of which are attitudes and motivation. As Siegel (2003) observed, motivation is considered to be "influenced by the learner's attitudes toward the L2, its speakers and culture, toward the social and practical value of using the L2, and toward his or her own language and culture" (p. 185). Because of the close connection between attitude and motivation, L2 researchers have studied them together, proposing a linear relationship in which attitude influenced motivation and motivation influenced L2 development (e.g., Gardner, 1985). There are others who have argued for the usefulness of separating them (e.g., Crookes & Schmidt, 1991).

2.3.4.1. Attitudes. *Attitudes* are one's evaluative responses to a person, place, thing or an event. According to social psychologists, attitudes are individually driven, that is, they are one's personal thoughts or feelings based on one's beliefs or opinions; therefore, different individuals develop different shades of attitudes toward the same stimuli (Eiser, 1987). Attitudes are also socially grounded, that is, they must be experienced as related to subjects or events in the external world. Attitude is intricately linked to language learning processes and practices because, as pointed out in the *Routledge Encyclopedia* (2000), it "affects the learner not only with respect to the processing of information and identification with people or groups, but also with respect to motives and the relationship between language and culture, and their place within the existing linguistic and cultural diversity" (p. 57).

In addition to the individual's personal dispositions, there are at least two external forces that appear to shape the learner's language-learning attitude: environmental and pedagogic. The environmental factor includes social, cultural, political and economic imperatives that shape the L2 educational milieu, and is explained in section 2.3.6. The pedagogic factor shapes how teachers, learners and the learning situation interact with each other to trigger positive or negative attitudes in the learner. The teacher's curricular objectives, classroom activities and even personal attitudes play a role in influencing the learner's attitude to language learning (Malcolm, 1987). In fact, the teachers' attitudes seem to have a greater influence on L2 development than even parental or community-wide attitudes (Tucker & Lambert, 1973). Similarly, as diary studies show, learners can hold negative attitudes toward the learning situation if there is a mismatch between their and their teacher's curricular objectives (Schumann & Schumann, 1977). It is in this context that Breen and Littlejohn (2000) advocated shared decision-making based on meaningful "discussion between all members of the classroom to decide how learning and teaching are to be organized" (p. 1).

Furthermore, learners' attitude toward the speakers of the TL and its impact on L2 development has been widely studied, resulting in conflicting findings. Early experiments conducted by Gardner and his colleagues (see, e.g., Gardner & Lambert, 1972) showed high correlation between learner's positive attitude toward the speakers of the TL and L2 development. Such a strong claim has been questioned (Cooper & Fishman, 1977; Oller, Baca, & Vigil, 1977). Later research, however, shows that although L2 learners might develop a negative attitude toward the TL community because of cultural or political reasons, a positive attitude toward the TL itself and its usefulness can contribute to L2 development (Berns, 1990). In sum, it is fair to assume that a positive attitude to language learning is a necessary but not a sufficient condition for success.

2.3.4.2. Motivation. Motivation provides "the driving force to sustain the long and often tedious learning process" (*Routledge Encyclopedia*, 2000, p. 425). It is perhaps the only intake variable that has been consistently found, in various contexts and at various levels of L2 development, to correlate positively with successful learning outcome. Most studies on motivation have been inspired by the distinction social psychologists Gardner and Lambert (1972) made between integrative and instrumental motivation. *Integrative motivation* refers to an interest in learning an L2 in order to socioculturally integrate with members of the TL community. *Instrumental motivation* refers to an interest in learning an L2 for functional purposes such as getting a job or passing an examination. In several studies, Gardner, Lambert and colleagues (see, e.g., Gardner, 1985) reported that integrative motivation is far superior to instrumental motivation.

Studies conducted in other learning and teaching contexts (Chihara & Oller, 1978; Lukmani, 1972) failed to show the superiority of integrative motivation. In fact, a comprehensive review of motivational studies found a wide range of correlations covering all possibilities: positive, nil, negative, and ambiguous (Au, 1988). Later studies by Gardner and his colleagues themselves (Gardner, 1988; Gardner & MacIntyre, 1991) clearly demonstrated that both integrative motivation and instrumental motivation have "consistent and meaningful effects on learning, and on behavioral indices of learning" (Gardner & MacIntyre, 1991, p. 69).

Unlike the binary approach proposed by social psychologists, cognitive psychologists have suggested three major types of motivation: intrinsic, extrinsic, and achievement motivation. *Intrinsic motivation* is the desire to engage in activities characterized by enjoyment (Csikszentmihalyi, 1975; Deci, 1975; Deci & Ryan, 1985). There is no apparent reward except the experience of enjoying the activity itself. According to Csikszentmihalyi (1975) true enjoyment accompanies the experience of what he calls *flow*, that peculiar, dynamic, holistic, sensation of total involvement with the activity itself. Thus, intrinsically motivated activities are ends in themselves rather than means to an end. Individuals seek out and engage in intrinsically motivated activities in order to feel competent and self-determining. Like basic human drives, intrinsic needs are innate to the human organism and function as an important energizer of behavior.

Extrinsic motivation can be triggered only by external cues that include gaining and maintaining peer, sibling, or adult approval, avoiding peer or sibling or adult disapproval, and gaining or losing specific tangible rewards. It is conditioned by practical considerations of life with all its attendant sense of struggle, success, or failure. Thus, extrinsic motivation is associated with lower levels of self-esteem and higher levels of anxiety compared to intrinsic motivation. *Achievement motivation*, on the other hand, refers to the motivation and commitment to excel. It is involved whenever there is competition with internal or external standards of excellence. It is a specific motive that propels one to utilize one's fullest potential. The driving force for achieving excellence can be either intrinsic, or extrinsic or a combination of both (Deci, 1975; Deci & Ryan, 1985; McClelland, Atkinson, Clark, & Lowell, 1953).

It may be assumed that all three types of motivation will influence L2 development in different degrees depending on individual dispositions and different environmental and pedagogic contexts. To be primarily motivated for intrinsic reasons, the learners have to get involved in continual cycles of seeking language-learning opportunities and conquering optimal challenges in order to feel competent and self-determining. They have to let their natural curiosity and interest to energize their language-learning endeavor and help them overcome even adverse pedagogic and environmental limitations. To be primarily motivated for achievement considerations, the learners have to strive to reach internally induced or externally imposed standards of excellence in a spirit of competition and triumph. It appears that a vast majority of L2 learners are primarily motivated for extrinsic reasons. In fact, extrinsic motivation accounts for most of what has been reported under integrative and instrumental motivation (van Lier, 1991).

The general trend of the experimental studies has been to suggest that motivation "involves all those affects and cognitions that initiate language learning, determine language choice, and energize the language learning process" (Dornyei, 2000, p. 425). It operates at the levels of language, learner, and learning situation. Over time, several intake factors, particularly individual, affective and environmental factors, contribute to determine the degree of motivation that a learner brings to the task of language learning.

2.3.5. Knowledge Factors

Knowledge factors refer to language knowledge and metalanguage knowledge. All adult L2 learners exposed to formal language education in their L1 inevitably bring with them not only their L1 knowledge/ability but also their own perceptions and expectations about language, language learning, and language use. Both language knowledge and metalanguage knowledge play a crucial role in L2 development.

2.3.5.1. Language Knowledge. Language knowledge represents knowledge/ability in the native language, in the still developing target language, and in other languages already known. By virtue of being members of their native language speech community and by virtue of their experience as language users, all adult L2 learners possess varying degrees of implicit and explicit knowledge/ability in their L1. Empirical studies show that L2 learners do not "effectively switch off the L1 while processing the L2, but has it constantly available" (V. Cook 1992, p. 571), and that prior linguistic knowledge functions as "some sort of anchor with which to ground new knowledge" (Gass, 1997, p. 17).

The influence and use of language knowledge can be a facilitating or a constraining factor in L2 development. As Corder (1983) suggests, prior language knowledge "created and remembered from the learner's own linguistic development" (p. 91) may very well provide the starting point (or what he calls "initial hypothesis") of the L2 developmental continuum. It forms the basis for initial comprehension of the linguistic input exposed to the learner. Prior knowledge may also impose a set of constraints on "the domains from which to select hypotheses about the new data one is attending to" (Schachter, 1983, p. 104). As Becker (1983) put it, the role of prior knowledge is to help the learner characterize the present in the past and "to make any new utterance reverberate with past ones, in unpredictable directions" (p. 218).

2.3.5.2. Metalanguage Knowledge.   *Metalanguage knowledge,* also known as metalinguistic awareness, refers to "one's ability to consider language not just as a means of expressing ideas or communicating with others, but also as an object of inquiry" (Gass & Selinker, 2001, p. 302). It ranges from making puns in casual conversations to possessing insights into what a language system is and what it is used (and misused) for. It also leads to a conscious perception and sensitivity in language learning, and language teaching. It is "an individual's ability to match, intuitively, spoken and written utterances with his/her knowledge of a language" (Masny & d'Anglejan, 1985, p. 176). It is considered to be an important factor in L2 development because it encompasses learners' knowledge/ability not only to think about language as a system but also to make comparisons between their L1 and L2, thus facilitating the psycholinguistic process of language transfer.

There seems to be a strong relationship between language experience and metalanguage knowledge. Studies reveal that prior language experience helps L2 learners develop an intuitive "feel" for the TL (Donato & Adair-Hauck 1992; Gass 1983). L2 learners have been shown to be able "to produce a correct correction when they have an incorrect explicit rule or no explicit rule at all" thereby demonstrating the presence of L2 intuitions (Green & Hecht 1992, p.176). Extending the role of metalanguage knowledge, V. Cook (1992, and elsewhere) proposed the concept of *multicompetence,* as we discussed in chapter 1. Cook hypothesized that a heightened metalinguistic awareness may impact other aspects of cognition thereby shaping the cognitive processes of L2 development and use.

2.3.6. Environmental Factors

Environmental factors refer to the wider milieu in which language learning and teaching take place. These include the global, national, social, cultural, political, economic, educational, and family contexts. The impact of these overlapping factors on L2 development is not fully known, partly because, as Siegel (2003) pointed out, "one shortcoming of the field of SLA is that generalizations have been made on the basis of research carried out in only a limited range of sociolinguistic settings and involving only standard varieties of language" (p. 183). However, even the limited knowledge we have suggests that environmental factors contribute to shape L2 development. Now, we focus on two closely connected factors: social and educational.

2.3.6.1. Social Context.   *Social context* refers to a range of language-learning environments such as the home, the neighborhood, the classroom, and the society at large. Recently, scholars such as Pavlenko (2002), Hall (2002) and Siegel (2003) suggested that the movement from the L1 to the L2 involves more than psycholinguistic abilities, because it depends on historical, political, and social forces as well. Such a conclusion echoes earlier studies reported in the 1980s that any serious attempt to study L2 development necessarily entails the study of social context as an important variable (Beebe 1985; Heath 1983; K. K. Sridhar & N. Sridhar 1986; Wong-Fillmore 1989). In fact, Beebe (1985) pointedly argued that the learner's choice of *what* input becomes intake is highly affected by social and situational contexts. Additionally, social context is critical because it shapes various learning and teaching issues such as (a) the motivation for L2 learning, (b) the goal of L2 learning, (c) the functions an L2 is expected to perform in the community, (d) the availability of input to the learner, (e) the variation in the input, and (f) the norms of proficiency acceptable to that particular speech community.

Specific social settings such as the neighborhood and the classroom, in which learners come into contact with the new language have also been found to influence L2 development. Studies conducted by Wong-Fillmore (1989) revealed that social settings create and shape opportunities for both learners and competent speakers of the L2 to communicate with each other, thereby maximizing learning potential. A study by Donato and Adair-Hauck (1992) concluded that the social and discursive context in which instructional intervention is delivered plays a crucial role in facilitating L2 development in the classroom.

The social context also shapes the role of the TL in a particular speech community and the nature of the linguistic input available for learners. Comparing the sociolinguistic profiles of English-language learning and use in India, West Germany, and Japan, Berns (1990) illustrated how these three different social contexts contribute to the emergence of various communicative competences and functions in these countries, thereby influencing L2 development and use in significantly different ways. In these and other similar contexts, the TL plays a role that is complementary or supplementary to local languages (Krishnaswamy & Burde, 1998). The competences and functions invariably determine the nature and quality of input that is available to the learner. Most often, the learner is not exposed to the full range of the TL in all its complexity that one would expect in a context where it is used as the primary vehicle of communication.

2.3.6.2. Educational Context.

Closely related to the social context is the educational context. Studies on educational contexts grounded in educational psychology emphasize the inseparability and reciprocal influence of educational institutions and settings in which learning and teaching operations are embedded (Bloome & Green, 1992). In the context of L2 development, it is the educational context that shapes language policy, language planning, and most importantly, the learning opportunities available to the L2 learner. It is impossible to insulate classroom life from the dynamics of political, educational, and societal institutions, because, as I have argued elsewhere (Kumaravadivelu, 2001), the experiences participants bring to the classroom are shaped not only by the learning and teaching episodes they have encountered in the classroom, but also by a broader social, economic, educational, and political environment in which they grow up. These experiences have the potential to affect classroom practices in ways unintended and unexpected by policy planners or curriculum designers or textbook producers.

As Tollefson (2002) and others pointed out, it is the educational context that determines the types as well as the goals of instructional programs made available to the L2 learner. For instance, the educational context will condition the relationship between the home language and the school language, between "standard" language and its "nonstandard" varieties. As a result of decisions made by educational policymakers, the L2 learners will have a choice between *additive bilingualism*, where they have the opportunity to become active users of the L2 while at the same time maintaining their L1, or *subtractive bilingualism*, where they gradually lose their L1 as they develop more and more competence and confidence in their L2. Similarly, as Norton (2000) and Pavlenko (2002) asserted, the educational context can also shape the complex relationship between power, status and identity by determining "how access to linguistic and interactional resources is mediated by nonnative speaker status, race, gender, class, age, and social status, and to ways in which discourses appropriated by L2 learners are linked to power and authority" (Pavlenko, 2002, p. 291).

To sum up this section on intake factors, all the six major intake factors already outlined—individual, negotiation, tactical, affective, knowledge, and environmental—appear to interact with each other in as yet undetermined ways. They also play a role in triggering and maximizing the operational effectiveness of intake processes, to which we turn now.

2.4. INTAKE PROCESSES

Intake processes are cognitive mechanisms that at once mediate between, and interact with, input data and intake factors. They consist of mental operations that are specific to language learning as well as those that are required for general problem-solving activities. As procedures and operations that are internal to the learner, intake processes remain the most vital and the least understood link in the input–intake–output chain. The intake processes that appear to shape L2 development may be grouped under three broad and overlapping categories: inferencing, structuring, and restructuring. These processes appear to govern what goes on in the learners' mind when they attempt to internalize the TL system, that is, infer the linguistic system of the TL from the available and accessible input data, structure appropriate mental representations of the TL system, and restructure the developing system in light of further exposure and experience. In the rest of this section, I briefly outline each of them.

2.4.1. Inferencing

The intake process of *inferencing* involves making a series of intelligent guesses to derive tentative hypotheses about various aspects of the TL system. Inferences are normally made by using all available, at times inconclusive, linguistic and nonlinguistic evidence based on the learner's implicit and explicit knowledge base. Implicit knowledge refers to information learners intuit about the TL, even though they cannot articulate that information in the form of rules or principles. *Explicit knowledge* refers to the learners' knowledge about the TL, their L1, and their knowledge of the world (see also section 2.3.5). Similarly, inferencing can be made using inductive as well as deductive reasoning. That is, learners can infer how a particular subsystem of language works by moving inductively from the particular to the general (i.e. from examples to rules), or moving deductively from the general to the particular.

Furthermore, L2 learners may benefit from the processes of *overgeneralization* and *language transfer* to make inferences about the TL system. Using intralingual cues, they may overgeneralize certain features of the TL system on the basis of any partial learning that may have already taken place. Some of the communication strategies such as paraphrase or word coinage (discussed in section 2.3.3) that learners employ in order to get across their message while using their still-developing interlanguage system are an indication of this process of overgeneralization. Similarly, using interlingual cues, learners may transfer certain phonological, morphological, syntactic, or even pragmatic features of their first language. Language transfer, as a cognitive process, has been considered to be essential to the formation of IL (Selinker, 1992).

Inferencing is particularly useful when the learners are able to pay attention to the new features presented in the input data in order to find the gap between what is already known and what needs to be learned anew. The process of inferencing can be expected to vary from learner to learner because it reflects individual cognitive capabilities involving the connections made by learners themselves and not the connections inherently found in the input data. It can lead to working hypotheses that in turn may lead to interim conclusions that are tested against new evidence and are subsequently rejected or refined. Inferencing thus may entail framing new insights or reframing what is already vaguely or partially known.

2.4.2. Structuring

I use the term *structuring* to refer to the complex process that governs the establishment of mental representations of the TL, and their evolution in the course of IL development. As Rivers (1991) argued, the notion of mental representation "is at the heart of the process of internalization of language" (p. 253). It refers to how the L2 system is framed in the mind of the learner. It combines elements of analysis and control proposed by Bialystok (1990, and elsewhere). Analysis is connected to language knowledge, and control is connected to language ability. As learners begin to understand how the L2 system works, and as their mental representations of the system become more explicit and more structured, they begin to see the relationships between various linguistic categories and concepts. Control is the process that allows learners "direct their attention to specific aspects of the environment or a mental representation as problems are solved in real time" (Bialystok, 2002, p. 153). In other words, the intake process of structuring helps learners construct, structure and organize the symbolic representational system of the TL by gradually making explicit the implicit knowledge that shape their IL performance. It also guides the gradual progress the learners make from unanalyzed knowledge, consisting of prefabricated patterns and memorized routines, to analyzed knowledge, consisting of propositions in which the relationship between formal and functional properties of the TL become increasingly apparent to the learners.

Compared to inferencing, structuring gives learners not only a deeper understanding of the properties and principles of the TL system, but also a greater control over their use for communicative purposes. It helps them pay selective attention to relevant and appropriate input data in order to tease out specific language problems. It can also regulate the flow of information between short-term and long-term memory systems, taking the responsibility for differential applicability of interim knowledge to various situations before interim knowledge gets fully established. The difference between inferenced knowledge/ability and structured knowledge/ability may contribute to the distinction Chaudron (1983) made between preliminary intake and final intake. The former relates to "perception and comprehension of forms" and the latter to "the incorporation of the forms in the learner's grammar" (pp. 438–439). Although inferenced knowledge/ ability and structured knowledge/ability are partially independent and partially interacting dimensions of intake processes, they may be seen as constituting two ends of a learning continuum.

2.4.3. Restructuring

The idea of *restructuring* as an intake process is derived from the work of Cheng (1985) and others in cognitive psychology and applied with some modification to L2 development by McLaughlin and his colleagues (McLaughlin, 1987; 1990; McLeod & McLaughlin 1986). Restructuring can be traced to the structuralist approach enunciated by Jean Piaget, who maintained that cognitive development is characterized by fundamental, qualitative change when a new internal organization is imposed for interpreting new information. In other words, restructuring denotes neither an incremental change in the structure already in place nor a slight modification of it but the addition of a totally new structure to allow for a totally new interpretation. It results in learners abandoning their initial hunch and opting for a whole new hypothesis. It marks a strategy shift that coordinates, integrates, and reorganizes task components resulting in more efficient intake processing. It can operate at phonological, morphological, syntactic, semantic, and pragmatic levels (McLaughlin, 1990).

Although most aspects of inferencing and structuring account for the reasons why intake processing requires selective attention and an extended time period of practice for the formation of mental representations of the TL system, restructuring as an intake process accounts for discontinuities in L2 development. It has been frequently observed that although some learning occurs continuously and gradually, as is true of the development of automaticity through practice, some learning occurs in discontinuous fashion, through restructuring (McLeod & McLaughlin, 1986). Restructuring is mostly a sudden, abstract, insight-forming phenomenon happening quickly and incidentally, taking very little processing time and energy.

To sum up this section, the intake processes of inferencing, structuring, and restructuring constitute the mental mechanisms governing L2 development. They work in tandem in as yet undetermined ways to facilitate or constrain the formation of mental representations of the TL system. They seem to operate at various points on the implicit–explicit continuum, triggering incidental learning at some times and intentional learning at some other times. In conjunction with various intake factors, these processes help learners synthesize the developing knowledge into grammar, and internalize it so as to effectively and efficiently access it in appropriate contexts of language use.

2.5. OUTPUT

Output refers to the corpus of utterances that learners actually produce orally or in writing. In addition to well-formed utterances that may have already been structured and/or restructured, the learner output will contain, as discussed in section 2.1, deviant utterances that cannot be traced to any of the three major sources of input because they are the result of an interplay between intake factors and intake processes.

Traditionally, output has been considered not as a mechanism for language learning but as evidence of what has already been learned. Research, however, indicates a larger role for output. Introducing the concept of *comprehensible output*, Merrill Swain (1985) argued that we need "to incorporate the notion of being pushed towards the delivery of a message that is not only conveyed, but that is conveyed precisely, coherently, and appropriately" (pp. 248–249). She further asserted that production "may force the learner to move from semantic processing to syntactic processing" (p. 249). In other words, an attempt to produce language will move learners from processing language at the level of word meaning (which can sometimes be done by guessing from the context or by focusing on just key words) to processing language at the level of grammatical structures (which requires a much higher level of cognitive activity).

In a later work, Swain (1995) identified three possible functions of output: the noticing function, the hypothesis-testing function, and the metalinguistic function. The *noticing function* relates to the possibility that when learners try to communicate in their still-developing target language, they may encounter a linguistic problem and become aware of what they do not know or know only partially. Such an encounter may raise their awareness, leading to an appropriate action on their part. The hypothesis-testing function of output relates to the possibility that when learners use their still-developing TL, they may be experimenting with what works and what does not work. Moreover, when they participate in negotiated interaction and receive negative feedback, they are likely to test different hypotheses about a particular linguistic system. Finally, the metalinguistic function of output relates to the possibility that learners may be consciously thinking about language and its system, about its phonological, grammatical, and semantic rules in order to guide them to produce utterances that are linguistically correct and communicatively appropriate.

2.6. AN INTERACTIVE FRAMEWORK OF INTAKE PROCESSES

Having briefly discussed various aspects of input, intake, intake factors, intake processes and output, I now attempt to pull these constructs together in order to make sense of how learners might internalize the L2 knowledge system. There is no clear consensus among SLA researchers about what plans or procedures learners use for thinking, remembering, understanding, and using language. There seems to be a general agreement, however, that "SLA is a terribly complex process, that understanding the process requires the contributions of numerous fields, from linguistic theory to anthropology to brain science, and that the process is not yet very well understood" (Gregg, 2003, p. 831). The primary reason why the process is not very well understood is that the phenomenon we wish to study—the underlying mental mechanism—is not directly available for empirical verification; it can be studied only through its external manifestation: spoken and/or written performance data produced by language learners and language users.

Despite the challenging nature of investigation and the limited tools available for the researcher, several exploratory models of cognition both in psychology and in SLA have been proposed. They include the monitor model (Krashen, 1981); the ACT* model (Adaptive Control of Thought, final version; Anderson, 1983); the language-processing model (Bialystok, 1983, 2002); the parallel distributed-processing model (McClelland, Rumelhart, & the PDP Research Group, 1986); the model for attention and processing (McLaughlin, 1987); the competition model (MacWhinney, 1987); and the model of input processing (van Patten, 1996). These are mainly descriptive models that are useful for explanation, not for prediction, of language learning. Although none of them fully and satisfactorily explains L2 development, each of them has contributed to partial understanding of certain aspects of it. Drawing from these models rather eclectically, I present below an interactive framework of intake processes, with particular reference to adult L2 development. Descriptive as well as speculative in nature, the framework seeks to highlight the intricate interplay of input, intake, intake factors, intake processes, and output.

Before I present the framework, it seems reasonable to posit two criteria that any framework of intake processes must necessarily satisfy: (a) it must be capable of including all the intake factors known to play a role in intake processes, and (b) it must reflect the interactive and parallel nature of intake processes. The first criterion is quite explicit in the SLA literature. As the discussion in section 2.3 amply shows, there are several learner internal and learner external intake factors of varying importance that, separately or in combination, facilitate or constrain L2 development. The issue facing the current scholarship is not whether any of the intake factors play any role in L2 development, but in what combination, in what learning context, and in what way.

The second criterion emerges from the insights derived from the models already cited. We now learn that processing goes on simultaneously in many areas of cognition and at many different levels. Language learning entails a nonlinear, parallel, interactive process rather than a linear, serial, additive process. It was earlier believed that learners internalize the TL system primarily by using either a *top–down processing*, a knowledge-governed system characterized by a step-by-step progression where output from one level acts as input for the next, or *a bottom-up processing*, an input-governed system characterized by a serial movement of information from the lower to the higher levels. It is now becoming increasingly clear that language learning is governed by interactive processing in which multiple operations occur simultaneously at multiple levels drawing evidence from multiple sources. In other words, from the perspective of the framework presented below, language processing is considered essentially interactive, involving intake factors and intake processes that operate in parallel and simultaneous ways, shaping and being shaped by one another.

As Fig. 2.5 indicates, the interactive framework consists of input, intake factors, a *central processing unit* (CPU), and output. The CPU consists of the cognitive processes of inferencing, structuring, and restructuring. The initial phase of intake processing is probably activated when learners begin to pay attention to the linguistic input they deem accessible or comprehensible. The input, with bits and pieces of information about the TL system, enters the CPU either directly or through any one or more intake factors. The

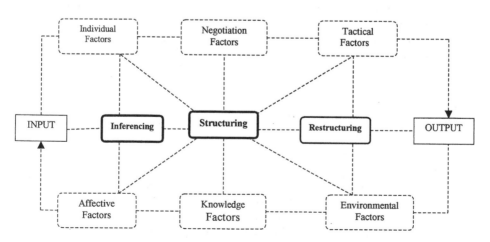

FIG. 2.5. An interactive framework of intake processes.

entry initiates the process of language construction. At this early stage, intake processing appears to operate at several layers, some of which may depend heavily on temporary, limited capacity, short-term working memory systems that in turn involve, to a large degree, prefabricated routines and idiomatic expressions.

An important task of the CPU at this stage appears to be to reduce the pressure on working memory systems by coding the incoming pieces of information into some meaningful organizational schemas. Such coding, which is probably a precursor to fully established mental representations, is assisted by the intake process of *inferencing*. Inferencing helps learners derive working hypotheses about syntactic, semantic and pragmatic aspects of the TL. Depending on the learning and teaching situation, learners might get various types of positive evidence, that is, well-formed utterances exposed to them, and negative evidence, that is, explicit corrections from their teachers or other competent speakers of the language, both of which will help them reject or refine their working hypotheses. This level of intake processing involving attention-allocation, short-term memory, and integration of pieces of information constitutes a part of what has been called *controlled information processing*.

If inferencing leads to the formation of working hypotheses, *structuring*, which is a higher level of processing, contributes to the establishment of mental representations. As we learn from schema theory, which explains how the human mind organizes knowledge in long-term memory (Schank & Abelson, 1977), the faster the testing and refinement of working hypotheses, the swifter the formation of mental representations and greater the chances of limited capacity, working-memory systems being purged and replaced by permanent long-term memory schemas. Memory schemas are responsible for storing incoming information, retrieving previously stored information, and pattern-matching mental representations (McClelland et al., 1986). This transition from working memory systems to permanent memory schemas is critical because, as we learn from schema theorists, language use requires that linguistic units such as phonemes, morphemes, words, phrases, syntactic patterns, and other discourse units be abstracted and stored in the form of memory schemas.

Repeated cycles of hypothesis formation, testing, and confirmation or rejection, and the construction of memory schemas mediated by intake processes, particularly by the process of structuring, result in the strengthening of mental representations of the TL, thereby considerably increasing the learners' ability to gain a greater analysis of and a better control over the properties and principles of the TL system. Any remaining gap in the establishment of mental representations is taken care of either by further opportunities for intentional corrective learning or by the activation of the process of restructuring. *Restructuring*, as mentioned earlier, represents quick insight formation that could result in incidental learning whereby complex and hitherto unclear language problems are teased out paving way for accurate decisions about the TL system. This level of intake processing, where the complex and combined processes of inferencing, structuring, and restructuring gradually assist the learners in internalizing the L2 system and in accessing the system for effective communicative use, constitutes a part of what has been called *automatic information processing*.

An important point to remember in the overall process of internalization of the L2 system is that each of the intake processes is facilitated as well as constrained, not merely by the availability and accessibility of linguistic input and the interplay of intake factors, but also by the role played by learner output. The arrows connecting input and output (Fig. 2.5) suggest that learner output is not a terminal point; it is rather a part in a cycle serving as an important source of input data for the learner thereby affecting the course of L2 development.

The interactive framework of intake processing described here incorporates several aspects of parallel distributed processing at both micro and macro levels. At the micro level, intake processing is considered to involve a large number of parallel, simultaneous, and interacting processes such as perception, syntactic parsing, and semantic interpretation, and the selection of whatever input information is relevant and useful, be it phonological, syntactic, semantic, or pragmatic. The development of a particular syntactic rule, for example, depends often on the development of a rule in some other domain, say a phonological or lexical rule, or vice versa (Ard & Gass, 1987; Klein, 1990). Following the *connectionist perspective*, the intake processing network is seen as a continual strengthening or weakening of interconnections in response to the language input encountered by learners, and to the language use employed by them.

At the macro level, the framework posits a criss-cross interplay among intake factors on one hand, and between them, and intake processes on the other hand. Most of the intake factors appear to interweave and interact with each other in a synergic relationship where the whole is greater than the sum of the parts. How the learner seeks, recognizes, attends to, and controls the input data depend to a large extent on the synergy of intake factors.

The interactive framework also suggests that the linguistic input is not processed linearly by proceeding step by step from one intake factor through another, or from one intake process through another. Instead, the entire operation is seen as interactive and parallel, responding simultaneously to all available factors and processes at a given point of time. In other words, none of the intake factors by themselves seems to be a *prerequisite* for another to be activated but each is considered to be a *corequisite*. The processing of input data is never consistent; it varies according to varying degrees of influence brought to bear on it by an unstable and as yet unknown configuration of intake factors and intake processes. Different intake factors and intake processes take on different statuses in different learning contexts, thereby significantly affecting the learners' working hypotheses about the TL and their strategies for learning and using it. The configuration also varies widely within an individual learner at different times and situations of learning, and also between learners, thereby accounting for wide variations in the degree of attainment reached by learners.

2.7. CONCLUSION

In this chapter, I explored the concepts of *intake*, *intake factors*, and *intake processes* in order to explain the factors and processes facilitating adult L2 development in formal contexts. I argued that any framework of intake processing must be capable of including multiple intake factors known to play a role in L2 development, and that it must reflect the interactive, parallel, and simultaneous nature of intake processes. Accordingly, I presented an interactive framework by synthesizing theoretical and empirical insights derived from interrelated disciplines such as second-language acquisition, cognitive psychology, information processing, schema theory, and parallel distributed processing.

In addition to input and output, the interactive framework of intake processes presented here consists of a cluster of intake factors (Individual, Negotiation, Tactical, Affective, Knowledge, and Environmental factors) and intake processes (inferencing, structuring, and restructuring). Interweaving and interacting in a synergic relationship, each intake factor shapes and is shaped by the other. The interactive nature of intake factors and intake processes suggests that input can be successfully converted into intake if and only if the intake factors and intake processes are optimally favorable and that consistent absence of one or a combination of these constructs may result in partial learning, or even nonlearning.

The interactive framework presented here casts doubts over the nature and scope of current research in L2 development. For the past 30 years or so, we have been focusing mostly upon narrowly circumscribed research problems within each intake variable, accumulating an impressive array of unrelated and unrelatable findings, which by the very nature of investigation can allow only a limited and limiting view of L2 development. If, as this chapter emphasizes, several intake factors facilitate the course of L2 development, if these factors shape and are shaped by each other, and if they are constantly acted upon by intake processes that are interactive, parallel, and simultaneous, then it is imperative that we reframe our research agenda by focusing on the synergic relationships between and within intake factors and processes in order to understand how they relate to each other, and how that relationship impacts on language learning.

Given the tentative and limited nature of knowledge that can be drawn from L2 research, the classroom teacher is faced with the task of making sense of such knowledge as well as with the task of making use of such knowledge for teaching purposes. In addition, the teacher has to take into account the dynamics of the classroom, which is the arena where learning and teaching is constructed. What is the nature of instructional intervention the teacher can profitably employ in order to construct a pedagogy that can accelerate language learning and accomplish desired learning outcome is the focus of the next chapter.

Chapter 3

Teaching: Input and Interaction

3. INTRODUCTION

We learned in chapter 2 how intake factors and intake processes interweave and interact with each other in as yet undetermined ways to convert parts of language input into learner intake. A crucial dimension of such a conversion, particularly in the context of classroom L2 development, is the relationship between teaching strategies and learning outcomes. Several studies have been conducted to investigate the role and relevance of instruction in the L2 classroom. One of the limitations of these studies is that they have focused narrowly on grammatical instruction rather than on any wider aspect of language teaching. In fact, as learned in chapter 2, this limitation is true not only of research related to teaching effectiveness but also research in second-language acquisition in general and, therefore, we should always keep in mind what Hatch (1978) said a quarter century ago about using research findings for pedagogic purposes: *Apply with caution.*

Systematic investigation into the effect of language teaching (read: grammar teaching) began as an offshoot of what came to be known as *morpheme studies* (Dulay & Burt, 1974; Larsen-Freeman, 1976). These studies attempted to assess whether, among other things, learning a language in classroom settings is different from learning a language in naturalistic environments. They revealed that the acquisition/accuracy order for various grammatical morphemes like singular copula (*'s/is*), plural auxiliary (*are*), possessive (*'s*), third person singular (*-s*), and so forth, is more or less the same regardless of the learner's L1 background, age, and learning environment (i.e., instructed or naturalistic). European researchers Wode (1976),

Felix (1981) and their colleagues also found that the acquisition sequences and strategies of L2 learners in classroom settings paralleled those followed by L2 learners in naturalistic settings. Although these and other studies of a similar kind dealt with only a handful of frequently occurring morphemes among a multitude of grammatical structures that constitute language, they hastily concluded that "the possibility of manipulating and controlling the students' verbal behavior in the classroom is in fact quite limited" (Felix, 1981, p. 109).

Such generalizations raised doubts about the effect of classroom instruction thereby prompting a very basic question: Does L2 instruction make any difference at all? In order to explore this question, Long (1983) reviewed 11 studies on instructed L2 development conducted up to that point and came out with ambiguous results. Six studies showed a positive effect of instruction, three showed minor or no effect, and two were unclear. Long, however, concluded that formal instruction has positive effects on (a) L2 developmental processes, (b) the rate at which learners acquire the language, and (c) their ultimate level of attainment. "Instruction is good for you," he declared rather encouragingly, "regardless of your proficiency level, of the wider linguistic environment in which you receive it, and of the type of test you are going to perform on" (1983, p. 379).

In spite of his encouraging conclusions, Long was concerned that the 11 studies available for his review were hardly the appropriate ones to shed any collective light on the effect of instruction on L2 development. The reason is threefold. First, the studies had very little research design in common to put together to seek any common wisdom. Taken together, they involved three types of learners (English as a second language, English as a foreign language, and Spanish as a second language), from three different age groups (children, adolescents, and adults) with varying proficiency levels (beginning, intermediate, and advanced), learning their target language in three different acquisition environments (rich, poor, and mixed), responding to two different tests (discrete and integrative) that sought to ascertain their learning outcomes. Secondly, as Long himself pointed out, most of the studies had failed to control for overall amount of combined contact and instruction considering the fact that they were conducted in environments where learners had access to the TL through both formal and natural exposure. Finally, and perhaps most importantly, the studies claiming to investigate the relationship between instruction and L2 development had bestowed only a scant attention on specific instructional strategies followed by classroom teachers who participated in the experiments. Besides, several teaching strategies were clubbed together under generic terms thereby ignoring the possible effects of specific classroom strategies. Thus, the early studies on the effect of instruction proved to be ineffectual, to say the least.

In retrospect, it appears that we were asking the wrong question. *Does instruction make a difference in L2 development?* is as pointless and purposeless as the question, *Does nutrition make a difference in human growth?* We can hardly answer the first question in the negative unless we propose and defend the untenable proposition that the human mind is untrainable. We all know through experience that learners do learn at least a part of what is taught and tested. The questions nutritionists normally ask are *What kind of nutrition makes a difference?* and *For who?* Likewise, we should have asked questions such as *What kind of instruction makes a difference? In what context?* and *Using what method?*

It comes as no surprise then that the initial inquiry into the effect of instruction has inevitably led to more focused studies with greater investigative rigor. Later studies (e.g., Donato & Adair-Hauck, 1992; Doughty, 1991; Lightbown, 1992; Pica, 1987; Spada, 1987; Van Patten & Cadierno, 1993) have not only sought to rectify some of the conceptual and methodological flaws found in the early attempts but have also started focusing on the impact of specific teaching strategies on learning-specified language items. Most of these studies, however, still suffered from the earlier drawback of dealing narrowly with grammatical instruction. Reviews of these and other recent studies have shown that instruction does have a role to play (see Doughty, 2003; Norris & Ortega, 2000). In her review of cases for and against L2 instruction, Doughty (2003), for instance, concluded that "instruction is potentially effective, provided it is relevant to learners' needs. However, we will be forced to acknowledge that the evidence to date for either absolute or relative effectiveness of L2 instruction is tenuous at best, owing to improving, but still woefully inadequate, research methodology" (p. 256).

Taken together, studies on L2 instruction suggest that proper instructional intervention at the proper time would be helpful for promoting desired learning outcomes in the L2 classroom. This, of course, is not a startling revelation because any language learning in a classroom context, as against learning a language in a naturalistic setting, inevitably involves some degree and some kind of intervention. We intervene by modifying the content and style of language input, and we intervene by modifying the nature and scope of interactional opportunities. Input modifications and interactional activities, then, constitute the foundational structure of any classroom learning and teaching operation.

3.1. INPUT MODIFICATIONS

It is generally agreed that language input has to be modified in order to make it available and accessible to the learner. What has been the source of disagreement is the type of modifications that should be brought about.

The bone of contention centers around three strands of thought that can be characterized as (a) form-based input modifications, (b) meaning-based input modifications, and (c) form- and meaning-based input modifications.

3.1.1. Form-Based Input Modifications

Historically and until very recently, input modifications have almost always been based on the formal (or structural) properties of the language, whether they relate to grammatical forms or communicative functions. Linguistic forms have been the driving force behind learning objectives, curriculum design, materials production, classroom procedures, and testing techniques. The essence of form-based input modifications, however, has not remained constant. The changing norms can best be captured by positing a product-oriented version and a process-oriented version of form-based input modifications.

The product-oriented version of form-based input modifications treats grammar as a product that can be analyzed, codified, and presented. It relates to the characteristics of grammar teaching as propagated and practiced during the heyday of audiolingualism (see chap. 5, this volume, for details). Within the audiolingual pedagogy, manipulating language input meant selecting grammatical features, sequencing them in some fashion, making them salient for the learner through a predominantly teacher-centered, metalinguistic, decontextualized instruction involving explicit pattern practice and explicit error correction. The learner was expected to observe the grammatical input, examine it, analyze it, imitate it, practice it, internalize it, use it. But, it became increasingly clear that confining the learner to an exclusively product-oriented, form-based language input not only distorted the nature of the target language exposed to the learner but also decreased the learner's potential to develop appropriate language knowledge/ability. In short, the product-oriented version of form-based input modifications turned out to be an extremist position.

The process-oriented version of form-based input modifications treats grammar as a network of systems to be interacted with rather than an objectified body of structures to be mastered. Instead of emphasizing memory, specific rules, and rule articulation, it focuses on understanding, general principles, and operational experience. The input modifications advocated here are still form-based but not based on teaching grammatical structures per se but on creating what Rutherford (1987) called consciousness raising. He explained that consciousness raising

> is the means to an end, not the end itself. That is, whatever it is that is raised to consciousness is not to be looked upon as an artifact or object of study to be committed to memory by the learner and thence recalled by him whenever

sentences have to be produced. Rather, what is raised to consciousness is not the grammatical product but aspects of the grammatical process . . . (p. 104)

In the specific context of L2 learning and teaching, it refers to the deliberate attempt to draw the learners' attention to the formal processes of their L2 in order to increase the degree of explicitness required to promote L2 development. Because *consciousness* is a loaded psychological term that cannot be easily defined, Sharwood-Smith (1991) suggested a more verifiable term, *input enhancement*, to refer to consciousness-raising activities. From a pedagogic point of view, input enhancement serves the purpose of drawing the learner's explicit attention to grammatical features by such activities as highlighting, underlining, rule-giving, and so forth.

The idea of grammatical process was recently expanded by Larsen-Freeman (2000, 2003), who introduced the term, *grammaring*, to refer to long-overlooked qualities of grammar such as that "it is a dynamic process in which forms have meanings and uses in a rational, discursive, flexible, interconnected, and open system" (Larsen-Freeman, 2003, p. 142). Grammaring is seen as the learner's knowledge/ability to use grammatical structures accurately, meaningfully, and appropriately. Language input introduced to the learner then should be modified in such a way as to make the reason underlying a structure transparent. For example, Larsen-Freeman suggests that when two different forms exist in a language, as in

There is a book on the table.

A book is on the table.

the underlying principle behind their variation in meaning or use must be presented. As she explains

the meaning of these two sentences is more less the same, but the sentence with *there* would be used to introduce new information in normal discourse. The second sentence is much more limited in frequency and scope. One of its functions is in giving stage directions to the director of a play, telling the director how to stage some scene in the play. While it may be difficult for students to figure this difference out on their own, the principle will help them learn to look for ways that particular grammar structures are distinctively meaningful and/or appropriate. (Larsen-Freeman, 2000, p. 11)

Although the process-oriented, form-based input modifications appear to have a greater intellectual appeal and instructional relevance than strictly product-oriented, form-based input modifications, it must be remembered that proponents of both subscribe to similar, linguistically motivated learning and teaching principles. That is, they believe that formal properties of the language, both structures and relations, can be systematically analyzed, selected, sequenced, and presented one by one to the learner. They both believe that the learner will be able to put these discrete items together in order to internalize the totality of language. Learners exposed to such input modifications may be able to develop higher levels of analysis of language as system but may not be able to understand the full implications of communicative use. In other words, predominantly form-based input modifications facilitate the development of linguistic knowledge/ability but not necessarily pragmatic knowledge/ability both of which, as we have seen in chapter 2, are required for successful language communication. As a response to this predicament, it was suggested that the focus be shifted from form to meaning.

3.1.2. Meaning-Based Input Modifications

A forceful articulation of the importance of meaning-based input modifications came a while ago from Newmark (1963/1970) who argued that "systematic attention to the grammatical form of utterances is neither a necessary condition nor a sufficient one for successful language learning" and that "teaching particular utterances in contexts which provide meaning and usability to learners is both sufficient . . . and necessary" (p. 217). Because these statements became very influential and are often misinterpreted, it is important to recall the context in which these were made, and also the caveat that accompanied them.

Newmark made these statements in a paper entitled "Grammatical Theory and the Teaching of English as a Foreign Language." The grammatical theory referred to here is Chomskyan transformational grammar, which was newly proposed and widely discussed at that time. Emphasizing the inapplicability of the theory of transformational grammar to language teaching, Newmark asked language teachers to resist the "great temptations" to write new language-teaching textbooks reflecting the "neat and precise" grammatical analysis offered by transformational grammar. It is in this context he suggested that, "we should liberate language teaching from grammatical theory, and should teach the natural use of language" (1963/1971, p. 218). In a follow-up paper, Newmark (1966/1970) further clarified his stand by saying that "the important point is that *the study of grammar as such* is neither necessary nor sufficient for learning to use a language" (p. 226, emphasis added). What he was objecting to is *the study of grammar as such* but was in favor of "a limited kind of structural drill" so long as it is "embedded in a meaningful context" (p. 226).

In spite of the context and the caveat, Newmark's argument formed one of the bases for an exclusively meaning-oriented input modification as exemplified, for instance, in Krashen's input hypothesis. To put it in a nutshell (see chap. 7, this volume, for details), the input hypothesis (Krashen,

1982 and elsewhere) claimed that we acquire language in only one way: by understanding messages, that is, by obtaining comprehensible input. Comprehensible input is defined as i + 1, structures that are a bit beyond the L2 learner's current level of knowledge/ability. It is considered to contain all the grammatical structures the acquirer is ready to acquire, in the right order and right quantity, as long as enough comprehensible input of consistently high quality is provided. Linguistic knowledge/ability is attained necessarily and sufficiently as the result of mere exposure to instances of comprehensible input, which can be provided through meaning-oriented activities such as language games and problem-solving tasks. Form-based language awareness does not play any direct role in L2 development. A similar argument was made by Prabhu (1987), who stated that "the development of competence in a second language requires not systematization of language inputs or maximization of planned practice, but rather the creation of conditions in an effort to cope with communication" (p. 1).

Language-teaching programs that have systematically followed some of the pedagogic features that later characterized the input hypothesis, and for which we have a considerable body of research literature, are the Canadian French immersion programs. These are public school programs in which speakers of English (the majority language) study in French (the minority language). The learners have very little interaction with native speakers of French other than their teachers, and exposure to French comes primarily from teachers and instructional materials. Although the learners seldom reach near native capability, they eventually emerge as competent L2 speakers (Swain & Lapkin, 1982). According to Krashen (1984), immersion "works" because it provides learners with a great deal of comprehensible input thereby proving that "subject-matter teaching *is* language teaching" (pp. 61–62, emphasis in original).

Krashen's enthusiastic endorsement notwithstanding, research based on immersion as well as nonimmersion programs shows that exclusively meaning-oriented input modifications do not lead to desired levels of grammatical accuracy. Several studies (Lightbown 1992; Lightbown & Spada, 1990; Schmidt, 1993; Van Patten 1990) have shown that even though learners exposed to meaning-based input modifications speak fluently and confidently, their speech is marked by numerous grammatical errors. In fact, there is little evidence to show that successful grammar construction can take place solely through meaning-based input modifications. Reviewing more than two decades of research in French immersion classes, Swain (1991) concluded that immersion students are able to understand much of what they hear and read even at early grade levels, and that, although they are well able to get their meaning across in their second language, even at intermediate and higher grade levels, they often do so with nontargetlike morphology and syntax. A probable reason is that language learners who are focusing on meaning may not have the processing space to attend to form at the same time because of limitations on the number of cognitive psychological operations learners can engage in. Whatever the reason, it is clear that "learners do not very readily infer knowledge of the language system from their communicative activities. The grammar, which they must obviously acquire somehow as a necessary resource for use, proves elusive" (Widdowson 1990, p. 161).

It turns out that it is not just grammatical knowledge/ability that proves elusive; there may be problems in developing pragmatic knowledge/ability as well. Citing examples from immersion studies, Swain (1991) argued that "by focusing entirely on meaning, teachers frequently provide learners with inconsistent and possibly random information about their target language use" (p. 241). A specific example she cites to show how meaning-based input modifications can be "functionally restricted" relates to the French pronouns *tu* and *vous,* which carry information about both grammatical concepts (*singular, plural,* or *generic*) and sociolinguistic use (*formal* or *informal*). An analysis of classroom input showed that the teachers used the pronouns largely to denote their grammatical uses; there was scarcely any use of *vous* in its sociolinguistic function marking politeness. This difference is considered the primary reason for the underuse of *vous* as a politeness marker by immersion students.

Furthermore, even if the language input introduced by the teacher is solely meaning-based, there is no way one can prevent learners from explicitly focusing on form, or vice versa. In other words, teachers may control input availability in the classroom; they certainly do not control input acceptability. That belongs to the realm of the learner. Learners may be focusing on both form and meaning regardless of teacher intention and intervention. There are scholars who believe that a combination of form- and meaning-based input is what is really needed.

3.1.3. Form- and Meaning-Based Input Modifications

Some of the carefully designed classroom-oriented experiments conducted in the late 80s and early 90s (Doughty, 1991; Lightbown & Spada, 1990; Spada, 1987; Van Patten & Cadierno, 1993) authenticated what the learners already seem to know, namely, focusing on form and meaning is more beneficial than focusing on either one of them.

In a study on the development of oral communicative skills, Spada (1987) investigated the relationships between instructional differences and learning outcomes in three intermediate level classes of a communicatively based ESL program. Class A received primarily form-based instruction, Class B received both form- and meaning-based instruction, and Class C received primarily meaning-based instruction. Her findings revealed that

Class B registered a significant improvement, and Classes A and C did not improve as much as Class B. She concluded that "neither form-based nor meaning-based instruction in itself is sufficient, but rather, both are required" (p. 153). Her study reinforced her earlier finding that learners require opportunities for both form-focused and function-focused practice in the development of particular skill areas, and if one or the other is lacking they do not appear to benefit as much (Spada, 1986).

In a related study, Lightbown and Spada (1990) investigated the effects of form-focused instruction and corrective feedback in communicative language teaching. Their study was part of a long-term project and the data came from more than a 1000 students in nearly 40 intensive ESL classes and from over 200 students in regular ESL programs. The instructional strategy consisted of meaning-based activities, opportunities for the negotiation of meaning in group work, and the provision of comprehensible input. The teachers who taught these classes differed from each other in terms of the total amount of time they gave to form-focused activities. The researchers analyzed the learners' listening and reading comprehension as well as their ability to speak. They found that form-based instruction within a communicative context contributes to higher levels of language knowledge/ability. Lightbown and Spada (1990) concluded that "accuracy, fluency, and overall communicative skills are probably best developed through instruction that is primarily meaning-based but in which guidance is provided through timely form-focused activities and correction in context" (p.443).

A similar conclusion was reached by Doughty (1991), who conducted an experiment focusing on one grammatical subsystem of English (restrictive relative clauses) with intermediate level international students from seven different L1 backgrounds. They had very little knowledge of English relativization as revealed through a pilot test. They were randomly assigned to one of three groups: two experimental groups (in addition to exposure to relative clauses, the group was provided with an instructional treatment aimed at improving their ability to relativize in English) and a control group (in which they were exposed to relative clauses but received no instruction). Of the two experimental groups, one group (MOG) was given meaning-oriented instruction along with the bringing to prominence of the structural elements of relativization, and the other group (ROG) was given exclusively rule-oriented instruction. The third group was called COG (control group). The study revealed that compared to the control group, both the MOG and ROG groups were equally effective with respect to gain in relativization, but the MOG alone demonstrated substantial comprehension of the overall input. Doughty attributes the overall superior performance of the MOG group to the successful combination of a focus on meaning and the bringing to prominence of the linguistic properties of relativization in the MOG treatment.

The findings of the three experiments just outlined lead us to an interesting proposition, namely, bringing linguistic properties to prominence within the purview of a meaning-focused instructional strategy may change the way language data are recognized by the learner as potential language input, thus favorably shaping intake factors and intake processes (see chap. 2). Such a proposition has been put to test by Van Patten and Cadierno (1993).

In a carefully designed study, Van Patten and Cadierno (1993) investigated the relationship between instructional modifications and *input processing*, a term they use to refer to the process of converting input into intake. Based on a pretest, they randomly selected three groups of learners studying Spanish as an L2 in the United States. The first group received "traditional" instruction on object pronouns and word order, the second received "processing" instruction on the same, and the third received no instruction at all on the targeted items. Traditional instruction involved presenting the learners with explicit explanations concerning the form and position of direct object pronouns within the sentence and then giving them sustained practice, which moved the learners gradually from mechanical drill to communicative drill. At all times, instruction focused on the production of the targeted items by the learners, in other words, on their output. In processing instruction, presentation was dominated by two types of activities that forged form-meaning connections. One type had subjects listening to or reading utterances and then demonstrating that they had correctly assigned argument structure to the targeted items. The second type of activity had subjects respond to the content of an utterance by checking "agree" or "disagree." At no point did processing instruction involve the production of the targeted items by the learners. The results of the experiment showed that unlike traditional instruction, processing instruction altered the way in which the learners recognized language input, which in turn had an effect on the developing knowledge/ability of the learners. Based on the results, Van Patten and Cadierno (1993) concluded that "instruction is more beneficial when it is directed toward how learners perceive and process input rather than when instruction is focused on having learners practice the language via output" (p. 54).

In the context of helping learners actively engage form and meaning in a principled way, Long (1991, 1996) proposed what is called *focus on form* (not to be confused with form-focused input already discussed for which Long uses the term *focus on forms*—note the plural. In order to avoid potential terminological confusion, I hereafter use its abbreviated version, FonF, as suggested by Doughty & Williams, 1998). According to Long, FonF "overtly draws students' attention to linguistic elements as they arise incidentally in lessons whose overriding focus is on meaning or communication" (Long, 1991, p. 46) and "consists of an occasional shift of attention to linguistic code features—by the teacher and/ or one or more students—triggered by perceived problems with comprehension or production. (Long & Robinson, 1998, p. 23). In other words, the learner's attention to linguistic features will be drawn explicitly if and only if it is necessitated by communicative demand.

The input modification required for FonF places emphasis on designing pedagogic tasks based on the future language needs of a particular group of learners, tasks such as attending a job interview, making an airline reservation, reading a restaurant menu or a journal abstract, writing a lab report, or taking a driving test. For instance, learners may be given a task the solution of which requires them

> to synthesize information on economic growth in Japan from two or more written sources and use it to graph trends in imports and exports over a 10-year period. Successful completions of the task involves them in reading (and rereading) brief written summaries of sales trends for different sectors of the Japanese economy, each of which uses such terms as *rose, fell, grew, sank, plummeted, increased, decreased, declined, doubled, deteriorated, and exceeded.* The frequency of these lexical items in the input, due to their repeated use in the different passages, and/or their being underlined or italicized, makes them more salient, and so increase the likelihood of their being noticed by students. (Long & Robinson, 1998, pp. 24–25)

A task like this, as Doughty (2003) pointed out, helps learners integrate forms and meaning, create their metalinguistic awareness, and increase their noticing capacity all of which, as we discussed in chapter 2, promote successful intake processing and ultimately language development.

An unmistakable lesson we learn from the aforementioned discussion is that language should be presented to learners in such a way that they recognize it as potential language input. We also learn that instruction should help learners obtain language input in its full functional range, relevant grammatical rules, and sociolinguistic norms in context along with helpful corrective feedback. In other words, both form- and meaning-based input modifications are essential for an effective L2 teaching program. Yet, just the input, however modified, is not sufficient. What is additionally required for learners to recognize and internalize form-meaning relationships is the opportunity for meaningful interaction, and hence the importance of interactional activities in classroom L2 learning and teaching.

3.2. INTERACTIONAL ACTIVITIES

Although the L2 literature presents several terms with attendant conceptual ambiguities to refer to conversation in the classroom, the two that have been widely used are *interaction* and *negotiation*. Both of them are used to mean something that is very different from their general usage involving intricate sociolinguistic norms governing communication (see, e.g., the discussion on Hymes' SPEAKING acronym in chap. 1, this volume). The term *interaction* or *negotiation* or *negotiated interaction* generally refers to conversational exchanges that arise when participants try to accommodate potential or actual problems of understanding, using strategies such as comprehension checks or clarification checks. Such an exercise is also perceived to promote the learners' processing capacity specifically by helping them with conscious noticing required to convert input into intake (Gass, 1997; Long, 1996).

Characterizing such a definition of interaction as limited and limiting, I have argued elsewhere (Kumaravadivelu, 2003a) that it is beneficial to isolate three interrelated dimensions of interaction and have discussed them using, although it is a little bit of a stretch, Halliday's macrofunctions of language: textual, interpersonal, and ideational (see chap. 1, this volume, for details). I have suggested that in the context of classroom communication, we should actually talk about interaction as a textual activity, interaction as an interpersonal activity, and interaction as an ideational activity. The first refers to the linguistic realizations that create coherent written or spoken texts that fit a particular interactional event, enabling L2 learners and their interlocutors to understand the message as intended. Specifically, it focuses on syntactic and semantic conversational signals, and its outcome is measured primarily in terms of linguistic knowledge/ability. The second refers to the participants' potential to establish and maintain social relationships and have interpersonal encounters, and its outcome is measured in terms of personal rapport created in the classroom. The third refers to an expression of one's self-identity based on one's experience of the real or imaginary world in and outside the classroom. Specifically, it focuses on ideas and emotions the participants bring with them, and its outcome is measured primarily in terms of pragmatic knowledge/ability. By introducing such a tripartite division, I am not suggesting that the three dimensions are equal or separate. Any successful interactional activity will mark the realization of all three dimensions in varying degrees of sophistication. This division is principally for ease of description and discussion. It is fair to say that so far, L2 interactional research has focused largely on interaction as a textual activity, and to some extent on interaction as interpersonal activity. It has almost completely ignored interaction as an ideational activity. Let us briefly consider each of them.

3.2.1. Interaction as a Textual Activity

Most L2 interactional studies treat interaction primarily as a textual activity in which learners and their interlocutors modify their speech phonologically, morphologically, lexically, and syntactically in order to maximize chances of mutual understanding, and minimize instances of communication breakdown. Such a seemingly excessive preoccupation with linguistic aspects of interaction can best be understood in a historical perspective. A major impetus for L2 interactional studies came from research on caretaker talk conducted in the context of first-language acquisition. Empirical studies carried out during the 1970s (R. Brown 1973; Snow 1972; Snow & Ferguson 1977, and others) showed that the mother's speech to the child contained remarkably well-formed utterances characterized by a number of formal adjustments in comparison to speech used in adult–adult conversations. The formal adjustments include: a lower mean length of utterances, the use of sentences with a limited range of syntactic–semantic relations, few subordinate and coordinate constructions, modified pitch, intonation and rhythm, and a high level of redundancy.

Extending the concept of *caretaker talk* to L2 learners, researchers studied modified speech used by competent speakers of a language to outsiders who were felt to have very limited or no knowledge/ability of it at all. This modified speech has been referred to as foreigner talk. Ferguson (1975) found that foreigner talk is very similar to caretaker talk. Specifically, he found that foreigner talk is characterized by a slow rate of delivery, clear articulation, pauses, emphatic stress, exaggerated pronunciation, paraphrasing, substitution of lexical items by synonyms, and omission, addition, and replacement of syntactic features. Hopping from foreigner talk to teacher talk was an easy and logical step. Not surprisingly then, teacher talk, that is, the language a teacher uses to talk to L2 learners, was found to contain characteristics of foreigner talk (Henzl, 1974). Further, it was found that teacher talk increased in linguistic complexity with the increasing proficiency level of the learners (Gaies, 1977).

Recognizing that L2 interactional studies so far had narrowly focused on input, be it foreigner talk or teacher talk, and hence had overlooked "the most important factor of all," Hatch (1978) observed: "it is not enough to look at input and to look at frequency; the important thing is to look at the corpus as a whole and examine the interactions that take place within conversations to see how that interaction, itself, determines frequency of forms and how it shows language functions evolving" (p. 403). The lead given by Hatch has spawned several studies on the role of interaction resulting in a substantial body of literature.

Foremost among the L2 interactionists is Long (1981, and elsewhere), who makes a distinction between modified input and modified interaction. The former involves a modification of language input that has short phrases and sentences, fewer embeddings, and greater repetition of nouns and verbs, whereas the latter involves a modification of the conversational structure that has a considerable number of comprehension checks, confirmation checks, and clarification checks. As paraphrased by Allwright and

Bailey (1991), a comprehension check is the speaker's query of the interlocutors to see if they have understood what was said: *Do you understand?* or *Do you get what I'm saying?* A confirmation check is the speaker's query as to whether or not the speaker's (expressed) understanding of the interlocutor's meaning is correct: *Oh, so are you saying you did live in London?* A clarification check is a request for further information or help in understanding something the interlocutor has previously said: *I don't understand exactly. What do you mean?*

Long found that although modified input is unquestionably important, it is participation in meaningful interaction made possible through modified interaction that significantly contributed to comprehension leading to L2 development. Based on his work, he proposed a two-part hypothesis: (a) interactional modifications geared to solving communication difficulties help to make input comprehensible, and (2) comprehensible input promotes L2 development. Subsequent research by Pica, Young, and Doughty (1987) and others confirmed the first, but not the second, part of the hypothesis. They found that learners who were exposed to linguistically unmodified input with opportunities to negotiate meaning understood it better than learners who were exposed to linguistically simplified version of the input but were offered no opportunity for such negotiation.

Studies on interaction as a textual activity have clearly demonstrated that interactional modifications help learners become aware of form-meaning relationships. Several studies have questioned the claim that modified input can be made comprehensible without any active participation on the part of the learner. For instance, in a comparative study on the effects of input modifications and of interactional modifications, Pica et al. (1987) found that comprehension was assisted by the interactional modifications, and that input modifications, even with reduced linguistic complexity, had no such effect.

One does not have to look far to see the reasons for this. Input modifications, though crucial, do not by themselves offer opportunities for interaction. They may make some of the structural–semantic features salient, but they do not make structural–semantic relationships transparent. In other words, input modifications may provide potentially acceptable input; but, they do not help learners learn the relationship between form and meaning in order to develop the necessary knowledge/ability to convey their intended meaning in an interactive speech event. It is the learner's interactional efforts that make form-meaning relationships in the TL data acceptable and internalizable. As Allwright and Bailey (1991) pointed out, "it is the work required to negotiate that spurs language acquisition, rather than the intended outcome of the work—comprehensible input" (p. 123). Interactional modifications help learners focus on the meaningful use of particular linguistic features, and practice the productive use of those features. They help learners stretch their limited linguistic repertoire, thereby resulting in opportunities for further L2 development (for more details, see Gass, 1997).

Although classroom interaction by definition includes learner production, the role of learner output in L2 development was not given any serious consideration for a long time. The scope of interaction as a linguistic activity has now been extended to include the effect of learner output, particularly after the emergence of two output-related hypotheses: the comprehensible output hypothesis (Swain, 1985) and the auto-input hypothesis (Schmidt & Frota, 1986). Both these hypotheses emphasize the role played by the learner's output in shaping L2 development. They highlight the importance of learner output produced in the process of meaningful interaction as it provides the learner with the opportunity to form and test initial hypotheses, and the opportunity to pay particular attention to the linguistic means of communicative expression. A study by Pica, Holliday, Lewis, and Morgenthaler (1989) found that comprehensible output was an outcome of linguistic demands placed on the learner in the course of interaction. Further research by Swain (1995) and others has confirmed the importance of output.

The precise role of interactional modifications in general has not been sufficiently investigated (see Gass, 2003, for a recent review). However, there seems to be a consensus among researchers that L2 learning environment must include opportunities for learners to engage in meaningful interaction with competent speakers of their L2 if they are to discover the formal and functional rules necessary for comprehension and production. As the studies cited earlier show, what enables learners to move beyond their current receptive and productive capacities when they need to understand unfamiliar language input or when required to produce a comprehensible message are opportunities to modify and restructure their interaction with their interlocutors until mutual comprehension is reached.

That meaningful interaction is crucial for L2 development has been widely recognized. There has not been adequate recognition, however, that providing interactional opportunities means much more than providing opportunities for an explicit focus on linguistic features or for a possible form-meaning relationships embedded in the input data. Studies that approach interaction primarily as a textual activity can offer only a limited perspective on the role of interaction in L2 development, for they treat interactional modifications as no more than conversational adjustments. Clearly, interaction is much broader a construct than that. It entails, minimally, a spectrum of linguistic, social, and cultural constructs that create the very context of language communication. Therefore, in order to facilitate an effective interplay of various intake factors and intake processes discussed in the previous chapter, we may have to go beyond the narrow confines of interaction as a textual activity, and consider the role of interaction as an interpersonal activity and also interaction as an ideational activity, among other yet unknown possibilities.

3.2.2. Interaction as an Interpersonal Activity

Unlike interaction as a textual activity that deals with conversational adjustments, interaction as an interpersonal activity deals with interpersonal communication. Classroom community is a minisociety nested within a larger society. It has its own rules, regulations, and role relationships. Interaction in such a minisociety is essentially a social process involving, as Breen (1985) pointed out, all its participants in verbal and nonverbal interaction that exists on a continuum from ritualized, predictable, phatic communion to dynamic, unpredictable, diversely interpreted communication, just as in any social interaction. Classroom community presents different contexts for different participants who bring different social realities with them. It also represents a tension between the internal world of the individual and the social world of the group. This tension requires individuals to adapt their learning process to the sociopsychological resources of the group, just as the group's psychic and social process unfolds from the individual contributions of a learner.

Interaction as an interpersonal activity, therefore, has the potential to create a conducive atmosphere in which the other two interactional activities—textual and ideational—can flourish. Such a potential has not been adequately explored, much less exploited. Studies conducted by Wong-Fillmore (e.g., 1989) reveal that social processes are as important as cognitive processes for successful L2 development. As we have seen in chapter 2, social processes are steps by which both the learners and competent speakers of the TL create and shape appropriate social settings in which it is possible and desirable to communicate by means of the TL. In a research study, Donato and Adair-Hauck (1992) showed how groups or dyads engaged in social interactions both in and outside the classroom foster the formation of linguistic awareness in learners. Taking a Vygotskyan perspective to social processes of language learning, they argue for an interactional approach in which social discourse is central to the teaching–learning relationship.

Vygotskyan sociocultural theory provides a richer and deeper interpretation of the role of interaction in the language classroom (Hall, 2002; Lantoff, 2000). It focuses on the construction of interpersonal interactions where participants actively and dynamically negotiate not just textual meaning, but also their social relationships. Such an approach treats interaction as a social practice that shapes and reshapes language learning. Thus, as Ellis (1999) explained, "socio-cultural theory has the greater potential as it emphasizes the collaborative nature in meaning making in discourse in general, not just in exchanges where communication breakdown occurs" (p. 224).

In fact, at the pedagogic core of interaction as an interpersonal activity are opportunities for increased learner–learner interaction and greater topic control on the part of the learner. Learner–learner interaction, otherwise known in the L2 literature as nonnative speaker/nonnative speaker (NNS/NNS) interaction, was initially thought to provide what is called "junky" input data, which can hardly help on successful L2 learning. However, Yule and Gregory (1989), for instance, found "sufficient evidence to suggest that the benefits of modified interaction, in terms of creating more comprehensible input, can actually be obtained in a situation which does not involve native speaking interlocutors" (p. 42). Similarly other studies on classroom interactional analysis demonstrate that NNS/NNS interactive discourse is equally beneficial in promoting L2 comprehension and production (see Gass, 1997). According to these studies, NNS/NNS partners produce more and frequent instances of interactional modifications, and employ more communication strategies than do NS/NNS partners thereby enhancing their chances of L2 comprehension.

Closely linked to the opportunity made available for learner–learner interaction is the flexibility given to learners in nominating topics for discussion in class. During the early part of interactional research, Hatch (1978) reported that giving the learners the freedom to nominate topics provided an effective basis for interactional opportunities. Although not enough work has been done on the effect of learner topic control, a study by Slimani (1989) found that learners benefited more from self- and peer-nominated topics than from teacher nominated topics. Reflecting on learner-topic control, Ellis (1992) rightly observes,

> Having control over the topic is also one way of ensuring that the linguistic complexity of the input is tailored to the learner's own level. Better opportunities for negotiating meaning when a communication problem arises are likely to occur. Topic control may also stimulate more extensive and more complex production on the part of the learner (p. 177)

3.2.3. Interaction as an Ideational Activity

Both interaction as textual and interaction as interpersonal activities can provide only a limited perspective because they do not take into account the social, cultural, political, and historical processes and practices that shape language learning and teaching. In other words, they both fail to recognize language as ideology (cf. chap. 1, this volume). Language, as Weeden (1997) so aptly stated, "is the place where actual and possible forms of social organization and their likely social and political consequences are defined and contested. Yet it is also the place where our sense of ourselves, our subjectivity, is constructed" (p. 21). Thus, language is not simply a network of interconnected linguistic systems; rather, it is a web of interlinked sociopolitical and historical factors that shape one's identity and voice. In such a context, the development of the ability to speak one's mind and "the ability to impose reception" (Bourdieu, 1991) are of paramount importance. It is, therefore, no longer sufficient if interactional modifications provide the learners only with the opportunity to fix communication breakdowns or to foster personal relationships in class. They must also provide them with some of the tools necessary for identity formation and social transformation.

Nobody emphasized this critical nature of education more and with greater conviction than critical pedagogists such as Giroux, Shor, Simon, and others who, influenced by the pioneering thoughts of Paulo Freire, looked at the classroom as an ideological site—a site that is socially constructed, politically motivated, and historically determined. Therefore, critical pedagogy has to empower classroom participants "to critically appropriate forms of knowledge outside of their immediate experience, to envisage versions of a world which is 'not yet' in order to alter the grounds on which life is lived" (Simon, 1988, p. 2). Such a pedagogy would take seriously the sociopolitical, historical conditions that create the cultural forms and interested knowledge that give meaning to the lives of teachers and learners. "In one sense, this points to the need to develop theories, forms of knowledge, and social practices that work with the experiences that people bring to the pedagogical setting" (Giroux, 1988, p.134).

Critical pedagogists call for an "empowering education" that relates "personal growth to public life by developing strong skills, academic knowledge, habits of inquiry, and critical curiosity about society, power, inequality, and change" (Shor 1992, p. 15); and one that helps students explore the subject matter in its sociopolitical, historical contexts with critical themes integrated into student language and experience. They consider contemporary language education "as somewhat bizarre in that it legitimates and limits language issues as technical and developmental" (Giroux & Simon, 1988, p. 131) and believe that language education must be "viewed as a form of learning that not only instructs students into ways of 'naming' the world but also introduces them to particular social relations" (Giroux & Simon, 1988, p. 131).

In the same vein, critical linguists argue that "all representation is mediated, moulded by the value-systems that are ingrained in the medium (language in this case) used for representation; it challenges common sense by pointing out that something could have been represented in some other way, with a very different significance" (Fowler, 1996, p. 4). Saying that ideology and power that constitute dominant discourses are hidden from ordinary people, critical linguists seek to make them visible by engaging in a type of critical discourse analysis that "is more issue-oriented than theory-oriented" (van Dijk, 1997, p. 22). By doing so, they hope to shed light on the way power relations work within the society. They thus move from the local to the global displaying "how discourse cumulatively contributes to the reproduction of macro structures . . ." (Fairclough, 1995, p. 42).

As can be expected, critical linguists pointedly emphasize the role of critical language awareness in developing sociopolitical consciousness. Fairclough, in particular, believes that critical language awareness "can lead to reflexive analysis of practices of domination implicit in the transmission and learning of academic discourse, and the engagement of learners in the struggle to contest and change such practices" (Fairclough, 1995, p. 222). He further points out that language learners can learn to contest practices of domination only if the relationship between language and power is made explicit to them.

Pointing out that researchers in L2 interactional analysis have shied away from any serious engagement with the ideological forces acting upon classroom discourse, I have proposed what is called *critical classroom discourse analysis* (CCDA; Kumaravadivelu, 1999a). The primary function of such an analysis is to play a reflective role, enabling teachers to reflect on and to cope with sociocultural and sociopolitical structures that directly or indirectly shape the character and content of classroom interaction. I have argued that

> language teachers can ill afford to ignore the sociocultural reality that influences identity formation in and outside the classroom nor can they afford to separate learners' linguistic needs and wants from their sociocultural needs and wants. Negotiation of discourse meaning and its analysis should not be confined to the acquisitional aspects of input and interaction, or to the instructional imperatives of form/function focused language learning activities or to the conversational routines of turn-taking and turn-giving sequences; instead, they should also take into account discourse participants' complex and competing expectations and beliefs, identities and voices, fears and anxieties. (Kumaravadivelu, 1999a, p. 472)

Drawing from the CCDA perspective, I suggest that interaction as an ideational activity must necessarily address questions such as:

- If classroom interaction is socially constructed, politically motivated, and historically determined, what are the ways in which we can study and understand the impact of these forces on interactional modifications?
- If discourse participants bring to the classroom their racialized, stratified, and gendered experiences, how can we identify the way(s) in

which these experiences motivate the style and substance of classroom interaction?

- If the objective of language education should not be merely to facilitate effective language use but also to promote critical engagement among discourse participants, then how can we analyze and assess the extent to which critical engagement is facilitated in the classroom?
- If the learner's voice has to be recognized and respected, how might their personal purposes, attitudes, and preferred ways of doing things be reconciled with interactional rules and regulations, and instructional aims and objectives?
- If negotiation of discourse meaning is not confined to the acquisitional aspects of input and interaction, but include expectations and beliefs, identities, and voices, fears and anxieties of the participants, how might such a comprehensive treatment help or hinder the proper management of classroom interaction?
- If classroom discourse lends itself to multiple perspectives depending on discourse participants' preconceived notions of learning, teaching, and learning outcomes, how can we identify and understand possible mismatches between intentions and interpretations of classroom aims and events?

Clearly, investigations of these and other related questions will provide additional insights necessary to determine the nature and scope of interaction as an ideational activity.

An increasing number of scholars in L2 learning and teaching have expressed similar critical thoughts about power and inequality in L2 education as well. For example, Norton (2000) introduced the concept of *investment,* which presupposes that when language learners interact, they are not only exchanging information but "are constantly organizing and reorganizing a sense of who they are and how they relate to the social world. Thus an investment in the target language is also an investment in a learner's own identity, an identity which is constantly changing across time and space" (pp. 10–11). Similarly, Benesch (2001), demonstrated how "all teaching is ideological, whether or not the politics are acknowledged" (p. 46), and has shown us how teaching English for academic purposes can usefully address students' multiple identities by engaging them in decisions affecting their lives in and out of school. Hall (2002) argued for a teaching agenda that is embedded in a sociohistorical and/or sociopolitical authority. Johnston (2003) called for a particular way of *seeing* the language classroom and has sought "to reveal the value-laden nature of our work in the language classroom and to provide tools for analyzing that work" (p. 5). A common thread that runs through all these works is an unfailing emphasis on interaction as an ideational activity.

To sum up this section on interactional activities, if interaction as a textual activity focuses on formal concepts, and interaction as an interpersonal activity focuses on social context, then interaction as an ideational activity may be said to focus on ideological content. If the first enables learners to modify conversational signals, the second encourages them to initiate interactional topics, the third empowers them to construct their individual identity. If first measures quality of interaction in terms of gains in linguistic knowledge, the second measures it in terms of gains in sociocultural knowledge. The three types of interaction may be said to produce three types of discourse: (a) interaction as a textual activity produces instructional discourse resulting in better conversational understanding; (b) interaction as an interpersonal activity produces informational discourse resulting in superior social communication; and (c) interaction as an ideational activity produces ideological discourse resulting in greater sociopolitical consciousness. These three types of activities, however, should not be viewed as hierarchical, that is, they should not be associated with the traditional levels of proficiency—beginning, intermediate, and advanced. From a language-acquisitional point of view, they make it easier for learners of various levels to notice potential language input, and recognize syntactic–semantic relationships embedded in the input, thereby maximizing their learning potential.

Instructional design that deals with the selection and sequencing of language content in order to maximize the interplay between input and interaction on one hand, and the learner and the learning process on the other hand, is yet another important piece of the pedagogic puzzle. In the next section, I turn to the design issues under the general rubric: content specifications.

3.3. CONTENT SPECIFICATIONS

One of the essential components of any language teaching program is *syllabus* or *curriculum,* which specifies the *what* or the content of language learning and teaching. The two terms are often used interchangeably although they may indicate a hierarchical relationship where curriculum refers broadly to all aspects of language policy, language planning, teaching methods, and evaluation measures, whereas syllabus relates narrowly to the specification of content and the sequencing of what is to be taught. This section is limited to syllabus as a content-specifier.

3.3.1. Syllabus Characteristics

A well-designed language teaching syllabus seeks mainly (a) to clarify the aims and objectives of learning and teaching, and (b) to indicate the classroom procedures the teacher may wish to follow. More specifically, any syllabus, according to Breen (2001, p. 151), should ideally provide the following:

- A clear framework of knowledge and capabilities selected to be appropriate to overall aims;
- continuity and a sense of direction in classroom work for teacher and students;
- a record for other teachers of what has been covered in the course;
- a basis for evaluating students' progress;
- a basis for evaluating the appropriateness of the course in relation to overall aims and student needs, identified both before and during the course;
- content appropriate to the broader language curriculum, the particular class of learners, and the educational situation and wider society in which the course is located.

Of course, the assumption behind this ideal list of syllabus objectives is that they will enable teaching to become more organized and more effective. In that sense, a syllabus is more a *teaching* organizer than a *learning* indicator, although a well-conceived and well-constructed syllabus is supposed to relate as closely as possible to learning processes.

But to expect any close connection between teaching design and learning device is to ignore the role of learner intake factors on intake processes that we discussed in chapter 2. It is precisely for this reason Corder (1967) talked about the notion of a "built-in-syllabus" that learners themselves construct based on the language content presented to them and in conjunction with intake factors and processes. As Corder rightly asserted, the learner syllabus is organic rather than linear, that is, learners appear to learn several items simultaneously rather than sequentially retaining some, rejecting others and reframing certain others. What is therefore needed is a psycholinguistic basis for syllabus construction.

A well-known work that attempted to determine a possible set of psycholinguistically valid criteria for syllabus construction was reported by Manfred Pienemann and his colleagues. In a series of empirical studies, Pienemann (1984, 1987) investigated the acquisitional sequence of German word order rules:

Stage 1: X = canonical order

Romance learners of German as a Second Language (GSL) start out with a subject–verb–object order as their initial hypothesis about German word order, for example, *die kinder spielen mit ball* ('the children play with the ball').

Stage 2: X + 1 adverb-preposing

For example, *da kinder spielen* ('there children play'). This preposing rule is optional in German. But once this rules is applied, Standard German requires a word order like 'there play children' (i.e., inversion).

Stage 3: X + 2 = verb separation

For example, *alle kinder muß die pause machen* ('all children must the break have'). Before the verb separation is acquired, the word order in the interlanguage is the same as in sentences with main verbs only (cf. the English equivalent—*all children must have a break*). Verb separation is obligatory in Standard German.

Stage 4: X + 3 = inversion

For example, *dann hat sie wieder die knoch gebringt* ('then has she again the bone bringed'). In Standard German, subject and inflected verbal element have to be inverted after preposing of elements.

From a group of Italian children learning German as a second language in a naturalistic environment, Pienemann selected 10 who were either at Stage 2 or Stage 3 in their L2 development. The subjects were given classroom instruction for 2 weeks on the structure from Stage 4, that is, inversion. When they were tested for the development of the newly instructed structure, Pienemann found that children who were at Stage 3 progressed to Stage 4, but children who were at Stage 2 remained at the same stage. The study, he surmised, demonstrated that the relevant acquisitional stages are interrelated in such a way that at each stage, the processing prerequisites for the following stage are developed.

Based on his findings, Pienemann proposed what he called a *learnability/ teachability hypothesis*. The learnability hypothesis states that learners can benefit from classroom instruction only when they are psycholinguistically ready for it. The learnability of a structure in turn constrains the effectiveness of teaching, which is the teachability hypothesis. The teachability hypothesis predicts that instruction can only promote language acquisition if the interlanguage of the L2 learner is close to the point when the structure to be taught is acquired in the natural setting so that sufficient processing prerequisites are developed.

Notice that the teachability hypothesis does not claim that teaching has no influence whatsoever on L2 development. Rather, it maintains that the influence of teaching is restricted to the learning items for which the learner is ready to process. Pienemann argued that, provided the learner is at the appropriate acquisitional stage, instruction can improve acquisition with respect to (a) the speed of acquisition, (b) the frequency of rule application, and (c) the different linguistic contexts in which the rule has to be applied. From his findings, Pienemann derived two general tenets for L2 teaching:

> The principles of L2 development are not only a more reliable background for psycholinguistically plausible simple–complex criteria in material grading than the present intuitive procedures, but they are a necessary background for grading, since formal L2 learning is subject to a set of learning principles which are shared by formal and natural L2 developments. Thus, teaching is only possible within the margin determined by these principles. As a consequence, any learning task which contradicts these principles is not-learnable; it would ask too much of the learner. (Pienamann, 1984, pp. 40–41)

The learnability/teachability hypothesis as an idea makes eminent sense and has pointed toward a fruitful line of research (see Pienamann, 2003, for a recent review of his and related works). However, its validity and its applicability have been questioned because of the small size of the sample and also because of practical problems, like identifying the learners' current state of grammar. Besides, further research by others (e.g., Lightbown, 1985) demonstrated that classroom learners develop their language in a sequence that has no bearing on the sequence introduced by the teacher. The general consensus now is that we just do not have adequate knowledge of the learner's language-processing capacity in order to coordinate the teaching sequence with learning sequence.

In spite of the advances made in psycholinguistic research, our rationale for selecting and grading language input presented to the learner is no more objective today than it was more than a quarter century ago when Mackay (1965) discussed the highly subjective notions of "difficulty" and "complexity." Pointing out that selection is an "inherent" characteristic of any language teaching enterprise because, "it is impossible to teach the whole of language," Mackey (1965) identified three major criteria for selection: *frequency, range,* and *availability.* Frequency refers to the items that occur the most often in the linguistic input that the learners are likely to encounter. It is, therefore, tied to the linguistic needs and wants of the learners. Range, on the other hand, is the spread of an item across texts or contexts. In other words, an item that is found and used in several communicative contexts is more important than the one that is confined to one or two contexts. Although frequency of an item answers the question how often it occurs, range answers the questions where it is used, by whom, and for what purposes. Availability relates to the degree to which an item is necessary and appropriate, and it also corresponds to the readiness with which it is remembered and used.

Gradation deals with sequencing (which comes before which) and grouping (what goes with what) of linguistic items. According to Kelly (1969), syllabus designers have historically used three basic principles for determining the sequencing of linguistic input: *complexity, regularity,* and *productivity.* The first principle suggests a movement from the easy to the difficult, the second from the regular to the irregular, and the third from the more useful to the less useful. Unlike sequencing, grouping is concerned with the systems of a language, and its structures (Mackey, 1965). Grouping attempts to answer the question: What sounds, words, phrases, or grammatical structures can be grouped and taught together? For instance, the simple present (habitual) may be grouped with words like *usually, often,* and *every,* as in *I go to the park every weekend.* Similarly, words may be grouped together by association (*chair, table, furniture, seat, sit,* etc.).

The putting together of the selected and graded language input is generally governed by the overall theoretical stance adopted by the syllabus designer. Once again, the L2 literature presents a plethora of syllabuses as reflected in labels such as the structural syllabus, the notional-functional syllabus, the task-based syllabus, the discourse syllabus, the skill-based syllabus, the content-based syllabus, the process-syllabus, the procedural syllabus, and so forth. Although one can discern subtle and sometimes significant variations among these in terms of content as well as method of teaching, there are certainly overlapping features among them. A fruitful way of understanding the basic philosophy governing these types of syllabus is to put them into broad classifications.

3.3.2. Syllabus Classifications

Nearly a quarter century ago, Wilkins (1976) proposed two broad classifications of syllabus: synthetic syllabus and analytic syllabus. The underlying assumption behind the synthetic syllabus is that a language system can be (a) analyzed into its smaller units of grammatical structures, lexical items, or functional categories; (b) classified in some manageable and useful way; and (c) presented to the learner one by one for their understanding and assimilation. The learners then are expected to synthesize all the separate elements in order to get the totality of the language. Because the synthesis is done by the learner, the syllabus is dubbed synthetic. The language-centered as well as learner-centered methods discussed in chapter 5 and chapter 6 follow the synthetic syllabus. As we see in much detail in those chapters, language-centered pedagogists devised suitable classroom procedures for teachers to present, and help learners synthesize, discrete items of grammar and vocabulary while learner-centered pedagogists did the same, adding notional and functional categories to the linguistic items.

In the analytic syllabus, the language input is presented to the learner, not piece by piece, but in fairly large chunks. These chunks will not have any specific linguistic focus; instead, they will bring the learner's attention to the communicative features of the language. They are connected texts in the form of stories, games, problems, tasks, and so forth. It is the responsibility of the learner to analyze the connected texts into its smaller constituent elements, hence the term, *analytic*. Learning-centered methods discussed in chapter 7 adhere to the analytic approach to syllabus construction.

It is not the purpose of this chapter to discuss in detail how these syllabus types are linked to other aspects of language teaching such as teaching strategies, textbook production, and evaluation measures. These will be explained with examples as we discuss different categories of method in Part II of the volume.

3.4. CONCLUSION

In this chapter, I focused on various aspects of input, interaction, and syllabus design as they impact on classroom instruction. In spite of the impressive knowledge we have gained on the nature and relevance of input and interactional modifications, we have only a limited understanding of their role in L2 learning and teaching. A primary reason is that, as mentioned earlier, studies on classroom instruction have focused generally and narrowly on the impact of grammatical instruction rather than on the intricate and intractable issue of the interplay between input and interaction on one hand and between them and intake factors and intake processes on the other hand. The fact that research on instructional modifications has not substantively addressed this crucial relationship should have a sobering influence on our readiness to draw implications for pedagogic purposes.

But still, applied linguists are left with no option but to make use of the still developing knowledge for drawing useful and useable ideas for language teaching. According to Corder (1984),

> There are those who believe that second language acquisition research is still at such a preliminary stage that it is premature to base any proposals for language teaching upon it yet. There are others, among whom I count myself, who believe that it is the task of the applied linguist to make practical use of whatever knowledge is available at the time. We cannot constantly be waiting to see what is around the next corner. (p. 58)

Indeed, without waiting to see what is around the next corner, applied linguists have, from time to time, readily conceived and constructed a succession of language-teaching methods based on insights from whatever research findings that were available to them. In the same way, I attempt to use the current state of knowledge to describe and evaluate their successes and failures in order to see what we can learn from them. More specifically, I use the features of language, learning, and teaching discussed so far to take a close and critical look at major categories of language teaching methods. With that objective in mind, let us turn to Part II.

Part Two

LANGUAGE TEACHING METHODS

Chapter 4

Constituents and Categories of Methods

4. INTRODUCTION

In Part One, I discussed the fundamental features of language, language learning, and language teaching that, I believe, have to be considered in conceiving, constructing, or critiquing any coherent and comprehensive L2 pedagogy. In this second part, I take a critical look at some established language teaching methods to see how far they address those fundamental features. But first, certain key terms and concepts constituting language teaching operations have to be explained. I also need to provide the rationale behind the categorization of language teaching methods presented in this book.

4.1. CONSTITUENTS OF LANGUAGE TEACHING METHODS

A variety of labels such as approach, design, methods, practices, principles, procedures, strategies, tactics, techniques, and so on are used to describe various elements constituting language teaching. A plethora of terms and labels can hardly facilitate a meaningful and informed discussion in any area of professional activity. In this section, I attempt to tease out some of the terminological and conceptual ambiguities surrounding some of the terms and concepts used in the field of second and foreign-language teaching.

4.1.1. Method and Methodology

Method is central to any language teaching enterprise. Many of us in the language teaching profession use the term, method, so much and so often that we seldom recognize its problematic nature. For instance, we are hardly aware of the fact that we use the same term, method, to refer to two different elements of language teaching: method as proposed by theorists, and method as practiced by teachers. What the teachers actually do in the classroom is different from what is advocated by the theorists. In fact, classroom-oriented research conducted by Kumaravadivelu (1993a), Nunan (1987), Thornbury (1996), and others clearly shows that even teachers who claim to follow a particular method do not actually adhere to the basic principles associated with it.

One way of clearing the confusion created by the indiscriminate use of the term, method, is to make a distinction between method and *methodology*. For the purpose of this book, I consistently use method to refer to established methods conceptualized and constructed by experts in the field (see text to come). I use the term, methodology, to refer to what practicing teachers actually do in the classroom in order to achieve their stated or unstated teaching objectives. This distinction is nothing new; it is implicit in some of the literature on language teaching. Such a distinction is, in fact, the basis by which Mackey (1965) differentiated what he called *method analysis* from *teaching analysis*. He rightly asserted:

> any meaning of method must first distinguish between what a teacher teaches and what a book teaches. It must not confuse the text used with the teacher using it, or the method with the teaching of it. Method analysis is one thing, therefore, teaching analysis, quite another. Method analysis determines how teaching is done by the book; teaching analysis shows how much is done by the teacher. (p. 138)

In other words, a teaching analysis can be done only by analyzing and interpreting authentic classroom data that include the methodological practices of the teacher as revealed through classroom input and interaction, and teacher intention and learner interpretation (see Kumaravadivelu, 2003a, chap. 13). A method analysis, on the other hand, can be carried out by merely analyzing and interpreting different constituent features of a method presented in standard textbooks on language teaching methods, using any appropriate analytical framework.

4.1.2. Approach, Method, and Technique

Antony (1963) was perhaps the first in modern times to articulate a framework for understanding the constituents of method. His purpose, a laudable one, was to provide much-needed coherence to the conception and representation of elements that constitute language teaching. He proposed a three-way distinction: *approach, method,* and *technique*. He defined approach as "a set of correlative assumptions dealing with the nature of language and the nature of language teaching and learning. It describes the nature of the subject matter to be taught. It states a point of view, a philosophy, an article of faith . . ." (Antony, 1963, pp. 63–64). Thus, an approach embodies the theoretical principles governing language learning and language teaching. A method, however, is "an overall plan for the orderly presentation of language material, no part of which contradicts, and all of which is based upon, the selected approach. An approach is axiomatic, a method is procedural" (p. 65). As such, within one approach there can be many methods. Methods are implemented in the classroom through what are called techniques. A technique is defined as "a particular trick, strategem, or contrivance used to accomplish an immediate objective" (p. 66). The tripartite framework is hierarchical in the sense that approach informs method, and method informs techniques.

When it was introduced, the Antony framework was welcomed as a helpful tool for making sense of different parts of language teaching operations, and it was in use for a long time. However, a lack of precise formulation of the framework resulted in a widespread dissatisfaction with it. Antony himself felt that modifications and refinements of his framework are "possible" and even "desirable" primarily because the distinction between approach and method on one hand, and method and technique on the other hand, was not clearly delineated. The way approach and method are used interchangeably in some of the literature on L2 teaching testifies to the blurred boundaries between the two. Secondly, the inclusion of specific items within a constituent is sometimes based on subjective judgments. For instance, Antony considered pattern practice a method, and imitation a technique when, in fact, both of them can be classified as classroom *techniques* because they both refer to a sequence of classroom activities performed in the classroom environment, prompted by the teacher and practiced by the learner.

The Antony framework is flawed in yet another way. It attempted to portray the entire language teaching operations as a simple, hierarchical relationship between approach, method, and technique, without in any way considering the complex connections between intervening factors such as societal demands, institutional resources and constraints, instructional effectiveness, and learner needs. After taking these drawbacks into consideration, Clarke (1983) summarized the inadequacy of the Antony framework thus:

> Approach, by limiting our perspective of language learning and teaching, serves as a blinder which hampers rather than encourages, professional growth. Method is so vague that it means just about anything that anyone wants it to mean, with the result that, in fact, it means nothing. And technique, by giving the impression that teaching activities can be understood as abstractions separate from the context in which they occur, obscures the fact that classroom practice is a dynamic interaction of diverse systems. (p. 111)

In short, the Antony framework did not effectively serve the purpose for which it was designed.

4.1.3. Approach, Design, and Procedure

To rectify some of the limitations of the Antony framework, Richards and Rodgers (1982) attempted to revise and refine it. They proposed a system that is broader in its scope and wider in its implications. Like Antony, they too made a three-part distinction—approach, design, and procedure—but introduced new terms to capture the refinements:

> The first level, *approach*, defines those assumptions, beliefs, and theories about the nature of language and the nature of language learning which operate as axiomatic constructs or reference points and provide a theoretical foundation for what language teachers ultimately do with learners in classrooms. The second level in the system, *design*, specifies the relationship of theories of language and learning to both the form and function of instructional materials and activities in instructional settings. The third level, *procedure*, comprises the classroom techniques and practices which are consequences of particular approaches and designs. (Richards & Rodgers, 1982, p. 154)

Notice that the term, method, does not figure in this hierarchy. That is because Richards and Rodgers preferred to use it as an umbrella term to refer to the broader relationship between theory and practice in language teaching.

As is evident, Richards and Rodgers retained the term, approach, to mean what it means in the Antony framework, that is, to refer primarily to the theoretical axioms governing language, language learning, and language teaching. They introduced a new term, design, to denote what Antony denoted by the term, method. Design, however, is broader than Antony's method as it includes specifications of (a) the content of instruction, that is, the syllabus, (b) learner roles, (c) teacher roles, and (d) instructional materials and their types and functions. Procedure, like technique in the Antony framework, refers to the actual moment-to-moment classroom activity. It includes a specification of context of use and a description of precisely what is expected in terms of execution and outcome for each exercise type. Procedure, then, is concerned with issues such as the following: the types of teaching and learning techniques, the types of exercises and practice activities, and the resources—time, space, equipment—required to implement recommended activities.

The three-tier system proposed by Richards and Rodgers (1982) is surely broader and more detailed than the Antony framework. However, a careful analysis indicates that their system is equally redundant and overlapping. For instance, while defining approach, the authors state that "theories at the level of approach relate directly to the level of design since they provide the basis for determining the goals and content of language syllabus" (p. 155). While defining design, they state that design considerations "deal with assumptions about the content and the context for teaching and learning . . ." (p. 158). The boundary between approach and design is blurred here because the operational definitions of both relate to theoretical assumptions that actually belong to the realm of approach.

Furthermore, the Richards and Rodgers framework suffers from an element of artificiality in its conception and an element of subjectivity in its operation. As the *Routledge Encyclopedia of Language Teaching and Learning* (2000) pointed out,

> at least some information on the three areas of analysis—approach, design, procedure—has to be inferred, because the proponents of each method do not always provide comprehensive outlines for the underlying theory and for all areas of practice. Therefore, determining some aspects may be a matter of interpretation of statements or materials and consequently carries the risk of misinterpretation. (p. 619)

This observation echoes a similar argument made much earlier by Pennycook (1989) who was "struck by a feeling of strain at attempts to fit disparate concepts into their framework. In many instances, their attempts to demonstrate conceptual unity for methods do not seem justifiable" (p. 602).

4.1.4. Principles and Procedures

An apparent and perhaps inherent drawback with a three-tier framework is that it is difficult to keep the boundaries separate without redundancy and overlapping. This is so particularly because we are dealing with different levels of organization, all of which form an integral part of an interdependent system. Furthermore, a three-tier framework opens the door for an interpretation that is unfortunate, and perhaps, unintended. That is, the framework appears to treat approach as a theorist/researcher activity, design as a syllabus designer/materials producer activity, and procedure as a classroom teacher/learner activity. As we saw in Part One, it is the theorist who engages in the sort of activities described under approach, activities such as providing a rationale and an account of psychosociolinguistic theories governing language learning and teaching. The activities described under method/design, which include syllabus construction, materials production, and the determination of learner/teacher roles are considered to be the responsibilities of the syllabus/materials designer and not of the classroom teacher. The teacher's task in the classroom is what is described under technique/procedure.

The division of labor among the three groups of people involved in language learning and teaching operations, the division implicit in the three-tier frameworks, is acceptable to some extent in a traditional educational system in which a centrally planned educational agenda was handed down to the teacher. It is inadequate in the current pedagogic environment in which the teacher is increasingly playing, at the local level, multiple roles of teacher, researcher, syllabus designer, and materials producer. Recent emphases on classroom decision making (Breen & Littlejohn, 2000), teacher and learner autonomy (Benson, 2001), teacher cognition (Woods, 1996), teacher inquiry (Johnson & Golombek, 2002), and action research (Edge, 2001) attest to the shifting responsibilities of various participants involved in the learning and teaching operations. It is certainly inadequate in the emerging postmethod era because, as we see in Part Three, one of the central objectives of postmethod pedagogy is to fundamentally restructure the reified relationship between the theorist and the teacher (Kumaravadivelu, 2001).

Besides, we need to keep in mind what we use such a framework for. Antony (1963) and Richards and Rodgers (1982) did not propose their frameworks with the same purpose in mind. Antony had a very limited aim of presenting "a pedagogical filing system within which many ideas, opposing or compatible, may be filed" (1963, p. 63). He merely hoped that his framework "will serve to lessen a little the terminological confusion in the language teaching field" (p. 67). In other words, his framework is meant to be a descriptive tool. Richards and Rodgers, however, had a higher goal. Their framework is an attempt to provide "insights into the internal adequacy of particular methods, as well as into the similarities and differences which exist between alternative methods" (1982, p. 168). They hoped that their framework "can be used to describe, evaluate, and compare methods in language teaching" (1982, p. 164). In other words, their framework is meant to be an evaluative tool as well.

In spite of the aforementioned claim, the Richards and Rodgers (1982) framework can be used only to describe the components of various methods as conceptualized by theorists, and as presented on paper, although, as we saw earlier, even such a limited description will be partly based on subjective interpretations. However, the framework can hardly be used to evaluate the relative effectiveness or usefulness of methods "in language teaching," assuming it refers to what teachers do in the classroom. It does not, for instance, take into consideration several variables that shape the success or failure of classroom language learning/teaching—variables such as intake factors and intake processes (cf. chap. 2, this volume) and input modifications and instructional activities (cf. chap. 3, this volume). In other words, the relative merits of methods cannot be evaluated on the basis of a checklist, however comprehensive it may be. Besides, as a major large-scale experimental study called the Pennsylvania Project revealed (Smith, 1970), comparison of language-teaching methods with the view to evaluating their classroom effectiveness is a notoriously treacherous task replete with experimental pitfalls (because not all the variables governing classroom learning and teaching can be effectively controlled in order to study the impact of a particular method on learning outcomes) and explanatory flaws (because any explanation of what is observed in the classroom has to be the result of subjective interpretation rather than objective evaluation).

A three-tier distinction has thus proved to be inadequate to "lessen a little the terminological confusion in the language-teaching field" (Antony, 1963, p. 65). The first of the triad—approach—refers to theoretical principles governing language learning and teaching. These principles are generally drawn from a number of disciplines: linguistics, psychology, sociology, anthropology, information sciences, conversational analysis, discourse analysis, and so forth. The second part of the triad—method or design— can be part of the first component because we can, by all means, think of principles of syllabus design, principles of materials production, principles of evaluation, and so forth. The third component, of course, refers to actual classroom-teaching strategies. In other words, two major components of any systematic learning/teaching operation are the principles that shape our concepts and convictions, and the procedures that help us translate those principles into a workable plan in a specific classroom context.

In light of the just-mentioned argument, it appears to me to be useful to simplify the descriptive framework and make a two-part distinction: *principles* and *procedures*. The term, principles, may be operationally defined as a set of insights derived from theoretical and applied linguistics, cognitive psychology, information sciences, and other allied disciplines that provide theoretical bases for the study of language learning, language planning, and language teaching. The term thus includes not only the theoretical assumptions governing language learning and teaching but also those governing syllabus design, materials production, and evaluation measures. Similarly, procedures may be operationally defined as a set of teaching strategies adopted/adapted by the teacher in order to accomplish the stated and unstated, short- and long-term goals of language learning and teaching in the classroom. Thus, certain elements of Antony's approach and method, and Richards and Rodgers' approach and design can be subsumed under principles. Classroom events, activities, or techniques can be covered under procedures. The terms principles and procedures are not new; they are implicit in the literature and are being used widely though not uniformly or consistently. In this book, I employ these two terms, keeping in mind that they are useful only for description of methods, and not for evaluation of classroom teaching.

4.2. CATEGORIES OF LANGUAGE TEACHING METHODS

Yet another source of tiresome ambiguity that afflicts language teaching is the absence of a principled way to categorize language teaching methods in a conceptually coherent fashion. This need has become even more acute because of what Stern (1985) called the "method boom" (p. 249) witnessed in the 1970s. The exact number of methods currently in use is unclear. It is easy to count nearly a dozen, ranging from Audiolingualism to Jazz chants. (I haven't found one beginning with a Z yet, unless we count the Zen method!)

It is not as if the existing methods provide distinct or discrete paths to language teaching. In fact, there is considerable overlap in their theoretical as well as practical orientation to L2 learning and teaching. It is therefore beneficial, for the purpose of analysis and understanding, to categorize established methods into (a) *language-centered methods*, (b) *learner-centered methods*, and (c) *learning-centered methods* (Kumaravadivelu, 1993b). This categorization, which seeks to provide conceptual coherence, is made based on theoretical and pedagogic considerations that are presented in a nutshell below. A detailed treatment of these three categories of method follows in chapters 5, 6, and 7.

4.2.1. Language-Centered Methods

Language-centered methods are those that are principally concerned with linguistic forms. These methods (such as Audiolingual Method) seek to provide opportunities for learners to practice preselected, presequenced linguistic structures through form-focused exercises in class, assuming that a preoccupation with form will ultimately lead to the mastery of the target language and that the learners can draw from this formal repertoire whenever they wish to communicate in the target language outside the class. According to this view, language development is more intentional than incidental. That is, learners are expected to pay continual and conscious attention to linguistic features through systematic planning and sustained practice in order to learn and to use them.

Language-centered pedagogists treat language learning as a linear, additive process. In other words, they believe that language develops primarily in terms of what Rutherford (1987) called "accumulated entities" (p. 4). That is, a set of grammatical structures and vocabulary items are carefully selected for their usability, and graded for their difficulty. The teacher's task is to introduce one discrete linguistic item at a time and help the learners practice it until they internalize it. Secondly, supporters of language-centered methods advocate explicit introduction, analysis, and explanation of linguistic systems. That is, they believe that the linguistic system is simple enough and our explanatory power clear enough to provide explicit rules of thumb, and explain them to the learners in such a way that they can understand and internalize them.

4.2.2. Learner-Centered Methods

Learner-centered methods are those that are principally concerned with learner needs, wants, and situations. These methods (such as Communicative Language Teaching) seek to provide opportunities for learners to practice preselected, presequenced linguistic structures *and* communicative notions/functions through meaning-focused activities, assuming that a preoccupation with form *and* function will ultimately lead to target language mastery and that the learners can make use of both formal and functional repertoire to fulfill their communicative needs outside the class. In this view, as in the previous case, language development is more intentional than incidental.

Learner-centered pedagogists aim at making language learners grammatically accurate and communicatively fluent. They keep in mind the learner's real-life language use in social interaction or for academic study, and present linguistic structures in communicative contexts. In spite of strong arguments that emphasize the cyclical and analytical nature of communicative syllabuses (Munby, 1978; Wilkins, 1976; see chap. 3, this volume, for more details), learner-centered methods remain, basically, linear and additive. Proponents of learner-centered methods, like those of language-centered methods, believe in accumulated entities. The one major difference is that in the case of language-centered methods, the accumulated entities represent linguistic structures, and in the case of learner-centered methods, they represent structures plus notions and functions. Furthermore, just as language-centered pedagogists believe that the linguistic structures of a language could be sequentially presented and explained, the learner-centered pedagogists also believe that each notional/functional category could be matched with one or more linguistic forms, and sequentially presented and explained to the learner.

4.2.3. Learning-Centered Methods

Learning-centered methods are those that are principally concerned with cognitive processes of language learning (see chap. 2, this volume, for details). These methods (such as the Natural Approach) seek to provide opportunities for learners to participate in open-ended meaningful interaction through problem-solving tasks in class, assuming that a preoccupation with meaning-making will ultimately lead to target language mastery and that the learners can deploy the still-developing interlanguage to achieve linguistic as well as pragmatic knowledge/ability. In this case, unlike in the other two, language development is more incidental than intentional. That is, grammar construction can take place when the learners pay attention to the process of meaning-making, even if they are not explicitly focused on the formal properties of the language.

According to learning-centered pedagogists, language development is a nonlinear process, and therefore, does not require preselected, presequenced systematic language input but requires the creation of conditions in which learners engage in meaningful activities in class. They believe that a language is best learned when the focus is not on the language, that is, when the learner's attention is focused on understanding, saying, and doing something with language, and not when their attention is focused explicitly on linguistic features. They also hold the view that linguistic systems are too complex to be neatly analyzed, explicitly explained, and profitably presented to the learner.

In seeking to redress what they consider to be fundamental flaws that characterize previous methods, learning-centered pedagogists seek to fill, what Long (1985) called a "psycholinguistic vacuum" (p. 79). That is, they claim to derive insights from psycholinguistic research on language development in an attempt to incorporate them in language teaching methods. As a result, the changes they advocate relate not just to syllabus specifications—as it happened in the case of the shift from language-centered to learner-centered methods—but to all aspects of learning/teaching operations: syllabus design, materials production, classroom teaching, outcomes assessment, and teacher education.

The categories of language teaching methods just described are summarized in Fig. 4.1. A word of caution about this figure is in order. The figure represents method analysis, not teaching analysis. From a classroom methodological point of view, the three categories do not represent distinct entities with clear-cut boundaries. They overlap considerably, particularly during the transitional time when dissatisfaction with one method yields slowly to the evolution of another.

4.3. DESIGNER NONMETHODS

Part of the method boom that Stern talked about has given us what are called *new methods*. They include *Community Language Learning*, the *Silent Way*, *Suggestopedia*, and *Total Physical Response*. All these new methods advocate a humanistic approach to language learning and teaching. Community Language Learning treats teachers as language counselors who are sensitive to the language learners' emotional struggle to cope with the challenges of language learning. They are supposed to create a nonthreatening atmosphere in the classroom, forming a community of learners who build trust among themselves in order to help each other. The Silent Way believes that teachers

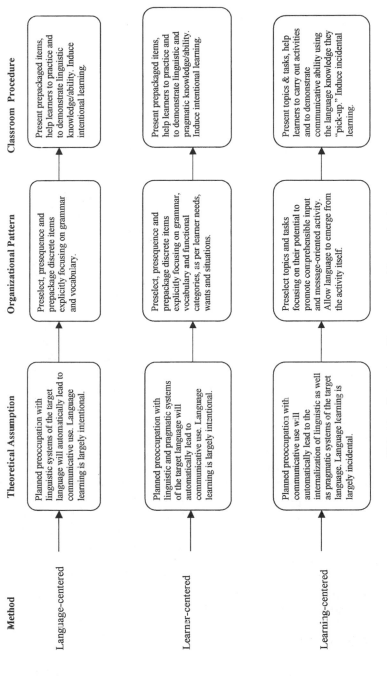

FIG. 4.1. Categories of language teaching methods.

should be silent in class and talk only when absolutely necessary. Using color charts and color rods as props, teachers are expected to encourage learners to express their thoughts, perceptions, and feelings, and in the process, learn the language. Suggestopedia, which now has even a fancier name, *Desuggestopedia*, aims at removing psychological barriers to learning through the psychological notion of "suggestion." Using fine arts such as music, art, and drama, teachers are advised to create a comfortable environment in class in order to eliminate any fear of failure on the part of the learners. Total Physical Response recommends that teachers activate their learners' motor skills through a command sequence in which learners perform an action, such as standing up, sitting down, walking to the board, and so forth.

These new methods have also been dubbed as *designer methods*. I prefer to call them *designer nonmethods* because none of them, in my view, deserves the status of a method. They are all no more than classroom procedures that are consistent with the theoretical underpinnings of a learner-centered pedagogy. From a classroom procedural point of view, they are highly innovative and are certainly useful in certain cases. But, they are not full-fledged methods. As I have argued elsewhere (Kumaravadivelu, 1995), a method, to be considered a method, must satisfy at least two major criteria. First, it should be informed by a set of theoretical principles derived from feeder disciplines and a set of classroom procedures directed at practicing teachers. Both the underlying principles and the suggested procedures should address the factors and processes governing learning and teaching (see Part One, this volume) in a coherent fashion. Second, a method should be able to guide and sustain various aspects of language learning and teaching operations, particularly in terms of curricular content (e.g., grammar and vocabulary), language skills (listening, speaking, reading, and writing), and proficiency levels (beginning, intermediate, and advanced).

None of the designer methods satisfies the just-cited criteria. In spite of their limitations, they have been wrongly treated as new methods, a treatment that really requires a stretch of interpretation, as seen in the case of Richards and Rodgers (1986) who attempted, rather laboriously, to fit the new methods into their tripartite framework of approach, design, and procedure. In fact, a reputed Canadian scholar expressed surprise at "the tolerant and positive reception the new methods were given by sophisticated methodologists and applied linguistics in North America. One could have expected them to be slaughtered one by one under the searing light of theory and research" (Stern, 1985, p. 249).

4.4. A SPECIAL TASK

Before concluding this section on categories of language teaching methods, a brief note on the status of Task-Based Language Teaching (TBLT) is in order. As the novelty of communicative language teaching is gradually wearing thin (see chap. 6, this volume, for details), TBLT is gaining ground. The word, "communicative," which was ubiquitously present in the titles of scholarly books and student textbooks published during the 1980s is being replaced by yet another word, "task." Since the late 1980s, we have been witnessing a steady stream of books on TBLT, in addition to numerous journal articles. There are research-based scholarly books on the nature and scope of pedagogic tasks (Bygate, Skehan, & Swain, 2001; Crookes & Gass, 1993; Skehan, 1998). There are books about task-based language learning and teaching in general (Ellis, 2003; Long, in press; Nunan, 2004; Prabhu, 1987). There are also specifically targeted books that provide tasks for language learning (Gardner & Miller, 1996; Willis, 1996), tasks for language teaching (Johnson, 2003; Nunan, 1989; Parrott, 1993), tasks for teacher education (Tanner & Green, 1998), tasks for classroom observation (Wajnryb, 1992), and tasks for language awareness (Thornbury, 1997).

In spite of the vast quantity of the published materials on TBLT, there is no consensus definition of what a *task* is. For instance, more than 15 years ago, Breen (1987) defined task as "a range of workplans which have the overall purpose of facilitating language learning—from the simple and brief exercise type to more complex and lengthy activities such as group problem-solving or simulations and decision-making" (p. 23). In a recent work on TBLT, Ellis (2003), after carefully considering various definitions available in the literature, synthesized them to derive a composite, lengthy definition:

> A task is a workplan that requires learners to process language pragmatically in order to achieve an outcome that can be evaluated in terms of whether the correct or appropriate propositional content has been conveyed. To this end, it requires them to give primary attention to meaning and to make use of their own linguistic resources, although the design of the task may predispose them to choose particular forms. A task is intended to result in language use that bears a resemblance, direct or indirect, to the way language is used in the real world. Like other language activities, a task can engage productive or receptive, and oral or written skills, and also various cognitive processes. (p. 16)

The definitions given not only bring out the complex nature of a task but it also signifies a simple fact. That is, as I pointed out more than a decade ago (Kumaravadivelu, 1993b), a language learning and teaching task is not inextricably linked to any one particular language teaching method. Task is not a methodological construct; it is a curricular content. In other words, in relation to the three categories of method outlined in this section, there can very well be *language-centered tasks, learner-centered tasks,* and *learning-centered tasks.* To put it simply, language-centered tasks are those that draw the learner's attention primarily and explicitly to the formal properties of the language. For instance, tasks presented in Fotos and Ellis (1991) and also in Fotos (1993), which they appropriately call *grammar tasks,* come under this category. Learner-centered tasks are those that direct the learner's attention to formal as well as functional properties of the language. Tasks for the communicative classroom suggested by Nunan (1989) illustrate this type. And, learning-centered tasks are those that engage the learner mainly in the negotiation, interpretation, and expression of meaning, without any explicit focus on form and/or function. Problem-solving tasks suggested by Prabhu (1987) are learning centered.

In light of the present discussion, I do not, in this book, treat the designer methods and TBLT as independent language teaching methods. I do, however, refer to them for illustrative purposes as and when appropriate.

4.5. CONCLUSION

In this chapter, I examined the use of terms and concepts that constitute language teaching operations in general. I argued that for the sake of simplicity and practicality, it is beneficial to have a two-tier system consisting of principles and procedures. I also presented a rationale for the classification of language-teaching methods into language-, learner-, and learning-centered methods. I shall henceforth be using these terms and categories as operationally defined and described in this chapter. The next three chapters in Part Two deal with the theoretical principles and classroom procedures of language-, learner-, and learning-centered methods.

Chapter 5

Language-Centered Methods

5. INTRODUCTION

Language teaching methods evolve and improve over time as their merits and demerits become more and more apparent with the accumulation of experience and experimentation, ultimately leading to the development of a new method with a new label. During the transitional time when dissatisfaction with one method results in the gradual development of another, there will necessarily be overlapping tendencies. Therefore, a method in a later phase of its life may appear to be slightly different from what it was in an earlier phase. But still, in order to fully understand the fundamental characteristics of any given category of method and to differentiate it meaningfully from other categories, it is necessary to go back to the foundational texts that provide what may be called a canonical description of the theoretical principles and classroom procedures of a method that may prototypically represent the category to which it belongs. With that understanding, I focus in this chapter on what is known as *audiolingual method*, which illustrates the essential characteristics of language-centered methods.

Although audiolingual method is considered to be "very much an American method" (Ellis, 1990, p. 21), some of its basics can be traced to almost simultaneous developments in Britain and the United States. Toward the second half of the 20th century, British applied linguists such as Hornby, Palmer, and West developed principles and procedures of what came to be called the *structural–situational method*. It primarily centered around the triple principles of *selection, gradation,* and *presentation*. Selection deals with the choice of lexical and grammatical content, gradation with the organization and sequencing of content, and presentation with the aims and activities of classroom teaching. As early as in 1936, Palmer, West, and their associates selected and graded a vocabulary list, which was later revised by West and published in 1953 with the title, *A General Service List of English Words*. The list consisted of a core vocabulary of about 2,000 words selected on the basis of such criteria as frequency, usefulness, and productivity and graded for complexity. Likewise, Palmer and Hornby attempted to classify major grammatical structures into sentence patterns and also sought to introduce them in situational dialogues. Hornby's book, *A Guide to Patterns and Usage of English,* published in 1954 became a standard reference book of basic English sentence patterns for textbook writers and classroom teachers.

As the British applied linguists were engaged in developing the structural–situational method, their American counterparts were called upon by their government already drawn into World War II to devise effective, short-term, intensive courses to teach conversational skills in German, French, Italian, Chinese, Japanese, and other languages to army personnel who could work as interpreters, code-room assistants, and translators. In response, American applied linguists established what was called Army Specialized Training Program (ASTP), which moved away from the prevailing reading/writing-oriented instruction to one that emphasized listening and speaking. After the war and by the mid-1950s, the program evolved into a full-fledged audiolingual method of teaching, and quickly became the predominant American approach to teaching English as second language.

A series of foundational texts published in the 1960s by American scholars provided the much needed pedagogic resources for language-centered methods. In an influential book titled *Language and Language Learning: Theory and Practice,* Brooks (1960) offered a comprehensive treatment of the audiolingual method. This was followed by Fries and Fries (1961), whose *Foundations of English Teaching* presented a corpus of structural and lexical items selected and graded into three proficiency levels—beginning, intermediate, and advanced. The corpus also included suggestions for designing contextual dialogues in which the structural and lexical items could be incorporated. Yet another seminal book, *Language Teaching: A Scientific Approach,* by Lado (1964) provided further impetus for the spread of the audiolingual method. Appearing in the same year was a widely acclaimed critical commentary on the audiolingual method titled *The Psychologist and the Foreign Language Teacher,* by Rivers (1964).

Although the British structural–situational method focused on the situational context and the functional content of language more than the American audiolingual method did, similarities between them are quite striking. Part of the reason is that linguists on both sides of the Atlantic were influenced by the tenets of structural linguistics and behavioral psychology. In view of that common ground, I combine the two traditions under one widely used label, *audiolingual method*, and discuss its theoretical principles and classroom procedures.

5.1. THEORETICAL PRINCIPLES

As mentioned, the fundamental principles of language-centered pedagogy are drawn from structural linguistics and behavioral psychology. These two schools of thought from sister disciplines have informed the theory of language, language learning, language teaching, and curricular specifications of language-centered pedagogy.

5.1.1. Theory of Language

Language-centered pedagogists believed in the theory of language proposed and propagated by American structural linguists during the 1950s. Structural linguists treated language as a system of systems consisting of several hierarchically linked building blocks: phonemes, morphemes, phrases, clauses, and sentences, each with its own internal structure. These subsystems of language were thought to be linearly connected in a structured, systematic, and rule-governed way; that is, certain phonemes systematically cluster together to form a morpheme, certain morphemes systematically cluster together to form a phrase, and so forth. Secondly, structural linguists viewed language as aural–oral, thus emphasizing listening and speaking. Speech was considered primary, forming the very basis of language. Structure was viewed as being at the heart of speech. Thirdly, every language was looked upon as unique, each having a finite number of structural patterns. Each structure can be analyzed, described, systematized, and graded, and by implication, can be learned and taught by taking a similar discrete path.

Structural linguists rejected the views of traditional grammarians, who depended on philosophical and mentalistic approaches to the study of language. Instead, structuralists claimed to derive their view of language through a positivist and empiricist approach. A scientific approach to the study of language, it was thought, would help identify the structural patterns of language in a more rigorous way. Such an emphasis on scientific methods of linguistic analysis dovetailed well with the views of behavioral psychologists whose antimentalist views of human learning informed the audiolingual theory of language learning.

5.1.2. Theory of Language Learning

Language-centered pedagogists derived their theory of language learning from *behaviorism*, a school of American psychology which was popular during the 1950s and '60s. Like structural linguists, behavioral psychologists too were skeptical about mentalism and rejected any explanation of human behavior in terms of emotive feelings or mental processes. They sought a scientifically based approach for analyzing and understanding human behavior. For them, human behavior can be reduced to a series of stimuli that trigger a series of corresponding responses. Consequently, they looked at all learning as a simple mechanism of stimulus, response, and reinforcement. Experience is the basis of all learning, and all learning outcomes can be observed and measured in the changes that occur in behavior.

Given their belief that all learning is governed by stimulus–response–reinforcement mechanisms, behaviorists did not make any distinction between general learning and language learning. Their theory of language learning can be summed up in a series of assumptions they made:

• First and foremost, learning to speak a language is the same as learning to ride a bicycle or drive a car. Language learning, then, is no different from the learning of other school subjects like math or science. It is no more than a systematic accumulation of consciously collected discrete pieces of knowledge gained through repeated exposure, practice, and application. This is a central belief that logically leads to all other assumptions of varying importance.

• Second, language learning is just a process of mechanical habit formation through repetition. Forming a habit, in the context of language learning, is described as developing the ability to perform a particular linguistic feature such as a sound, a word, or a grammatical item automatically, that is, without paying conscious attention to it. Such a habit can be formed only through repeated practice aided by positive reinforcement. Bloomfield (1942), a prominent structural linguist, in his *Outline Guide for the Practical Study of Foreign Language,* articulated the structuralist's view of language learning very succinctly: "The command of a language is a matter of practice. . . . practice everything until it becomes second nature" (p. 16). He also emphasized that "Language learning is overlearning: Anything else is of no use" (p. 12).

• Third, habit formation takes place by means of analogy rather than analysis. Analysis involves problem solving, whereas analogy involves the perception of similarities and differences. In the context of language learning, this means an inductive approach, in which learners themselves identify the underlying structure of a pattern, is preferable to a deductive approach. Pattern practice, therefore, is an important tool of language learning.

• Fourth, language learning is a linear, incremental, additive process. That is, it entails mastering of one discrete item at a time, moving to the next only after the previous one has been fully mastered. It also involves gradually adding one building block after another, thus accumulating, in due course, all the linguistic elements that are combined to form the total-ity of a language. Because speech is primary, discrete items of language can be learned effectively if they are presented in spoken form before they are seen in the written form.

• Finally, discrete items of language should be introduced in carefully constructed dialogues embedded in a carefully selected linguistic and cul-tural context. Language should not be separated from culture, and words should be incorporated in a matrix of references to the culture of the target language community.

These fundamental assumptions about language learning deeply influ-enced the theory of language teaching adopted by language-centered pedagogists.

5.1.3. Theory of Language Teaching

Audiolingual theory of language teaching is, in fact, a mirror image of its theory of language learning. Because learning a language is considered to involve forming habits in order to assimilate and use a hierarchical system of systems, language teaching is nothing more than a planned presentation of those (sub)systems combined with provision of opportunities for repeti-tion. The purpose of teaching, therefore, is twofold: In the initial stage, the teacher, using a textbook, serves as a model providing samples of linguistic input, and then in the later stage, acts as a skillful manipulator of questions, commands, and other cues in order to elicit correct responses from the learner. Linguistic input is, of course, presented in the form of dialogues because they involve

> a natural and exclusive use of the audio-lingual skills. All the elements of the sound-system appear repeatedly, including the suprasegmental phonemes, which are often the most difficult for the learner. All that is learned is mean-ingful, and what is learned in one part of a dialogue often makes meaning clear in another. (Brooks, 1964, p. 145)

The emphasis on dialogues also takes care of the primacy of speech as well as the strict sequencing of four language skills in terms of listening, speak-ing, reading, and writing.

Given the preference of analogy over analysis, pattern practice was con-sidered to be the most important aspect of teaching, because it "capitalizes on the mind's capacity to perceive identity of structure where there is differ-ence in content and its quickness to learn by analogy" (Brooks, 1964, p. 146). Besides, teaching the basic patterns helps the learner's performance become habitual and automatic. The teacher's major task is to drill the basic patterns. Learners "require drill, drill, and more drill, and only enough vocabulary to make such drills possible" (Hockett, 1959). During the process of drilling, the learners should be carefully guided through a series of carefully designed exercises, thereby eliminating the possibility for making errors. As the learners are helped to perform the drills, they are supposed to inductively learn the grammatical structure being practiced.

Language-centered pedagogists thus drew heavily from structural linguistics and behavioral psychology in order to conceptualize their principles of language teaching. And, in tune with the spirit that prevailed in these two disciplines at that time, they dubbed their approach to language teaching "scientific," as reflected in the title of Lado's 1964 book, mentioned earlier.

5.1.4. Content Specifications

Language-centered methods adhere to the synthetic approach to syllabus design in which the content of learning and teaching is defined in terms of discrete items of grammatical and lexical forms of the language that are presented to the learners (see chap. 3, this volume, for details). In other words, linguistic forms constitute the organizing principle for syllabus construction. Drawing from the available inventory of linguistic forms compiled by grammarians through standard linguistic analyses, the syllabus designer selects and sequences the phonological, lexical, and grammatical elements of the language that can be included in graded textbooks used for classroom teaching. The teacher presents the elements of language forms (in terms of nouns, verbs, adjectives, articles, relative clauses, subordinate clauses, etc.) one by one to the learners, who are then supposed to put them together to figure out the totality of the language system. The primary task of the learner is to synthesize the discrete items of language in order to develop adequate knowledge/ability in the language.

Selection and *gradation*, that is, what items to select and in what sequence to present them are but two challenges facing the syllabus designer. Language-centered pedagogists implicitly followed the frequency, range, and availability criteria for selection identified by Mackey (1965). Recall from chapter 3 that *frequency* refers to the items that the learners are likely to encounter most, whereas *range* refers to the spread of an item across texts or contexts. Frequency relates to where the item is used, by whom, and for what purposes. Availability is determined by the degree to which an item is necessary and appropriate. Similarly, for gradation purposes, language-centered pedagogists followed the criteria of complexity, regularity, and productivity (cf. chap. 3, this volume). Recall that the first principle deals with a movement from the easy to the difficult, the second from the regular to the irregular, and the third from the more useful to the less useful.

Although the principles of selection and gradation have been found to be useful for organizing language input presented to the learner in a classroom context, critics have been skeptical about the rationale governing the principles. It is difficult to establish usable criteria for selection and gradation that are pedagogically and psychologically sound. As Corder (1973) rightly observed, "we simply do not know to what extent linguistic categories have psychological reality, and therefore to what extent what might be a logical linguistic sequencing of items in a syllabus is psychologically logical, and therefore the optimum ordering from a learning point of view" (p. 308). The paradox, however, is that "in spite of doubts about the feasibility of a sequential arrangement, the grammar of a language cannot be taught all at once. Some sort of selection and sequencing is needed, and therefore a grammatical syllabus must be provided" (Stern, 1992, pp. 139–140). In order to address this imperative, language-centered pedagogists posited what they considered to be a reasonable and workable set of criteria.

This section on the theoretical principles briefly dealt with the conceptual underpinnings of language, language learning, language teaching, and curricular specifications of language-centered methods. As we will see, these theoretical beliefs are very much reflected in the classroom procedures that practicing teachers are advised to follow.

5.2. CLASSROOM PROCEDURES

The aims and activities of any language teaching method can be analyzed and understood, in part, by studying the input and interactional modifications that the teachers are advised to carry out for promoting desired learning outcomes in the classroom (see chap. 3, this volume, for details). In the following sections, we consider the nature and relevance of input and interactional modifications with reference to language-centered methods.

5.2.1. Input Modifications

Of the three types of input modifications discussed in chapter 3, language-centered methods adhere almost exclusively to form-based input modifications. The other two types (i.e., meaning-based and form- and meaning-based input) rarely figure in language-centered methods because, as we saw in the earlier sections of this chapter, linguistic form has been the driving force behind their learning and teaching operations, and the idea of negotiated meaning in a communicative context was not of any considerable importance. Language-centered pedagogists believe that form-based input modifications are not only necessary and but also sufficient for the development of linguistic as well as pragmatic knowledge/ability in the L2. For them, manipulating input entails selecting grammatical items, grading them in a principled fashion, and making them salient for the learner through a predominantly teacher-fronted instruction that explicitly draws the learner's attention to grammar. Such form-focused instruction is coupled with clear explanation and conscious error correction.

The grammatical items of the target language are introduced to the learners mostly through structural patterns. In a popular handbook of the times, Paulston and Bruder (1975) provided a comprehensive, 145-page long index of structural patterns arranged in alphabetical order. The first two entries, for instance, are about adjectives and adverbs. The grammatical forms listed are as follows (p. 51):

ADJECTIVES
    Adjective comparison
        1. (*as* Adj. *as*; *the same* X *as*)
        2. (adj. *-er than*; *more/less -ly than*; *more/less* Noun *than*)
        3. (adj. *-est*; *most/least -ly*; *most/least* Noun)
    Demonstrative
    Indefinite
        much/ many
        other/ another
        some/ any
    Phrases
    Possessive

ADVERBS
    already/ yet
    Comparison
    Frequency
    here/ there
    Manner
        by + Noun/Verb/*-ing*
        -ly
        with + Noun
    too/ enough
    Place and time of expressions

For purposes of teaching and testing linguistic forms such as the two just shown, Paulston and Bruder suggested three types of drills: mechanical, meaningful, and communicative. As the following examples indicate, me-

chanical drills are automatic manipulative patterns aimed at habit formation. The learner response is fully controlled and there is only one correct
way of responding. Meaningful drills have the same objective of mechanical habit formation, but the responses may be correctly expressed in more
than one way. Communicative drills are supposed to help learners transfer structural patterns to appropriate communicative situations; but, in
reality, it is still "a drill rather than free communication because we are
still within the realm of the cue-response pattern" (Paulston & Bruder,
1975, p. 15).

Paulston and Bruder also give examples of what kind of linguistic input
that will be provided by the teacher in a classroom context. For instance,
to teach the first of the three patterns of adjective comparison already
listed, the authors provide the following substitution drills (adapted from
pp. 55–56):

Pattern: Adjective Comparison 1 (Adj. *as*; *the same* X *as*)
(a) Mechanical drill: Teaching Point: *Practice Pattern*
   Model: Teacher (T): Our winter is as long as theirs.
                      (summer/warm)
          Students (S): Our summer is as warm as theirs.
   T: city/polluted   S: Our city is as polluted as theirs.
      lake/cold   Our lake is as cold as theirs.
      work/difficult   Our work is as difficult as theirs.
      apartment/big   Our apartment is as big as theirs.
(b) Meaningful drill: Teaching Point: *Use of Pattern*
   Model: T: VW's in my country --------------------.
          S: VW's in my country are (not as cheap as here)
                                    (not the same price as here)
          T: The winter in A --------------------.
             Women's style in A --------------------.
             The seasons in A --------------------.
             Houses in A are --------------------.
(c) Communicative drill: Teaching Point: *Communicative Use*
          T: Compare with your country. Pollution.
          S: (The pollution here is as bad as in my country.)
          T: traffic
             drivers
             prices
             cars
             TV
             newspapers

As these examples clearly show, the linguistic input exposed to the learners in the classroom are all carefully controlled. As we see in the following section, the use of such a carefully engineered and exclusively grammar-oriented language input cannot but limit the nature and scope of interaction in the classroom.

5.2.2. Interactional Activities

The interactional activities of teachers and learners in a typical audio-lingual classroom are characterized in terms of three Ps—*presentation, practice,* and *production.* At the presentation stage, the already selected and graded linguistic items are introduced through a carefully constructed dialogue that contains several examples of the new items. The dialogue may also provide, if set in a specific sociocultural context, new insights into the culture of the target language community. Learners hear the tape recording of the model dialogue (or hear a reading of it by their teacher), repeat each line, and sometimes act out the dialogue. They are also encouraged to memorize the dialogue. At this stage, the learners are supposed to begin to grasp, mostly through analogy, how a particular structure works. Where necessary, the teacher acts as the language informant, providing additional information or explanation about relevant grammatical rules.

At the second stage, the learners practice the new linguistic items through mechanical, meaningful, or communicative drills. The pattern practice consists of isolated, decontextualized sentences, with the same grammatical structure but different lexical items. They are also given substitution tables (see boxed examples to come), which help them see the pattern governing the grammatical structure involved. As Chastain (1971) correctly observed, during this whole process of drilling the dialogue and the structures,

> the students are carefully led in minimal steps through a series of exercises in which the possibility of error is almost eliminated, and the opportunity for practice is expanded to the fullest. The students are not supposed to analyze and search for answers, but to respond immediately to the stimulus of the teacher. . . . (pp. 34–35)

The learners are then sent to language lab (if available) for further drills in sentence patterns as well as in stress, rhythm, and intonation. This is usually followed by exercises in reading and writing, which also involve the use of the grammar and vocabulary already familiarized. Thus, the language skills are presented and practiced in isolation and in rigid sequence: listening, speaking, reading, and writing.

At the production stage, the learners are given the opportunity to role-play dialogues similar to the ones introduced in class or in the language lab.

They are supposed to modify the language they have memorized in order to vary their production. They are also encouraged to talk about a selected topic in a carefully controlled context. Once this is all done, they are believed to have developed adequate linguistic and pragmatic knowledge/ ability to use the newly learned language for communicative purposes outside the classroom. The assumption here is that they will be able to successfully transfer their linguistic knowledge of discrete items of grammar into communicative use in appropriate contexts, a questionable assumption that we revisit shortly.

A recent rendering of audiolingual teaching taken from Johnson (2001, pp. 173–174) illustrates some of the features of input and interactional modifications already described. Johnson provides an example of part of a lesson dealing with two sentence patterns: *HAVE + just + -ed,* and *HAVE + not + -ed + yet.* The use of capitals for *HAVE* indicates that the reference is to the verb as a whole, including all its constituent forms such as *has, have,* and others, and *-ed* refers to the past participle of verbs.

Objectives: to teach the present perfect tense, with *just* and *yet.* Some examples:

I have just picked up the pen.   *I haven't picked up the pen yet.*
She has just opened the door.   *She hasn't opened the door yet.*
They have just read the book.   *They haven't read the book yet.*

Step 1   Demonstrating the sentence pattern HAVE + just + -ed

Actions are done in front of the class, sometimes by the teacher and sometimes by a pupil. For example, the teacher picks up a pen and says *I have just picked up the pen.* Then a pupil opens the door and the teacher says *She has just opened the door.*

Step 2   Practicing HAVE + just +- ed
(a) Drill   Pupils form sentences from a table:

I			
We			(to close) the window
			(to switch on) the light
They	(to have)	Just	
			(to play) football
He/she			(to walk) home
You			

(b) Drill   The teacher says sentences like the ones on the left below. Chosen pupils make **HAVE + just + -ed** sentences (as in the example on the right):

She's closing the window.   *She's just closed the window.*
She's going to switch on the light.
They will play football.

Step 3   Demonstrating and practicing HAVE + not + -ed + yet
(a) Demonstration   Show a diary for the day:

7.30	get up	10.00	phone Bill
8.00	wash	12.00	visit Jane (for lunch)
9.00	eat breakfast	2.00	take dog for walk

Teacher says:
It's 8.30. I'm late. I haven't washed yet.
It's 9.30. Mary's late. She hasn't eaten breakfast yet.

(b) Drill   Pupils form sentences from the table:

I We They He/she You	(to have) not	(to eat) (to phone) (to visit) (to take)	John The dog for a walk Dinner Mary	yet

This is only part of a lesson. Think of what is needed to finish it . . .

To conclude this section, the classroom procedures explained and illustrated bring out the limitations of input as well as interactional modifications associated with language-centered methods. With regard to input, the emphasis has been on form-based modifications to the neglect of meaning-based activities. Likewise, the interactional modifications have been confined to interaction as a textual activity, which focuses on syntactic aspects of language. What has not been seriously taken into account is interaction as interpersonal activity, which focuses on establishing and maintaining social relationships, and interaction as ideational activity, which focuses on expression, interpretation, and negotiation of one's own experience.

5.3. A CRITICAL ASSESSMENT

Audiolingual method represents a milestone in the annals of language teaching for one good reason: Unlike earlier methods (such as Grammar-Translation method), it was based on well-articulated and well-coordinated theories of language, language learning, and language teaching, prompting its proponents to call it a "scientific" method. Although the method can hardly be called scientific in the normal sense of the term, there is no doubt that its proponents adhered to a highly rational view of learning and advocated a highly systematic way of teaching, both derived from the linguistic and psychological knowledge-base available at that time.

The systematic nature of language-centered methods proved to be immensely helpful to the classroom teacher. The entire pedagogic agenda was considered to be teacher friendly, as it provided a neat rules-of-thumb framework for teachers with which to work. It could be used at all proficiency levels. It was blessed with a narrowly defined objective of mastery of grammatical structures, aided by coherently designed syllabuses with preselected and presequenced items, and clearly delineated evaluation measures that focus on assessing the learning of discrete items of language. The presentation–practice–production sequence put the teacher firmly in charge of classroom proceedings, as it "is relatively easy to organize, and comes bundled with a range of techniques which, besides having the potential to organize large groups of students efficiently, also demonstrate the power relations within the classroom, since the teacher is the centre of what is happening at all times" (Skehan, 1998, p. 94). In addition, it was easy to train a large number of teachers in the principles and procedures of language-centered methods of teaching in a fairly short period of time.

Being systematic is, of course, different from being successful. How can the merits and demerits of language-centered methods be estimated? In the preface to the second edition of his authoritative book on audiolingual method, Brooks (1964) declared: "the comfortable grammar-translation days are over. The new challenge is to teach language as communication, face-to-face communication between speakers and writer-to-reader communication in books" (p. vii). As this statement clearly indicates, the central goal of language-centered methods, in spite of their unmistakable emphasis on the mastery of grammatical structures, is indeed "to teach language as communication." It is, therefore, only proper to assess whether language-centered pedagogists achieved the goal they set for themselves.

What does it mean "to teach language as communication" and to what extent are the language-centered methods conceptually and procedurally equipped to deal with it? Interestingly, although the phrase "teaching language as communication" was coined by language-centered pedagogists, it was later appropriated by learner-centered pedagogists and was used as a slogan for communicative language teaching (see chap. 6, this volume, for details). In a pioneering book on communicative language teaching titled, appropriately, *Teaching Language as Communication,* Widdowson (1978) made a useful distinction between language usage and language use:

> The first of these is the citation of words and sentences as manifestations of the language system, and the second is the way the system is realized for normal communicative purposes. Knowing a language is often taken to mean having a knowledge of correct usage but this knowledge is of little utility on its own: it has to be complemented by a knowledge of appropriate use. A knowledge of use must of necessity include a knowledge of usage but the reverse is not the case: it is possible for someone to have learned a large number of sentence patterns and a large number of words which can fit into them without knowing how they are actually put to communicative use. (pp. 18–19)

Widdowson goes on to argue that the teaching of usage does not guarantee a knowledge of use, implying that any teaching of language as communication entails the teaching of language use, not just language usage. In a later work, he states the problem of language-centered methods succinctly: "the structural means of teaching would appear to be inconsistent with the communicative ends of learning" (Widdowson, 1990, p. 159).

Experiential as well as empirical evidence on the effectiveness of language-centered methods revealed that the learners, at the end of their language learning, were better at language usage than at language use. To put it differently, they were able to develop linguistic knowledge/ability but not pragmatic knowledge/ability. There are several factors that contributed to this less-than-desirable outcome. First, language-centered pedagogists failed to recognize that superficial linguistic behavior in terms of structures and vocabulary, even if it becomes habitual, does not in any way entail the internalization of the underlying language system required for effective communication. Second, they seldom acknowledged that communicative situations are far more complex and that, as V. Cook (1991) pointed out, "if communication is the goal of language teaching, its content needs to be based on an analysis of communication itself, which is not covered properly by structures and vocabulary" (p. 137). Finally, they assumed, wrongly, that the learners will be able to successfully transfer their knowledge of isolated items of grammar and vocabulary and automatically apply it to real-life communicative situations outside the classroom. The transfer did not occur primarily because, as Rivers (1972) argued, skill getting is fundamentally different from skill using.

The theoretical bases of language-centered pedagogy signify at once its strengths as well as its weaknesses. Although the solid, theoretical foundation governing its orientation to language, language learning, and language teaching gave language-centered pedagogy a principled, systematic, and coherent base, it also contributed to its demise. Its theory turned out to be flawed, and a flawed theory can hardly result in a flawless outcome. Severe criticism about its theory came from the two disciplines that the pedagogy was totally dependent upon: psychology and linguistics.

The advent of cognitive psychology and Chomskyan linguistics shed new insights that shook the very foundation of the psychological and linguistic principles upon which the language-centered pedagogy was based. Taking a mentalistic approach, cognitive psychologists focused on the role of the human mind and its capacity to form insights, and rejected the stimulus–response mechanism and habit-formation advocated by behaviorists. They emphasized the active mental processes governing learning rather than the passive techniques of repetition and reinforcement. Similarly, Chomskyan linguistics with its emphasis on transformational generative rules effectively questioned the hierarchical system of structural linguistics.

From an acquisitional point of view, Chomsky persuasively argued that the behavioristic approach is woefully inadequate to account for first-language development. As discussed in chapter 1, this volume, he hypothesized that a child is born with an innate ability, and using that ability, the child acquires the first language by formulating rules, testing them out, and confirming or reformulating them rather than by merely responding to the linguistic stimuli available in the environment. Language acquisition is largely a developmental process of insight formation grounded in the cognitive capacity of the human mind. Language behavior, then, is a rule-governed creative activity and not a habit-induced mechanical one. Extending the Chomskyan notion of language acquisition, sociolinguists such as Hymes pointed out that communicative capability does not merely include grammatical knowledge but also, more importantly, knowledge of sociocultural norms governing day-to-day communication. A detailed discussion of these developments and their implications for language teaching will be given in chapter 6. Suffice it to say here that the new developments cast doubts virtually on every aspect of language-centered pedagogy.

While the theoretical base of language-centered pedagogy was completely undermined by the new developments in psychology and linguistics, its classroom application did not fare any better. Both teachers and learners were losing interest in it mainly because of its failure to achieve its stated objectives. As Ellis (1990) pointed out in a review of research, "many learners found pattern practice boring . . . Even learners who were 'motivated' to persevere found that memorizing patterns did not lead to fluent and effective communication in real-life situations" (p. 30). The theoretical as well as classroom drawbacks of language-centered pedagogy resulted in a sharp decline in its popularity.

The loss of popularity of language-centered pedagogy does not, however, mean that it has no redeeming features. Highlighting the positive aspects of the pedagogy, several reputed scholars have, for instance, suggested that

- "Language learning does involve learning individual items" (Spolsky, 1989, p. 61) just the way behaviorists advocated.
- An explicit focus on the formal properties of the language might help the learner systematically examine, understand, and organize the linguistic system of the language (Bialystok, 1988).
- Explicit teaching of forms or structures of the target language is beneficial to learners at a particular point in their acquisition of the target language (Stern, 1983).
- A manipulative, repetition-reinforcement instructional procedure may be adequate at the early stages of second and foreign language learning (Rivers, 1972).
- "There must be some aspects of language learning which have to do with habit formation" (Widdowson, 1990, p. 11).

Considering these and other positive features, Widdowson (1990) cautioned wisely that "total rejection of behaviouristic theory is no more reasonable than total acceptance" (p. 11).

Cautioning against the developing tendency to throw out the baby with the bathwater, several scholars suggested that suitable modifications should be introduced in the classroom procedures of language-centered pedagogy in order to reduce its excessive system dependence and to make it more discourse oriented. Such a change of course was well articulated by none other than Lado, one of the leading proponents of language-centered pedagogy. When asked by a leading German professional journal, more than 20 years after the publication of his seminal book on what he called the "scientific approach" to language teaching, to look back and say which basic ideas of the audiolingual approach he would no longer stress, Lado responded:

First, I do not consider necessary the verbatim memorization of dialogues. In fact, it may be more effective to allow changes in what I would call a "creative memory" mode, that is, having the students remember the context and the ideas but encouraging them to communicative needs. Second, I no longer use pattern practice out of context. Third, I no longer limit the students to the vocabulary introduced in the text. I encourage them to introduce or ask for additional words and expressions relevant to the context. Fourth, I no longer limit myself to helping them master the language, leaving it up to them to use the language according to their needs. Finally, I give more attention to features of discourse. (Translated by and cited in Freudenstein, 1986, pp. 5–6)

5.4. CONCLUSION

In this chapter, I discussed the historical, psychological, and linguistic factors that shaped the language-centered pedagogy. I also explored its theoretical principles and classroom procedures with particular reference to the audiolingual method. Being a theory-driven, systematically organized, and teacher-friendly pedagogy, language-centered pedagogy began its life well but failed to deliver on its central promise of developing effective communicative ability in the learner.

The widespread dissatisfaction with the language-centered pedagogy coupled with the new developments in the fields of psychology and linguistics ultimately motivated the search for a better method. The result is the advent of what is called communicative language teaching, which is normally treated as a prototypical example of a learner-centered pedagogy. To what extent the new pedagogy addressed the drawbacks of the one it sought to replace and to what degree it achieved its stated objectives are the focus of chapter 6.

Learner-Centered Methods

6. INTRODUCTION

The theoretical principles and classroom procedures of the language-centered pedagogy we discussed in the previous chapter shaped language teaching and teacher education for nearly a quarter century. However, by the late 1960s and early 1970s, researchers and teachers alike became increasingly skeptical about the effectiveness of the pedagogy to realize its stated goal of fostering communicative capability in the learner. The skepticism was grounded in the growing realization that the knowledge/ability required to correctly manipulate the structures of the target language is only a part of what is involved in learning and using it.

Although several applied linguists wrote about the state of language teaching, it was perhaps Newmark's seminal paper, "How Not to Interfere With Language Learning," published in 1966, that epitomized the doubts that prevailed among language teaching professionals, and opened up new avenues of pedagogic thought. He doubted whether language learning can be additive and linear as was steadfastly maintained by language-centered pedagogists. He asserted that

> if each phonological and syntactic rule, each complex of lexical features, each semantic value and stylistic nuance—in short, if each item which the linguist's analysis leads him to identify had to be acquired one at a time, proceeding from simplest to most complex, and then each had to be connected to specified stimuli or stimulus sets, the child learner would be old before he could say a single appropriate thing and the adult learner would be dead. (Newmark, 1966, p. 79)

So arguing, Newmark (1966) adopted the view that complex bits of language are learned a whole chunk at a time rather than learned as an assemblage of constituent items. He declared that language-centered pedagogy with its emphasis on sequential presentation, practice, and production of isolated linguistic items "constitutes serious interference with the language learning process" (p. 81). In making such a bold declaration, he was clearly ahead of his time. Although his provocative thoughts had to wait for full deployment until the advent of learning-centered methods (see chap. 7, this volume), they certainly highlighted the inadequacy of language-centered methods, and prompted the search for an alternative method.

The search was accelerated by a congruence of important developments in social sciences and humanities. Interestingly, almost all of the developments either occurred or became prominent in the 1960s, precisely when dissatisfaction with language-centered pedagogy was growing. As we saw in chapter 1, in linguistics, Chomsky demonstrated the generative nature of the language system and hypothesized about the innate ability of the human mind to acquire it. Halliday provided a different perspective to language, highlighting its functional properties. In sociolinguistics, Hymes proposed a theory of communicative competence incorporating sociocultural norms governing language communication. Austin's speech act theory elaborated on how language users perform speech acts such as requesting, informing, apologizing, and so forth. In psychology, behaviorism was yielding its preeminence to cognitivism, which believed in the role of human cognition as a mediator between stimulus and response. Sociologists were developing communication models to explain how language is used to construct social networks.

A development that was unrelated to the academic disciplines just mentioned, but one that hastened the search for an alternative method, was the formation of European Economic Community (EEC), a common market of Western European countries, a precursor to the current European Union (EU). By deliberate policy, the EEC eased trade and travel restrictions within multilingual Europe, which in turn provided an impetus for greater interaction among the people of the Western European countries and, consequently, provided a *raison d'etre* for developing a function-oriented language teaching pedagogy in order to meet their specific communicative needs. In 1971, the Council of Europe, a wing of EEC, commissioned a group of European applied linguists and entrusted them with the task of designing a new way to teach foreign languages.

Learning from the shortcomings of language-centered pedagogy and drawing from the newly available psychological and linguistic insights, Wilkins, a British applied linguist who was a member of the group commissioned by the Council of Europe, proposed a set of syllabuses for language teaching. Originally published as a monograph in 1972, a revised and expanded version of his proposals appeared in 1976 as a book titled *Notional Syllabuses*. Instead of merely a grammatical core, the new syllabus consisted of categories of notions such as time, sequence, quantity, location, and frequency, and categories of communicative functions such as informing, requesting, and instructing. The notional/functional syllabus, as it was known, provided a new way of exploiting the situational dialogue inherited from the past by indicating that formal and functional properties can after all be gainfully integrated. Thus began a language teaching movement which later became well-known as *communicative method* or *communicative approach* or simply *communicative language teaching*. The watchword here is, of course, communication; there will be more on this later.

It should be kept in mind that communicative language teaching is not a monolithic entity; different teachers and teacher educators offered different interpretations of the method within a set of broadly accepted theoretical principles so much so that it makes sense to talk about not one but several communicative methods. In what follows, I look at, in detail, the theoretical principles and classroom procedures associated with communicative language teaching, treating it as a prototypical example of a learner-centered pedagogy.

6.1. THEORETICAL PRINCIPLES

The conceptual underpinnings of learner-centered pedagogy are truly multidisciplinary in the sense that its theory of language, language learning, and language teaching came not only from the feeder disciplines of linguistics and psychology, but also from anthropology and sociology as well as from other subdisciplines such as ethnography, ethnomethodology, pragmatics, and discourse analysis. The influence of all these areas of inquiry is very much reflected in the theory of language communication adopted by learner-centered pedagogists.

6.1.1. Theory of Language

In order to derive their theory of language, learner-centered pedagogists drew heavily from Chomskyan formal linguistics, Hallidayan functional linguistics, Hymsian sociolinguistics, and Austinian speech act theory. In chapter 1, we discussed how these developments contributed to our understanding of the nature of language. Let us briefly recall some of the salient features.

Criticizing the basic tenets of structural linguistics, Chomsky pointed out that language constitutes not a hierarchical structure of structures as viewed by structuralists, but a network of transformations. He demonstrated the inadequacy of structuralism to account for the fundamental characteristics of language and language acquisition, particularly their creativity and uniqueness. Whereas structuralists focused on "surface" features of phonology and morphology, Chomsky was concerned with "deep" structures, and the way in which sentences are produced. Chomskyan linguistics thus fundamentally transformed the way we look at language as system. However, preoccupied narrowly with syntactic abstraction, it paid very little attention to meaning in a communicative context.

Going beyond the narrowness of syntactic abstraction, Halliday emphasized the triple macrofunctions of language—textual, interpersonal, and ideational. The textual function deals with the phonological, syntactic, and semantic signals that enable language users to understand and transmit messages. The interpersonal function deals with sociolinguistic features of language required to establish roles, relationships, and responsibilities in a communicative situation. The ideational function deals with the concepts and processes underlying natural, physical, and social phenomena. In highlighting the importance of the interplay between these three macrofunctions of language, Halliday invoked the "meaning potential" of language, that is, sets of options or alternatives that are available to the speaker–hearer.

It was this concern with communicative meaning that led Hymes to question the adequacy of the notion of grammatical competence proposed by Chomsky. Unlike Chomsky who focused on the "ideal" native speaker–hearer and an abstract body of syntactic structures, Hymes focused on the "real" speaker–hearer who operates in the concrete world of interpersonal communication. In order to operate successfully within a speech community, a person has to be not just grammatically correct but communicatively appropriate also, that is, a person has to learn what to say, how to say it, when to say it, and to whom to say it.

In addition to Hallidayan and Hymsian perspectives, learner-centered pedagogists benefited immensely from Austin's work. As we know, he looked at language as a series of speech acts we perform rather than as a collection of linguistic items we accumulate, an idea that fitted in perfectly with the concept of *language as communication*. We use language, Austin argued, to perform a large number of speech acts: to command, to describe, to agree, to inform, to instruct, and so forth. The function of a particular speech act can be understood only when the utterance is placed in a communicative context governed by commonly shared norms of interpretation. What is crucial here is the illocutionary force, or the intended meaning, of an utterance rather than the grammatical form an utterance may take.

By basing themselves on speech-act theory and discourse analysis, and by introducing perspectives of sociolinguistics, learner-centered pedagogists attempted to get closer to the concreteness of language use. Accordingly, they operated on the basis of the following broad principles:

- Language is a system for expressing meaning;
- the linguistic structures of language reflect its functional as well as communicative import;
- basic units of language are not merely grammatical and structural, but also notional and functional;
- the central purpose of language is communication; and
- communication is based on sociocultural norms of interpretation shared by a speech community.

In short, unlike language-centered pedagogists who treated language largely as system, learner-centered pedagogists treated it both as system and as discourse, at least some of the features of the latter (cf. chap. 1, this volume).

6.1.2. Theory of Language Learning

Learner-centered pedagogists derived their language learning theories mainly from cognitive psychologists, who dismissed the importance given to habit formation by behaviorists, and instead focused on insight formation. They maintained that, in the context of language learning, the learner's cognitive capacity mediates between teacher input (stimulus) and learner output (response). The learner, based on the data provided, is capable of forming, testing, and confirming hypotheses, a sequence of psychological processes that ultimately contribute to language development. Thus, for cognitive psychologists, mental processes underlying response is important, not the response itself. They also believed in developmental stages of language learning and, therefore, partial learning on the part of the learner is natural and inevitable. Because of the active involvement of the learner in the learning process, only meaningful learning, not rote learning, can lead to internalization of language systems (for more details, see the section on intake processes in chap. 2, this volume).

Consistent with the theory of language just discussed, learner-centered pedagogists looked at language communication as a synthesis of textual, interpersonal, and ideational functions. These functions, according to Breen and Candlin (1980), involve the abilities of interpretation, expression, and negotiation, all of which are intricately interconnected with one another during communicative performance. They suggest that language learning

is most appropriately seen as communicative interaction involving all the participants in the learning and including the various material resources on which the learning is exercised. Therefore, language learning may be seen as a process which grows out of the interaction between learners, teachers, texts and activities. (p. 95)

It must not be overlooked that in foregrounding the communicative abilities of interpretation, expression, and negotiation, learner-centered pedagogists did not neglect the importance of grammar learning. As Widdowson (2003) recently lamented, the concern for communicative function was misconstrued by some as a justification for disregarding grammar. "But such a view runs directly counter to Halliday's concept of function where there can be no such disjunction since it has to do with semantically encoded meaning *in form*. This concept of function would lead to a renewed emphasis on grammar, not to its neglect" (p. 88, emphasis in original). As a matter of fact, learner-centered pedagogists insisted that language learning entails the development of both accuracy and fluency, where accuracy activity involves conscious learning of grammar and fluency activity focuses on communicative potential (Brumfit, 1984).

In a recent interpretation of the learning objectives of communicative language teaching, Savignon (2002, pp. 114–115) considers the five goal areas, (known as Five Cs: communication, cultures, connections, comparisons, and communities) agreed upon as National Standards for Foreign Language Learning in the United States as representing a holistic, communicative approach to language learning:

- The *communication* goal area addresses the learner's ability to use the target language to communicate thoughts, feelings, and opinions in a variety of settings;
- the *cultures* goal area addresses the learner's understanding of how the products and practices of a culture are reflected in the language;
- the *connections* goal area addresses the necessity for learners to learn to use the language as a tool to access and process information in a diversity of contexts beyond the classroom;
- the *comparisons* goal area are designed to foster learner insight and understanding of the nature of language and culture through a comparison of the target language and culture with the languages and cultures already familiar to them; and
- the *communities* goal area describes learners' lifelong use of the language, in communities and contexts both within and beyond the school setting itself.

These learning goals, Savignon rightly asserts, move the communicative language teaching toward a serious consideration of the discoursal and sociocultural features of language use.

6.1.3. Theory of Language Teaching

As can be expected, learner-centered pedagogists took their pedagogic bearings from the theories of language and language learning outlined above. Consequently, they recognized that it is the responsibility of the language teacher to help learners (a) develop the knowledge/ability necessary to manipulate the linguistic system and use it spontaneously and flexibly in order to express their intended message; (b) understand the distinction, and the connection, between the linguistic forms they have mastered and the communicative functions they need to perform; (c) develop styles and strategies required to communicate meanings as effectively as possible in concrete situations; and (d) become aware of the sociocultural norms governing the use of language appropriate to different social circumstances (Littlewood, 1981, p. 6).

In order to carry out the above responsibilities, it was argued, language teachers must foster meaningful communication in the classroom by

- Designing and using information-gap activities where when one learner in a pair-work exchange knows something the other learner does not;
- offering choice of response to the learner, that is, open-ended tasks and exercises where the learner determines what to say and how to say it;
- emphasizing contextualization rather than decontextualized drills and pattern practices;
- using authentic language as a vehicle for communication in class;
- introducing language at discoursal (and not sentential) level;
- tolerating errors as a natural outcome of language development; and
- developing activities that integrate listening, speaking, reading, and writing skills.

These and other related measures recognize the importance of communicative abilities of negotiation, interpretation, and expression that are considered to be the essence of a learner-centered pedagogy.

Such recognition also entailed a reconsideration of the role played by teachers and learners in a communicative classroom. Breen and Candlin (1980) identified two main roles for the "communicative" teacher.

The first role is to facilitate the communicative process between all participants in the classroom, and between those participants and the various activities and texts. The second role is to act as an *interdependent* participant within the learning-teaching group. This latter role is closely related to the objective of the first role and it arises from it. These roles imply a set of secondary roles for the teacher: first, as an organizer of resources and as a resource himself. Second, as a guide within the classroom procedures and activities. In this role the teacher endeavors to make clear to the learners what they need to do in order to achieve some specific activity or task, if they indicate that such guidance is necessary. (p. 99, emphasis as in original)

The learners have to take an active role too. Instead of merely repeating after the teacher or mindlessly memorizing dialogues, they have to learn to navigate the self, the learning process, and the learning objectives.

6.1.4. Content Specifications

In order to meet the requirements of the learning and teaching principles they believed in, learner-centered pedagogists opted for a product-oriented syllabus design just as their language-centered counterparts did before them, but with one important distinction: Whereas the language-centered pedagogists sought to select and sequence grammatical items, learner-centered pedagogists sought to select and sequence grammatical as well as notional/functional categories of language. Besides, they put a greater premium on the communicative needs of their learners. It is, therefore, only natural that a learner-centered curriculum is expected to provide a framework for identifying, classifying, and organizing language features that are needed by the learners for their specific communicative purposes. One way of constructing a profile of the communicative needs of the learners is "to ask the question: Who is communicating with whom, why, where, when, how, at what level, about what, and in what way?" (Munby, 1978, p. 115).

The 1970s witnessed several frameworks for content specifications geared toward a learner-centered pedagogy. As mentioned earlier, Wilkins (1972) proposed a notional/functional syllabus containing an inventory of semantico-grammatical notions such as duration, frequency, quantity, dimension, and location, and communicative functions such as greeting, warning, inviting, requesting, agreeing, and disagreeing. His syllabus was further expanded by another member of the Council of Europe, van Ek (1975) who, based on a detailed needs analysis, identified the basic communicative needs of European adult learners, and produced an inventory of notions, functions and topics as well as grammatical items required to express them. Munby's (1978) book titled *Communicative Syllabus Design* contains an elaborate taxonomy of specifications of communicative functions, discourse features and textual operations along with micro- and macroplanning.

Any textbook writer or language teacher can easily draw from such inventories and taxonomies to design a syllabus that addresses the specific needs and wants of a given group of learners. Finocchiaro and Brumfit (1983) in their well-known book, *The Functional-Notional Approach: From Theory to Practice,* provided detailed guidelines for teachers. Here is part of a sample "mini-curriculum" adapted from their work:

Title and Function	Situation	Communicative Expressions	Structures	Nouns	Verbs	Adj.	Adv.	Structure Words	Activities
Apologizing	Theater (asking someone to change seats)	Excuse me. Would you mind . . . ? I'm very grateful.	V + *ing*	seat place friend	move change				Dialogue study Roleplay Paired practice
Apologizing	Department store (Returning something)	I'm sorry. Would it be possible . . . ?	Simple past Present perfect	shirt	buy wear	small	too	you	Aural comprehension Indirect speech
Requesting directions	At the bus stop	I beg your pardon. Could you tell me . . . ?	Interrogatives (simple present) Modal *must*	names of places	must get to get off take		how where	us	Reading Questions and answers Cloze procedure Dictation

(Adapted from Finocchiaro & Brumfit, 1983, p. 38)

The sample units make it clear to the teacher and the learner what communicative function (e.g., apologizing) is highlighted and in what context (e.g., theater, store, etc.) as well as what grammatical structures/items and vocabulary are needed to carry out the function. They also indicate to the teacher possible classroom activities that can be profitably employed to realize the learning and teaching objectives.

The focus on the learner's communicative needs, which is the hallmark of a learner-centered pedagogy, has positive as well as problematic aspects to it. There is no doubt that identifying and meeting the language needs of specific groups of learners will be of great assistance in creating and sustaining learner motivation, and in making the entire learning/teaching operation a worthwhile endeavor. Besides, a need-based, learner-centered curriculum will give the classroom teachers a clear pathway to follow in their effort to maximize learning opportunities for their learners. Such a curriculum easily facilitates the designing of specific purpose courses geared to the needs of groups of learners having the same needs (such as office secretaries, air traffic controllers, lawyers, or engineers). However, as Johnson (1982) correctly pointed out, if we are dealing with, as we most often do, groups of learners each of whom wishes to use the language for different purposes, then, it may be difficult to derive a manageable list of notions and functions. The Council of Europe attempted to tackle this practical problem by identifying a "common core" of functions such as greeting, introducing, inviting, and so forth associated with the general area of social life alongside other specialized, work-related units meant for specific groups of learners.

Yet another serious concern about specifying the content for a learner-centered class is that there are no criteria for selecting and sequencing language input to the learner. Johnson (1982), for instance, raised a few possibilities and dismissed all of them as inadequate. The criterion of simplicity, which was widely followed by language-centered pedagogists, is of little use here because whether a communicative function or a speech act is simple or complex does not depend on the grammatical and discoursal features of a function but on the purpose and context of communication. A second possible criterion—priority of needs—is equally problematic because, as Johnson (1982) observed, "questions like 'Do the students need to learn how to *apologize* before learning how to *interrupt*?' have no clear answer" (p. 71). Practical difficulties such as these notwithstanding, the learner-centered syllabus provided a clear statement of learning/teaching objectives for classroom teachers to pursue in their classroom.

6.2. CLASSROOM PROCEDURES

The content specifications of learner-centered pedagogy are a clear and qualitative extension of those pertaining to language-centered pedagogy, an extension that can make a huge difference in the instructional design.

But, from a classroom procedural point of view, there is no *fundamental* difference between language-centered pedagogy and learner-centered pedagogy. The rationale behind this rather brisk observation will become apparent as we take a closer look at the input modifications and interactional activities recommended by learner-centered pedagogists.

6.2.1. Input Modifications

Unlike the language-centered pedagogist, who adopted an almost exclusive form-based approach to input modifications, learner-centered pedagogists pursued a form- and meaning-based approach. Recognizing that successful communication entails more than structures, they attempted to connect form and meaning. In a sense, this connection is indeed the underlying practice of any method of language teaching for, as Brumfit and Johnson (1979) correctly pointed out,

> no teacher introduces "shall" and "will" (for example) without relating the structure implicitly or explicitly to a conceptual meaning, usually that of futurity; nor would we teach (or be able to teach) the English article system without recourse to the concepts of countableness and uncountableness. (p. 1)

What learner-centered pedagogists did, and did successfully, was to make this connection explicit at the levels of syllabus design, textbook production, and classroom input and interaction. Notice how, for example, the minicurriculum cited (section 6.1.4) focuses on the communicative function of "apologizing," while at the same time, identifying grammatical structures and vocabulary items needed to perform that function.

In trying to make the form-function connection explicit, language-centered pedagogists assumed that contextual meaning can be analyzed sufficiently and language input can be modified suitably so as to present the learner with a useable and useful set of form- and meaning-based learning materials. Such an assumption would have been beneficial if there is a one-to-one correspondence between grammatical forms and communicative functions. We know that a single form can express several functions just as a single function can be expressed through several forms. To use an example given by Littlewood (1981)

> the speaker who wants somebody to close the door has many linguistic options, including "Close the door, please," "Could you please close the door?," "Would you mind closing the door?," or "Excuse me, could I trouble you to close the door?" Some forms might only perform this directive function in the context of certain social relationships—for example, "You've left the door open!" could serve as a directive from teacher to pupil, but not from teacher to principal. Other forms would depend strongly on shared situational knowl-

edge for their correct interpretation, and could easily be misunderstood (e.g. "Brrr! It's cold, isn't it?"). (p. 2)

Similarly, a single expression, "I've got a headache" can perform the functions of a warning, a request, or an apology depending on the communicative context.

Language input in learner-centered pedagogy, then, can only provide the learner with standardized functions embedded in stereotypical contexts. It is almost impossible to present language functions in a wide range of contexts in which they usually occur. It is, therefore, left to the learner to figure out how the sample utterances are actually realized and reformulated to meet interpretive norms governing effective communication in a given situation. Whether the learner is able to meet this challenge or not depends to a large extent on the way in which interactional activities are carried out in the classroom.

6.2.2. Interactional Activities

To operationalize their input modifications in the classroom, learner-centered pedagogists followed the same presentation–practice–production sequence popularized by language-centered pedagogists but with one important distinction: Whereas the language-centered pedagogists presented and helped learners practice and produce grammatical items, learner-centered pedagogists presented and helped learners practice and produce grammatical as well as notional/functional categories of language. It must, however, be acknowledged that learner-centered pedagogists came out with a wide variety of innovative classroom procedures such as pair work, group work, role-play, simulation games, scenarios and debates that ensured a communicative flavor to their interactional activities.

One of the sources of communicative activities widely used by English language teachers during the 1980s is *Communicative Language Teaching—An Introduction,* by Littlewood (1981). In it, he presents what he calls a "methodological framework," consisting of precommunicative activities and communicative activities diagrammatically represented as

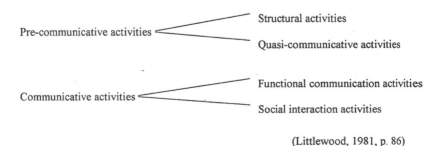

(Littlewood, 1981, p. 86)

Stating that these categories and subcategories represent differences of emphasis and orientation rather than distinct divisions, Littlewood explains that through precommunicative activities, the teacher provides the learners with specific knowledge of linguistic forms, and gives them opportunities to practice. Through communicative activities, the learner is helped to activate and integrate those forms for meaningful communication. The teacher also provides corrective feedback at all stages of activities, because error correction, unlike in the language-centered pedagogy, is not frowned upon.

Littlewood suggests several classroom activities that are typical of a learner-centered pedagogy. For example, consider the following activity:

Discovering Missing Information

Learner A has information represented in tabular form. For example, he may have a table showing distances between various towns or a football league table showing a summary of each team's results so far (how many games they have played/won/lost/drawn, how many goals they have scored, etc.). However, some items of information have been deleted from the table. Learner B has an identical table except that different items of information have been deleted. Each learner can therefore complete his own tale by asking his partner for the information that he lacks.

As with several previous activities, the teacher may (if he wishes) specify what language forms are to be used. For example, the distances table would require forms such as "How far is . . . from . . . ?" "Which town is . . . miles from . . . ?," while the league table would require forms such as "How many games have . . . played?" and "How many goals have . . . scored?."

(Littlewood, 1981, p. 26)

And another:

Pooling Information to Solve a Problem

Learner A has a train timetable showing the times of trains from X to Y. Learner B has a timetable of trains from Y to Z. For example:

Learner A's information:

Newtown dep.	:	11.34	13.31	15.18	16.45
Shrewsbury arr.	:	12.22	14.18	16.08	18.25

Learner B's information:

Shrewsbury dep.   :   13.02   15.41   16.39   18.46
Swansea arr.   :   17.02   19.19   20.37   22.32

Together, the learners must work out the quickest possible journey from Newtown to Swansea. Again, of course, it is important that they should not be able to *see* each other's information.

(Littlewood, 1981, pp. 34–35)

These two examples illustrate functional communication activities. The idea behind them is that "the teacher structures the situation so that learners have to overcome an information gap or solve a problem. Both the stimulus for communication and the yardstick for success are thus contained within the situation itself: learners must work towards a definite solution or decision" (Littlewood, 1981, p. 22). The activities are intended to help the learner find the language necessary to convey an intended message effectively in a specific context. The two sample activities show how two learners in a paired-activity are required to interact with each other, ask questions, seek information, and pool the information together in order to carry out the activities successfully.

Social interaction activities focus on an additional dimension of language use. They require that earners take into consideration the social meaning as well as the functional meaning of different language forms. Consider the following activities:

Role Playing Controlled Through Cues and Information

Two learners play the roles of a prospective guest at a hotel and the hotel manager.

Student A: You arrive at a small hotel one evening. In the foyer, you meet the manager(ess) and:

Ask if there is a room vacant.
Ask the price, including breakfast.
Say how many nights you would like to stay.
Ask where you can park your car for the night.
Say what time you would like to have breakfast.

Student B: You are the manager(ess) of a small hotel that prides itself on its friendly atmosphere. You have a single and a double room vacant for tonight. The prices are: £8.50 for the single room, £15.00 for the double room. Breakfast is £1.50 extra per person. In the street behind the hotel, there is a free car park. Guests can have tea in bed in the morning, for 50p.

(Littlewood, 1981, pp. 52–53)

As Littlewood (1981) explains,

the main structure for the interaction now comes from learner A's cues. A can thus introduce variations and additions without throwing B into confusion. For the most part, B's role requires him to respond rather than initiate, though he may also introduce topics himself (e.g. by asking whether A would like tea). (p. 53)

In carrying out this social interaction activity, learners have to pay greater attention to communication as a social behavior, as the activity approximates a communicative situation the learners may encounter outside the classroom. The focus here is not just formal and functional effectiveness, but also social appropriateness.

As these examples indicate, classroom procedures of learner-centered pedagogy are largely woven around the sharing of information and the negotiation of meaning. This is true not only of oral communication activities, but also of reading and writing activities. Information-gap activities, which have the potential to carry elements of unpredictability, freedom of choice, and appropriate use of language, were found to be useful and relevant. So were role-plays, which are supposed to help the learners get ready for the "real world" communication outside the classroom. One of the challenges facing the classroom teacher, then, is to prepare the learners to make the connection between sample interactions practiced in the classroom and the communicative demands outside the classroom. Whether this transfer from classroom communication to "real world" communication can be achieved or not depends to a large extent on the role played by the teachers as well as the learners.

To sum up this section and to put it in the framework of the three types of interactional activities discussed in chapter 3, learner-centered pedagogists fully endorsed interaction as a textual activity by emphasizing form-based activities, that is, by encouraging conscious attention to the formal properties of the language. They also facilitated interaction as an interpersonal activity by opting for meaning-based activities, by attempting to make the connection between form and function explicit, and by helping the learner establish social relationships in the classroom through collaborative pair and group work. To a limited extent, they promoted interaction as an ideational activity, which focuses on the learner's social awareness and identity formation by encouraging learners at the higher levels of proficiency to share with others their life experiences outside the classroom and by organizing activities such as debates on current affairs. The degree to which the objectives of these types of activities were fully realized is bound to vary from class to class and from context to context.

6.3. A CRITICAL ASSESSMENT

Perhaps the greatest achievement of learner-centered pedagogists is that they successfully directed the attention of the language-teaching profession to aspects of language other than grammatical structures. By treating language as discourse, not merely as system, they tried to move classroom teaching away from a largely systemic orientation that relied upon a mechanical rendering of pattern practices and more toward a largely communicative orientation that relied upon a partial simulation of meaningful exchanges that take place outside the classroom. By considering the characteristics of language communication with all earnestness, they bestowed legitimacy to the basic concepts of negotiation, interpretation, and expression. They highlighted the fact that language is a means of conveying and receiving ideas and information as well as a tool for expressing personal needs, wants, beliefs, and desires. They also underscored the creative, unpredictable, and purposeful character of language communication.

Of course, the nature of communication that learner-centered pedagogists assiduously espoused is nothing new. It has long been practiced in other disciplines in social sciences such as communication studies. But what is noteworthy is that learner-centered pedagogists explored and exploited it seriously and systematically for the specific purpose of learning and teaching second and foreign languages. It is to their credit that, although being critical of language-centered pedagogy, they did not do away with its explicit focus on grammar but actually extended it to include functional features as well. In doing so, they anticipated some of the later research findings in second-language acquisition, which generally supported the view that

> form-focused instruction and corrective feedback provided within the context of a communicative program are more effective in promoting second language learning than programs which are limited to an exclusive emphasis on accuracy on the one hand or an exclusive emphasis on fluency on the other. (Lightbown & Spada, 1993, p. 105)

The explicit focus on grammar is not the only teaching principle that learner-centered pedagogists retained from the discredited tradition of audiolingualism. They also retained, this time to ill-effect, its cardinal belief in a linear and additive way of language learning as well as its presentation–practice–production sequence of language teaching. In spite of their interest in the cognitive–psychological principles of holistic learning, learner-centered pedagogists preselected and presequenced grammatical, lexical, and functional items, and presented to the learners one cluster of items at a time hoping that the learners would learn the discrete items in a linear and additive manner, and then put them together in some logical fashion in order get at the totality of the language as communication. As Widdowson (2003) recently reiterated,

> although there are differences of view about the language learning process, there is a general acceptance that whatever else it might be, it is not simply additive. The acquisition of competence is not accumulative but adaptive: learners proceed not by adding items of knowledge or ability, but by a process of continual revision and reconstruction. In other words, learning is necessarily a process of recurrent unlearning and relearning, whereby encoding rules and conventions for their use are modified, extended, realigned, or abandoned altogether to accommodate new language data." (pp. 140–141)

As mentioned earlier, and it is worth repeating, from a classroom methodological point of view, there are no *fundamental* differences between language-centered and learning-centered pedagogies. They adhere to different versions of the familiar linear and additive view of language learning and the equally familiar presentation–practice–production vision of language teaching. For some, this is too difficult and disappointing an interpretation to digest because for a considerable length of time, it has been propagated with almost evangelical zeal and clock-work regularity that communicative language teaching marked a revolutionary step in the methodological aspects of language teaching. The term, *communicative revolution*, one often comes across in the professional literature is clearly an overstatement. Those who make such a claim do so based more on the array of innovative classroom procedures recommended to be followed in the communicative classroom (and they indeed are innovative and impressive) than on their conceptual underpinnings.

I use the phrase, "recommended to be followed," advisedly because a communicative learning/teaching agenda, however well-conceived, cannot by itself guarantee a communicative classroom because communication "is what may or may not be achieved through classroom activity; it cannot be embodied in an abstract specification" (Widdowson, 1990, p. 130). Data-based classroom-oriented investigations conducted in various contexts by various researchers such as Kumaravadivelu (1993a), Legutke and Thomas (1991), Nunan (1987), and Thornbury (1996) revealed without any doubt that the so-called communicative classrooms are anything but communicative. Nunan observed that, in the classes he studied, form was more prominent in that function and grammatical accuracy activities dominated communicative fluency ones. He concluded, "there is growing evidence that, in communicative class, interactions may, in fact, not be very communicative after all" (p. 144). Legutke and Thomas (1991) were even more forthright: "In spite of trendy jargon in textbooks and teachers' manuals, very little is actually communicated in the L2 classroom. The way it is structured does not seem to stimulate the wish of learners to say something, nor does it tap what they might have to say . . ." (pp. 8–9). My research confirmed these findings, when I analyzed lessons taught by those claiming to follow communicative language teaching, and reached the conclusion: "Even teachers who are committed to CLT can fail to create opportunities for genuine interaction in their classroom" (Kumaravadivelu, 1993a, p. 113).

Yet another serious drawback that deserves mention is what Swan (1985) dubbed the "tabula rasa attitude" of the learner-centered pedagogists. That is, they firmly and falsely believed that adult L2 learners do not possess normal pragmatic skills, nor can they transfer them, from their mother tongue. They summarily dismissed the L1 pragmatic knowledge/ability L2 learners bring with them to the L2 classroom. Swan (1985) draws attention to the fact that adult second-language learners know how to negotiate meaning, convey information, and perform speech acts. "What they do not know" he declares rightly, "is what words are used to do it in a foreign language. They need lexical items, not skills . . ." (p. 9). In other words, L2 learners, by virtue of being members of their L1 speech community, know the basic rules of communicative use. All we need to do is to tap the linguistic and cultural resources they bring with them. This view has been very well supported by research. Summarizing nearly two decades of studies on pragmatics in second language learning and teaching, Rose and Kasper (2001) stated unequivocally, "adult learners get a considerable amount of L2 pragmatic knowledge for free. This is because some pragmatic knowledge is universal . . . and other aspects may be successfully transferred from the learners' L1" (p. 4). In a similar vein, focusing generally on the nonuse of L1 in the L2 classroom, Vivian Cook (2002) has all along questioned the belief that learners would fare better if they kept to the second language, and has recently recommended that teachers "develop the systematic use of the L1 in the classroom alongside the L2 as a reflection of the realities of the classroom situation, as an aid to learning and as a model for the world outside" (p. 332).

6.4. CONCLUSION

In this chapter, I outlined the theoretical principles and classroom procedures of learner-centered pedagogy with particular reference to communicative language teaching. By citing extensively from the works of Finnocchiaro and Brumfit, and Littlewood, I have tried to illustrate the pedagogy both from its earlier and its later versions. It is apparent that by focusing on language as discourse in addition to language as system, learner-centered pedagogists made a significant contribution to furthering the cause of principled language teaching. It is also clear that they introduced highly innovative classroom procedures aimed at creating and sustaining learner motivation. The focus on the learner and the emphasis on communication have certainly made the pedagogy very popular, particularly among language teachers around the world, some of whom take pride in calling themselves "communicative language teachers."

The popularity of the learner-centered pedagogy started fading at least among a section of the opinion makers of the profession when it became more and more clear that, partly because of its linear and additive view of language learning and its presentation–practice–production sequence of language teaching, it has not been significantly different from or demonstrably better than the language-centered pedagogy it sought to replace. Swan (1985) summed up the sentiments prevailed among certain quarters of the profession, thus:

> If one reads through the standard books and articles on the communicative teaching of English, one finds assertions about language use and language learning falling like leaves in autumn; facts, on the other hand, tend to be remarkably thin on the ground. Along with its many virtues, the Communicative Approach unfortunately has most of the typical vices of an intellectual revolution: it over-generalizes valid but limited insights until they become virtually meaningless; it makes exaggerated claims for the power and novelty of its doctrines; it misrepresents the currents of thought it has replaced; it is often characterized by serious intellectual confusion; it is choked with jargon. (p. 2)

These and other valid criticisms resulted in a disillusionment that eventually opened the door for a radical refinement of communicative language teaching, one that focused more on the psycholinguistic processes of learning rather than the pedagogic products of teaching. This resulted in what was called a "strong" or a "process-oriented" version of communicative language teaching. The original "weak" version merely tinkers with the traditional language-centered pedagogy by incorporating a much-needed communicative component into it, whereas the "strong" version "advances the claim that language is acquired through communication, so that it is not merely the question of activating an existing but inert knowledge of the language, but of stimulating the development of the language system itself. If the former could be described as 'learning to use' English, the latter entails 'using English to learn it'" (Howatt, 1984, p. 279).

But, such a "strong" version has to be so radically different both in theory and in practice that it would lead to terminological and conceptual confusion to continue to call it *communicative* method or *learner-centered* pedagogy. A more apt description would be *learning-centered* pedagogy, to which we turn next.

Chapter 7

Learning-Centered Methods

7. INTRODUCTION

In chapter 5 and chapter 6, we learned how language- and learner-centered methods are anchored primarily in the linguistic properties of the target language, the former on formal properties and the latter on formal as well as functional properties. We also learned that they both share a fundamental similarity in classroom methodological procedures: presentation, practice, and production of those properties. In other words, they are grounded on the linguistic properties underlying the target language rather than on the learning processes underlying L2 development. This is understandable partly because, unlike the advocates of learning-centered methods, those of language- and learner-centered methods did not have the full benefit of nearly a quarter century of sustained research in the psycholinguistic processes of L2 development. Studies on intake factors and intake processes governing L2 development (cf. chap. 2, this volume), in spite of their conceptual and methodological limitations, have certainly provided a fast-expanding site on which the edifice of a process-based method could be constructed.

During the 1980s, several scholars experimented with various process-oriented approaches to language teaching. These approaches include: comprehension approach (Winitz, 1981), natural approach (Krashen & Terrell, 1983), proficiency-oriented approach (Omaggio, 1986), communicational approach (Prabhu, 1987), lexical approach (Lewis, 1993; Willis, 1990) and process approach (Legutke & Thomas, 1991). In addition, there is a host of other local projects that are little known and less recognized (see Hamilton, 1996, for some). All these attempts indicate a rare convergence of ideas and interests in as wide a geographical area and as varied a pedagogical context as North America, Western Europe and South Asia. In this chapter, I focus on two learning-centered methods, mainly because both of them have been widely recognized and reviewed in the L2 literature: the Natural Approach, and the Communicational Approach.

The Natural Approach (NA) was originally proposed by Terrell at the University of California at Irvine initially for teaching beginning level Spanish for adult learners in the United States. It was later developed fully by combining the practical experience gained by Terrell and the theoretical constructs of the Monitor Model of second language acquisition proposed by Krashen, an applied linguist at the University of Southern California. The principles and procedures of the approach have been well articulated in Krashen and Terrell (1983). In addition, Brown and Palmer (1988) developed language specifications and instructional materials for applying Krashen's theory. The NA is premised on the belief that a language is best acquired when the learner's focus is not directly on the language.

The Communicational Approach, very much like the NA, is based on the belief that grammar construction can take place in the absence of any explicit focus on linguistic features. It was developed through a long-term project initiated and directed by Prabhu, who was an English Studies Specialist at the British Council, South India. Reviews of the project that have appeared in the literature call it the Bangalore Project (referring to the place of its origin), or the Procedural Syllabus (referring to the nature of its syllabus), but the project team itself used the name Communicational Teaching Project (CTP). The need for the project arose from a widespread dissatisfaction with a version of language-centered pedagogy followed in Indian schools. It was also felt that the learner-centered pedagogy with its emphasis on situational appropriacy might not be relevant for a context where English is taught and learned more for academic and administrative reasons than for social interactional purposes. The project was carried out for 5 years (1979–1984) in large classes in South India (30 to 45 students per class in primary schools, and 40 to 60 students per class in secondary schools). Few classes used teaching aids beyond the chalkboard, paper, and pencil. Toward the end of the project period and at the invitation of the project team, a group of program evaluators from the University of Edinburgh, U.K. evaluated the efficacy of the approach (see, e.g., Beretta & Davies, 1985). Thus, among the known learning-centered methods, the CTP is perhaps the only one that enjoys the benefits of a sustained systematic investigation as well as a formal external evaluation.

In the following sections of this chapter, I take a critical look at the theoretical principles and classroom procedures associated with learning-centered methods with particular reference to the NA and the CTP.

7.1. THEORETICAL PRINCIPLES

The theoretical foundations of learning-centered pedagogy are guided by the theory of language, language learning, language teaching, and curricular specifications that the proponents of the pedagogy deemed appropriate for constructing a new pedagogy.

7.1.1. Theory of Language

Although learning-centered pedagogists have not explicitly spelled out any specific theory of language that governs their pedagogy, their principles and procedures imply the same theory that informs the learner-centered pedagogy (see chap. 6, this volume, for details). They have drawn heavily from the Chomskyan cognitive perspective on language learning, and from the Hallidayan functional perspective on language use. They particularly owe a debt to Halliday's concept of *learning to mean* and his observation that language is learned only in relation to use. They have, however, been very selective in applying the Hallidayan perspective. For instance, they have emphasized the primacy of meaning and lexicon while, unlike Halliday, minimizing the importance of grammar. There is also an important difference between the NA and the CTP in terms of the theory of language: while the NA values sociocultural aspects of pragmatic knowledge, the CTP devalues them. The reason is simple: unlike the NA, the CTP is concerned with developing linguistic knowledge/ability that can be used for academic purposes rather than developing pragmatic knowledge/ability that can be used for social interaction.

7.1.2. Theory of Language Learning

Both the NA and the CTP share a well-articulated theory of language learning partially supported by research in L2 development. They both believe that L2 grammar construction can take place incidentally, that is, even when the learners' conscious attention is not brought to bear on the grammatical system. There is, however, a subtle difference in their approach to language learning. The NA treats L2 grammar construction as *largely* incidental. That is, it does not rule out a restricted role for explicit focus on grammar as part of an institutionalized language learning/teaching program or as part of homework given to the learner. The CTP, however, treats L2 grammar construction as *exclusively* incidental. That is, it rules out any role for explicit focus on grammar even in formal contexts. In spite of this difference, as we shall see, there are more similarities than differences between the two in terms of their theoretical principles and classroom procedures.

The language learning theory of learning-centered pedagogy rests on the following four basic premises:

1. Language development is incidental, not intentional.
2. Language development is meaning focused, not form focused.
3. Language development is comprehension based, not production based.
4. Language development is cyclical and parallel, not sequential and additive.

I briefly discuss each of these premises below, highlighting the extent to which the NA and the CTP converge or diverge.

Language development is incidental, not intentional. In the context of L2 development, the process of incidental learning involves the picking up of words and structures, "simply by engaging in a variety of communicative activities, in particular reading and listening activities, during which the learner's attention is focused on the meaning rather than on the form of language" (Hulstijn, 2003, p. 349). The incidental nature of language development has long been a subject of interest to scholars. As early as in the 17th century, philosopher Locke (1693) anticipated the basic principles of learning-centered methods when he said:

> learning how to speak a language . . . is an intuitive process for which human beings have a natural capacity that can be awakened provided only that the proper conditions exist. Put simply, there are three such conditions: someone to talk to, something to talk about, and a desire to understand and make yourself understood. (cited in Howatt, 1984, p. 192)

Much later, Palmer (1921) argued that (a) in learning a second language, we learn without knowing that we are learning; and (b) the utilization of the adult learner's conscious attention on language militates against the proper functioning of the natural capacities of language development.

Krashen has put forth similar arguments in three of his hypotheses that form part of his Monitor Model of second-language acquisition. His input hypothesis states "humans acquire language in only one way—by understanding messages, or by receiving comprehensible input. . . . If input is understood, and there is enough of it, the necessary grammar is automatically provided" (Krashen, 1985, p. 2). His acquisition/learning hypothesis states that adults have two distinct and independent ways of developing L2 knowledge/ability. One way is *acquisition*, a process similar, if not identical, to the way children develop their knowledge/ability in the first language. It is a subconscious process. Acquisition, therefore, is "picking-up" a language incidentally. Another way is *learning*. It refers to conscious knowledge of an

L2, knowing the rules, being aware of them, and being able to talk about them. Learning, therefore, is developing language knowledge/ability intentionally. His monitor hypothesis posits that acquisition and learning are used in very specific ways. Acquisition "initiates" our utterances in L2 and is responsible for our fluency. Learning comes into play only to make changes in the form of our utterance, after it has been "produced" by the acquired system. Together, the three hypotheses claim that incidental learning is what counts in the development of L2 knowledge/ability. It must, however, be noted that Krashen does not completely rule out intentional learning which, he believes, may play a marginal role.

Unlike Krashen, Prabhu claims that language development is exclusively incidental. He dismisses any explicit teaching of descriptive grammar to learners, not even for monitor use as advocated by Krashen. He rightly points out that the sequence and the substance of grammar that is exposed to the learners through systematic instruction may not be the same as the learners' mental representation of it. He, therefore, sees no reason why any structure or vocabulary has to be consciously presented by the teacher or practiced by the learner. The CTP operates under the assumption that

> while the conscious mind is working out some of the meaning-content, a subconscious part of the mind perceives, abstracts, or acquires (or recreates, as a cognitive structure) some of the linguistic structuring embodied in those entities, as a step in the development of an internal system of rules. (Prabhu, 1987, pp. 69–70)

The extent to which learning-centered pedagogists emphasize incidental learning is only partially supported by research on L2 learning and teaching. As discussed in chapter 2 and chapter 3, research makes it amply clear that learners need to pay conscious attention to, and notice the linguistic properties of, the language as well. It has been argued that there can be no L2 learning without attention and noticing although it is possible that learners may learn one thing when their primary objective is to do something else (Schmidt, 1993). As Hulstjin (2003) concluded in a recent review,

> on the one hand, both incidental and intentional learning require some attention and noticing. On the other hand, however, attention is deliberately directed to committing new information to memory in the case of intentional learning, whereas the involvement of attention is not deliberately geared toward an articulated learning goal in the case of incidental learning. (p. 361)

Language development is meaning focused, not form focused. Closely linked to the principle of incidental learning is the emphasis placed by learning-centered methods on meaning-focused activities. This principle, which is in fact the cornerstone of learning-centered methods, holds that L2 development is not a matter of accumulation and assimilation of phonological, syntactic and semantic features of the target language, but a matter of understanding the language input "where 'understand' means that the acquirer is focused on the meaning and not the form of the message" (Krashen, 1982, p. 21). Learning-centered pedagogists point out the futility of focusing on form by arguing that

> the internal system developed by successful learners is far more complex than any grammar yet constructed by a linguist, and it is, therefore, unreasonable to suppose that any language learner can acquire a deployable internal system by consciously understanding and assimilating the rules in a linguist's grammar, not to mention those in a pedagogic grammar which represent a simplification of the linguist's grammars and consequently can only be still further removed from the internally developed system. (Prabhu, 1987, p. 72)

These statements clearly echo an earlier argument by Newmark (1966) that "the study of grammar as such is neither necessary nor sufficient for learning to use a language" (p. 77).

The emphasis on an exclusively meaning-focused activity ignores the crucial role played by language awareness (see section 2.3.5 on knowledge factors) and several other intake factors and intake processes in L2 development. What is more, it even ignores the active role played by learners themselves in their own learning effort (see section 2.3.3 on tactical factors). Even if the textbook writer or the classroom teacher provides modified input that makes meaning salient, it is up to the learner to recognize or not to recognize it as such. As Snow (1987) perceptively observed, what learners have in mind when they are asked to do meaning-focused activities is more important than what is in the mind of the teacher. She goes on to argue, "learners might be doing a good deal of private, intra-cerebral work to make sense of, analyze, and remember the input, thus in fact imposing considerable intentional learning on a context that from the outside looks as if it might generate mostly incidental learning" (p. 4).

Snow's observations are quite revealing because, during the course of the CTP project, Prabhu (1987) had seen that

> individual learners became suddenly preoccupied, for a moment, with some piece of language, in ways apparently unrelated to any immediate demands of the on-going activity in the classroom. . . . It is possible to speculate whether such moments of involuntary language awareness might be symptoms (or "surfacings") of some internal process of learning, representing, for instance, a conflict in the emerging internal system leading to system revision. (p. 76)

What Prabhu describes may perhaps be seen as one indication of learners doing the kind of private, intracerebral work to which Snow alerted us.

Prabhu (1987) counters such learner behavior by arguing that "if the instances of involuntary awareness are symptoms of some learning process, any attempt to increase or influence them directly would be effort misdirected to symptoms, rather than to causes" (p. 77). This argument, of course, assumes that any "involuntary language awareness" on the part of the learner is only a symptom and not a cause. Our current state of knowledge is too inadequate to support or reject this assumption.

Language development is comprehension based, not production based. It makes sense empirically as well as intuitively to emphasize comprehension over production at least in the initial stages of L2 development. Comprehension, according to several scholars (see Krashen, 1982; Winitz, 1981, for earlier reports; Gass, 1997; van Patten, 1996, for later reviews), has cognitive, affective, and communicative advantages. Cognitively, they point out, it is better to concentrate on one skill at a time. Affectively, a major handicap for some learners is that speaking in public, using their still-developing L2, embarrasses or frightens them; they should therefore have to speak only when they feel ready to do so. Communicatively, listening is inherently interactive in that the listeners try to work out a message from what they hear; speaking can be, at least in the initial stages, no more than parrotlike repetitions or manipulations of a cluster of phonological features.

Learning-centered pedagogists believe that comprehension helps learners firm up abstract linguistic structures needed for the establishment of mental representations of the L2 system (see Section 2.4 on intake processes). Prabhu (1987, pp. 78–80), lists four factors to explain the importance of comprehension over production in L2 development:

- Unlike production, which involves public display of language causing a sense of insecurity or anxiety in the learner, comprehension involves only a safe, private activity;
- unlike production, which involves creating and supporting new language samples on the part of the learner, comprehension involves language features that are already present in the input addressed to the learner;
- unlike production, which demands some degree of verbal accuracy and communicative appropriacy, comprehension allows the learner to be imprecise, leaving future occasions to make greater precision possible;
- unlike production, over which the learner may not have full control, comprehension is controlled by the learner and is readily adjustable.

Prabhu also points out that learners can draw on extralinguistic resources, such as knowledge of the world and contextual expectations, in order to comprehend.

Learning-centered pedagogists also believe that once comprehension is achieved, the knowledge/ability to speak or write fluently will automatically emerge. In accordance with this belief, they allow production to emerge gradually in several stages. These stages typically consist of (a) response by nonverbal communication; (b) response with single words such as *yes, no, there, OK, you, me, house, run,* and *come*; (c) combinations of two or three words such as *paper on table, me no go, where book,* and *don't go*; (d) phrases such as I *want to stay, where you going, boy running*; (e) sentences; and finally (f) more complex discourse (Krashen &Terrell, 1983).

Because of their emphasis on comprehension, learning-centered pedagogists minimize the importance of learner output. Krashen (1981) goes to the extent of arguing that, in the context of subconscious language acquisition, "theoretically, speaking and writing are not essential to acquisition. One can acquire 'competence' in a second language, or a first language, without ever producing it" (pp. 107–108). In the context of conscious language learning, he believes that "output can play a fairly direct role . . . although even here it is not necessary" (1982, p. 61). He has further pointed out that learner production "is too scarce to make a real contribution to linguistic competence" (Krashen, 1998, p. 180). The emphasis learning-centered methods place on comprehension, however, ignores the role of learner output in L2 development. We learned from Swain's comprehensible output hypothesis and Schmidt's auto-input hypothesis that learner production, however meager it is, is an important link in the input–intake–output chain (see chap. 2 and chap. 3, this volume).

Language development is cyclical and parallel, not sequential and additive. Learning-centered pedagogists believe that the development of L2 knowledge/ability is not a linear, discrete, additive process but a cyclical, holistic process consisting of several transitional and parallel systems—a view that is, as we discussed in chapter 2, quite consistent with recent research in SLA. Accordingly, they reject the notion of linearity and systematicity as used in the language- and learner-centered pedagogies. According to them linearity and systematicity involve two false assumptions: "an assumption of isomorphism between the descriptive grammar used and the internal system, and an assumption of correspondence between the grammatical progression used in the teaching and the developmental sequence of the internal system" (Prabhu, 1987, p. 73). These assumptions require, as Widdowson (1990) observed, reliable information "about cognitive development at different stages of maturation, about the conditions, psychological and social, which attend the emergence in the mind of general problem-solving capabilities" (p. 147). Such information is not yet available.

In fact, the natural-order hypothesis proposed by Krashen as part of his Monitor Model states that the acquisition of grammatical structures proceeds in a predictable order. Based on this claim, Krashen originally advocated adherence to what he called *natural order sequence*, but has softened his position saying that the natural order hypothesis "does not state that every acquirer will acquire grammatical structures in the exact same order" (Krashen & Terrell, 1983, p. 28). Learners may tend to develop certain structures early and certain other structures late. In other words, learner performance sequence need not be the same as language learning sequence, and the learning sequence may not be the same as teaching sequence. Therefore, any preplanned progression of instructional sequence is bound to be counterproductive. In this respect, learning-centered pedagogists share the view expressed earlier by Newmark and Reibel (1968): "an adult can effectively be taught by grammatically unordered materials" and that such an approach is, indeed, "the only learning process which we know for certain will produce mastery of the language at a native level" (p. 153).

7.1.3. Theory of Language Teaching

In accordance with their theory of L2 development, learning-centered pedagogists assert that "language is best taught when it is being used to transmit messages, not when it is explicitly taught for conscious learning" (Krashen & Terrell, 1983, p. 55). Accordingly, their pedagogic agenda centers around what the teacher can do in order to keep the learners' attention on informational content rather than on the linguistic form. Their theory of language teaching is predominantly teacher-fronted, and therefore best characterized in terms of teacher activity in the classroom:

1. The teacher follows meaning-focused activities.
2. The teacher provides comprehensible input.
3. The teacher integrates language skills.
4. The teacher makes incidental correction.

Let us briefly outline each of the four.

The teacher follows meaning-focused activities. In keeping with the principle of incidental learning, learning-centered pedagogy advocates meaning-focused activities where the learner's attention is focused on communicative activities and problem-solving tasks, and not on grammatical exercises. Instruction is seen as an instrument to promote the learner's ability to understand and say something. Interaction is seen as a meaning-focused activity directed by the teacher. Language use is contingent upon task completion and the meaning exchange required for such a purpose. Any attention to language forms as such is necessarily incidental to communication. In the absence of any explicit focus on grammar, vocabulary gains importance because with more vocabulary, there will be more comprehension and with more comprehension, there will be, hopefully, more language development.

The teacher provides comprehensible input. In order to carry out meaning-focused activities, it is the responsibility of the teacher to provide comprehensible input that, according to Krashen, is $i + 1$ where i represents the learner's current level of knowledge/ability and $i + 1$, the next higher level. Because it is the stated goal of instruction to provide comprehensible input, and move the learner along a developmental path, "all the teacher need to do is make sure the students understand what is being said or what they are reading. When this happens, when the input is understood, if there is enough of input, $i + 1$ will usually be covered automatically" (Krashen & Terrell, 1983, p. 33). Prabhu uses the term, *reasonable challenge,* to refer to a similar concept. In order then to provide reasonably challenging comprehensible input, the teacher has to exercise language control, which is done not in any systematic way, but naturally, incidentally by regulating the cognitive and communicative complexity of activities and tasks. Regulation of reasonable challenge should then be based on ongoing feedback. Being the primary provider of comprehensible input, the teacher determines the topic, the task, and the challenge level.

The teacher integrates language skills. The principle of comprehension-before-production assumes that, at least at the initial level of L2 development, the focus is mainly on listening and reading. Therefore, learning-centered pedagogists do not believe in teaching language skills—listening, speaking, reading and writing—either in isolation or in strict sequence, as advocated by language-centered pedagogists. The teacher is expected to integrate language skills wherever possible. In fact, the communicative activities and problem-solving tasks create a condition where the learners have to draw, not just from language skills, but from other forms of language use, including gestures and mimes.

The teacher makes incidental correction. The learning-centered pedagogy is designed to encourage initial speech production in single words or short phrases thereby minimizing learner errors. The learners will not be forced to communicate before they are able, ready, and willing. However, they are bound to make errors particularly because of the conditions that are created for them to use their limited linguistic repertoire. In such a case, the learning-centered pedagogy attempts to avoid overt error correction. Any correction that takes place should be incidental and not systematic. According to Prabhu (1987, pp. 62–63), incidental correction, in contrast to systematic correction, is (a) confined to particular tokens (i.e. the error itself is corrected, but there is no generalization to the type of error it represents); (b) only responsive (i.e., not leading to any preventive or preemptive action); (c) facilitative (i.e. regarded by learners as a part of getting objective and not being more important than other aspects of the activity);

and (d) transitory (i.e., drawing attention to itself only for a moment—not for as long as systematic correction does).

7.1.4. Content Specifications

The theoretical principles of learning-centered pedagogy warrant content specifications that are very different from the ones we encountered in the case of language- and learner-centered pedagogies. As discussed in earlier chapters, language- and learner-centered methods adhere to a product-based syllabus, whereas learning-centered methods adhere to a process-based syllabus. Unlike the product-based syllabus, where the content of learning/teaching is defined in terms of linguistic features, the process-based syllabus defines it exclusively in terms of communicative activities. In other words, a learning-centered pedagogic syllabus constitutes an indication of learning tasks, rather than an index of language features, leaving the actual language to emerge from classroom interaction.

Because the process syllabus revolves around unpredictable classroom interaction rather than preselected content specifications, learning-centered pedagogists do not attach much importance to syllabus construction. In fact, the NA has not even formulated any new syllabus; it borrows the notional/functional component of the semantic syllabus associated with learner-centered pedagogies, and uses it to implement its own learning-centered pedagogy, thereby proving once again that syllabus specifications do not constrain classroom procedures (see chap. 3, this volume, for a detailed discussion on method vs. content). Unlike the NA, the CTP has formulated its own syllabus known as the *procedural syllabus*. According to Prabhu (1987), the term procedure is used in at least two senses: (a) a specification of classroom activities (including their meaning-content), which bring about language learning; and (b) a specification of procedures (or steps) of classroom activity, but without any implications with respect to either language content or meaning content.

In spite of the terminological differences (i.e. semantic vs. procedural), learning-centered pedagogists advocate a syllabus that consists of open-ended topics, tasks, and situations. The following fragments of a learning-centered syllabus provide some examples:

Students in the classroom (from Krashen & Terrell, 1983, pp. 67–70)

1. Personal identification (name, address, telephone number, age, sex, nationality, date of birth, marital status).
2. Description of school environment (identification, description, and location of people and objects in the classroom, description and location of buildings).
3. Classes.
4. Telling time.

Personal details (From Prabhu, 1987, pp. 138–143)

a. Finding items of information relevant to a particular situation in an individual's curriculum vitae.

b. Constructing a curriculum vitae from personal descriptions.

c. Organizing/reorganizing a curriculum vitae for a given purpose/audience.

d. Working out ways of tracing the owners of objects, from information gathered from the objects.

Role-plays (From Brown & Palmer, 1988, p. 51)

a. Ask directions.

b. Shop: for food, clothing, household items.

c. Get a hotel room.

d. Deal with bureaucrats: passport, visa, driver's license.

As the examples show, the syllabus is no more than an open-ended set of options, and as such, gives teachers the freedom and the flexibility needed to select topics and tasks, to grade them, and to present them in a sequence that provides a reasonable linguistic and conceptual challenge.

In any pedagogy, instructional textbooks are designed to embody the principles of curricular specifications. The purpose of the textbook in a learning-centered pedagogy, then, is to provide a context for discourse creation rather than a content for language manipulation. The context may be created from various sources such as brochures, newspaper ads, maps, railway timetables, simulation games, etc. Using these contexts, the teacher makes linguistic input available for and accessible to the learner. It is, therefore, the responsibility of the teacher to add to, omit, adapt, or adopt any of the contexts created by the materials designer depending on specific learning and teaching needs, wants, and situations.

In spite of such a responsibility thrust on the classroom teacher in selecting, grading, and sequencing topics and tasks, the learning-centered pedagogists provide very little guidance for the teacher. Krashen (1982) suggests that the teacher should keep in mind three requirements in the context of syllabus specifications: they can only teach what is learnable, what is portable (i.e. what can be carried in the learner's head), and what has not been acquired. A practical difficulty with this suggestion is that we do not at present know, nor are we likely to know any time soon, how to determine what is learnable, what is portable, or what has been acquired by the learner at any given time.

In addition, in the absence of any objective criteria, determining the linguistic, communicative and cognitive difficulty of learning-oriented tasks in an informed way becomes almost impossible. As Candlin (1987) rightly observed, "any set of task-based materials runs the risk of demoralizing as well as enhancing the self-confidence of learners, in that it is impossible for task designers to gauge accurately in advance the thresholds of competence of different learners" (p. 18). In this context, Prabhu (1987, pp. 87–88) has suggested five "rough measures" of task complexity. According to him, we should take into account: (a) The amount of information needed for the learner to handle a task; (b) the "distance" between the information provided and information to be arrived at as task outcome; (c) the degree of precision called for in solving a task; (d) the learner's familiarity with purposes and constraints involved in the tasks; and (e) the degree of abstractness embedded in the task. Even these "rough measures" require, as Widdowson (1990) pointed out, reliable information about "cognitive development at different stages of maturation, about the conditions, psychological and social, which attend the emergence in the mind of general problem-solving capabilities" (pp. 147–148). Clearly, in terms of the current state of our knowledge, we are not there yet.

Anticipating some of the criticisms about sequencing, learning-centered pedagogists argue that a lack of informed and clear criteria for sequencing linguistic input through communicative tasks need not be a hindrance. Sequencing becomes crucial only in language- and learner-centered pedagogies, which are predominantly content-driven. In a predominantly activity-driven pedagogy, the question of sequencing is only of peripheral interest because what is of paramount importance are classroom procedures rather than language specifications. What the teacher does in the classroom to provide reasonably challenging, comprehensible, meaning-focused input is more important than what the syllabus or the textbook dictates. Consequently, the right place where decisions concerning sequencing should be made is the classroom, and the right person to make those decisions is the practicing teacher.

7.2. CLASSROOM PROCEDURES

How do the theoretical principles of learning-centered pedagogy get translated into classroom procedures? In the following section, I deal with this question under two broad headings: input modifications and interactional activities.

7.2.1. Input Modifications

The primary objective of learning-centered pedagogy in terms of classroom procedures is the creation of optimum learning conditions through input modifications with the view to encouraging learners to have intense contact with reasonably challenging, comprehensible input. In that sense, a learning-centered pedagogy is essentially an input-oriented pedagogy, and as such, input modifications assume great significance in its planning and implementation. Of the three types of input modifications—form-based, meaning-based, and form-and meaning-based—discussed in chapter 3, learning-centered pedagogy rests exclusively upon meaning-based input modification with all its merits and demerits. As input-oriented pedagogic programs, learning-centered methods seem to follow classroom procedures that take the form of problem-posing, problem-solving, communicative tasks. They also seem to follow, with varying emphases, a particular pattern in their instructional strategy: They all seek to use a broad range of themes, topics and tasks, give manageable linguistic input, and create opportunities for the learner to engage in a teacher-directed interaction.

The meaning-focused activities advocated by learning-centered pedagogists include what Prabhu (1987, p. 46) has called (a) information-gap, (b) reasoning-gap, and (c) opinion-gap activities:

- Information-gap activity involves a transfer of given information generally calling for the decoding or encoding of information from one form to another. As an example, Prabhu suggests pair work in which each member of the pair has a part of the information needed to complete a task, and attempts to convey it verbally to the other.
- Reasoning-gap activity "involves deriving some new information from given information through the processes of inference, deduction, practical reasoning or perception of relationships and patterns" (Prabhu, 1987, p. 46). An example is a group of learners jointly deciding on the best course of action for a given purpose and within given constraints.
- Opinion-gap activity "involves identifying and articulating a personal preference, feeling or attitude" (p. 46) in response to a particular theme, topic or task. One example is taking part in a debate or discussion of a controversial social issue.

While the NA followed all these types of activities, the CTP preferred reasoning-gap activity, which proved to be most satisfying in the classroom. In addition, the NA, in accordance with its principle of lowering the affective filters, deliberately introduced an affective-humanistic dimension to classroom activities for the specific purpose of creating or increasing learners' emotional involvement.

The underlying objective of all these activities is, of course, to provide comprehensible input in order to help learners understand the message. The NA believes that comprehensibility of the input will be increased if the teacher uses repetition and paraphrase, as in:

There are two men in this picture. Two. One, two (counting). They are young. There are two young men. At least I think they are young. Do you think that they are young? Are the two men young? Or old? Do you think that they are young or old? (Krashen & Terrell, 1983, p. 77)

The teacher is expected to weave these repetitions naturally into classroom discourse so that they do not sound like repetitions. This procedure not only helps the learner understand the message but it also tends to minimize errors because the learner is expected to respond in single words or short phrases. In the CTP, the language necessary for the learner to accomplish a task emerges through what is called the pre-task. During the pre-task stage, the teacher provides appropriate linguistic assistance by paraphrasing or glossing expressions, by employing parallel situations or diagrams, or by re-organizing information (see the classroom transcript to come). What is achieved through the pre-task is the regulation of comprehensible input.

It is in the context of regulating language input that Prabhu introduces the concept of *reasonable challenge*. The concept relates to both the cognitive difficulty and the linguistic complexity of the task, and, therefore, it is something that the teacher has to be aware of through ongoing feedback from learners. When classroom activities turn out to be difficult for learners, the teacher should be able "to guide their efforts step by step, making the reasoning explicit or breaking it down into smaller steps, or offering parallel instances to particular steps" (Prabhu, 1987, p. 48). Such a regulation of input is deemed necessary to make sure that the learner perceives the task to be challenging but attainable.

Within such a context, the linguistic input available in the classroom comes mostly from the teacher. The teacher speaks only the target language while the learners use either their first language or the second. If the learners choose to respond in the still-developing target language, their errors are not corrected unless communication is seriously impaired, and even then, only incidental correction is offered. There is very little interactive talk among the learners themselves because the learners' output is considered secondary to L2 development.

Learning-centered pedagogists contend that regulating input and teacher talk in order to provide reasonably challenging, comprehensible input is qualitatively different from systematized, predetermined, linguistic input associated with language- and learner-centered pedagogies. The language that is employed in learning-centered tasks, they argue, is guided and constrained only by the difficulty level of the task on hand. However, regardless of the pedagogic intentions, the instructional intervention and the control of language in the way just characterized appears to bear a remarkable resemblance to the methods that the learning-centered pedagogy is quite explicitly intended to replace (Beretta, 1990; Brumfit, 1984; Widdowson, 1990).

Furthermore, as the experimental studies reviewed in chapter 3 show, meaning-focused input modifications by themselves do not lead to the development of desired levels of language knowledge/ability. Learners should be helped to obtain language input in its full functional range, relevant grammatical rules and sociolinguistic norms in context, and helpful corrective feedback. The studies also show that it is the meaningful interaction that accelerates the learning process. Besides, the input modifications advocated by learning-centered pedagogies create a classroom atmosphere that can only lead to limited interactional opportunities, as we see next.

7.2.2. Interactional Activities

In spite of the underlying theoretical principle that it is through meaningful interaction with the input, the task, and the teacher that learners are given the opportunity to explore syntactic and semantic choices of the target language, learning-centered pedagogists attach a very low priority to negotiated interaction between participants in the classroom event. According to them, two-way interaction is not essential for language development. What is essential is the teacher talk. When we "just talk to our students, if they understand, we are not only giving a language lesson, we may be giving the best possible language lesson since we will be supplying input for acquisition" (Krashen & Terrell, 1983, p. 35). Even watching television, if it is comprehensible, is considered more helpful than two-way interaction. In chapter 3, we discussed how the three interrelated, overlapping dimensions of classroom interaction—interaction as a textual activity, interaction as an interpersonal activity, and interaction as an ideational activity—make it easier for learners to notice potential language input and recognize form-function relationships embedded in the input. Let us see how these dimensions of interactional modifications are realized in the learning-centered pedagogy.

7.2.2.1. Interaction as a Textual Activity.   From the perspective of interaction as a textual activity, the learning-centered class offers considerable evidence for the predominance of the teacher's role in providing, not only reasonably challenging input, but also linguistic and conversational cues that help the learner participate in classroom interaction. Although the explicit focus of the interaction is supposed to be on understanding the intended message, it has not been possible to fully ignore the textual realization of the message content in general, and the syntactic and semantic features of the language input in particular.

To encourage learner participation and early production, Krashen and Terrell (1983) suggested several procedures including what they call open-ended sentence, open dialogue, and association. In open-ended sentence, the learners are given a sentence with an open slot provided "for their contribution." For example:

> "In this room there is a _____. I am wearing a _____. In my
>   purse there is a _____.
> In my bedroom I have a _____. After class I want to _____. (p.
>   84).

The open dialogue provides two and three line dialogues to lead learners "to creative production." The dialogues are practiced in small groups. For example:

> Where are you going?
> To the _____
> What for?
> To _____ (p. 84).

Association activities are intended to get students to participate in conversation about activities they enjoy doing. Besides, the meaning of a new item "is associated not only with its target language form but with a particular student." For example:

> I like to _____
> you like to _____
> he likes to _____
> she likes to _____ (p. 85).

All these procedures involve prefabricated patterns that are "memorized 'chunks' that can be used as unanalyzed pieces of language in conversation" (p. 85). The teacher is expected to make comments and ask simple questions based on the learner's response. Once again, the focus has been teacher input rather than learner output.

At a later stage in learner production, interaction as a textual activity goes beyond memorized chunks and unanalyzed pieces. Consider the following episode from a typical CTP class during the pre-task stage, in which the teacher is expected to provide reasonably challenging linguistic input. The episode deals with the timetable for an express train:

> *Teacher*:   That is Brindavan Express which goes from Madras to Bangalore. Where does it stop on the way?

Students: Katpadi.

Teacher: Katpadi and . . .

Students: Jolarpet.

Teacher: Jolarpet, yes. What time does it leave Madras?

Students: Seven twenty-five a.m.

Teacher: Seven twenty-five . . .

Students: . . . a.m.

Teacher: Yes, seven twenty-five a.m. What time does it arrive in Bangalore?

Students: Ninc . . . One

Teacher: What time does it arrive . . .

Students: (severally) One p.m. . . . One thirty p.m. . . . One p.m.

Teacher: Who says one p.m.? . . . Who says one thirty p.m.? (pause) Not one thirty p.m. One p.m. is correct. One p.m. When does it arrive in Katpadi?

Students: Nine fifteen a.m. . . . Nine fifteen a.m.

Teacher: . . . arrive . . . arrive in Katpadi.

Students: Nine fifteen a.m.

Teacher: Nine fifteen a.m. Correct . . . When does it leave Jolarpet? Don't give the answer, put up your hands. When does it leave Jolarpet? When does it leave Jolarpet? When does it leave Jolarpet? When does it leave Jolarpet? (pause) Any more . . . ? [indicates student 11].

Student 11: Ten thirty p.m.

Student: Leaves Jolarpet at ten thirty . . .

Student 11: a.m.

Teacher: a.m. yes. Ten thirty a.m. correct . . . Now you have to listen carefully. For how long . . . for how long does it stop at Katpadi? How long is the stop in Katpadi . . . [indicates student 4].

Student 4:   Five minutes.

Teacher: Five minutes, yes. How do you know?

Student X: Twenty . . .

Student 4:   Twenty minus fifteen.

Teacher: Fifteen . . . nine fifteen arrival, nine twenty departure . . . twenty minus fifteen, five, yes . . . How long is the stop at Jolarpet? How long is the stop at Jolarpet? [After a pause, the teacher indicates student 12].

Student 12: Two minutes.

Teacher: Two minutes, yes. Thirty minus twenty-eight, two minutes, yes, correct.

(Prabhu, 1987, pp. 126–127)

Here, the teacher leads the learners step by step to the desired outcome through a series of meaning-oriented exchanges, each step requiring a greater effort of cognitive reasoning than the previous one. The teacher also simplifies the linguistic input to make it more comprehensible when the learner's response indicates the need for such simplification. In the absence of memorized chunks, learners are forced to use their limited repertoire in order to cope with the developing discourse. They have been observed to adopt various strategies such as

> using single words, resorting to gestures, quoting from the blackboard or the sheet which stated the task, waiting for the teacher to formulate alternative responses so that they could simply choose one of them, seeking a suggestion from a peer, or, as a last resort, using the mother tongue. (Prabhu, 1987, p. 59)

As the aforementioned examples show, interaction in the meaning-oriented, learning-centered class does involve, quite prominently, characteristics of interaction as a textual activity, that is, interactional modifications initiated and directed by the teacher in order to provide linguistic as well as conversational signals that directly or indirectly sensitize the learner to the syntactic and semantic realizations of the message content. There are critics who, not without justification, consider that this kind of interaction implicitly involves a focus on the form characteristic of language- and learner-centered methods (e.g., Beretta, 1990).

7.2.2.2. Interaction as an Interpersonal Activity. Interaction as an interpersonal activity offers participants in the L2 class opportunities to establish and maintain social relationships and individual identities through pair and/or group activities. It enhances personal rapport and lowers the affective filter. Of the two learning-centered methods considered here, the NA has deliberately introduced what are called affective-humanistic activities involving the learner's wants, needs, feelings, and emotions. These activities are carried out mainly through dialogues, role-plays, and interviews. At the initial stages of language production, these activities begin with short dialogues that contain a number of routines and patterns although more open-ended role-plays and interviews are used at later stages. Consider the following:

1. Dialogue:
    Student 1: What do you like to do on Saturdays?
    Student 2: I like to —————.
    Student 1: Did you ————— last Saturday?
    Student 2: Yes, I did.
        (No, I didn't. I —————.) (p. 100)
2. Role-play:
    You are a young girl who is sixteen years old. You went out with a friend at eight o'clock. You are aware of the fact that your parents require you to be at home at 11:00 at the latest. But you return at 12:30 and your father is very angry.

    Your father: Well, I'm waiting for an explanation.
                     Why did you return so late?
    You: ————————— (p. 101).
3. Interview:
    When you were a child, did you have a nickname? What games did you play? When during childhood did you first notice the difference between boys and girls? What is something you once saw that gave you a scare? (p. 102)

These affective-humanistic activities, as Krashen and Terrell (1983) pointed out, have several advantages: they have the potential to lower affective filters, to provide opportunities for interaction in the target language, to allow the use of routines and patterns, and to provide comprehensible input. Once again, even though dialogues, role-plays and interviews have been used in language- and learner-centered pedagogies, the affective-humanistic activities advocated by learning-centered pedagogists are supposed to form the center of the program and are expected to help learners regulate input and manage conversations.

Unlike the NA, the CTP does not, by design, promote interaction as an interpersonal activity. The CTP treats affective-humanistic activities as incidental to teacher-directed reasoning. In that sense, it is relatively more teacher fronted than the NA. Interaction as an interpersonal activity through pair and group work is avoided mainly because of "a risk of fossilization—that is to say of learners' internal systems becoming too firm too soon and much less open to revision when superior data are available" (Prabhu, 1987, p. 82). Empirical evidence, however, suggests that the fear of fossilization is not really well-founded. A substantial body of L2 interactional studies demonstrates that pair and group activities produce more interactional opportunities than teacher-fronted activities. They also show that learner–learner interaction produces more opportunities for negotiation of meaning than do teacher–learner interactions, thus contributing to better comprehension and eventually to quicker system development (see chap. 3, this volume, for details). Besides, avoiding learner–learner interaction may be depriving the learner of language output that can feed back into the input loop (see chap. 2, this volume).

7.2.2.3. Interaction as an Ideational Activity. Interaction as an ideational activity is an expression of one's own experience of the real or imaginary world inside, around, and beyond the classroom. It pertains to sharing personal experiences learners bring with them and is measured in terms of cultural and world knowledge. Believing as it does in meaningful interaction, learning-centered pedagogy should provide opportunities for learners to discuss topics that are relevant and interesting to them, to express their own opinions and feelings, and to interpret and evaluate the views of others.

As mentioned in the previous subsection, the affective-humanistic activities advocated by the NA follow, to a large degree, the characteristics of interaction as an interpersonal activity. They also carry an element of interaction as an ideational activity to the extent that activities involve the learner's past and present experiences. However, the affective-humanistic activities do not sufficiently address the issue of interaction as an ideational activity. There is, of course, meaning-based interaction, but not genuine communication that can result in the sharing of personal experience and world knowledge. In an evaluation of the NA, Krashen himself laments that the "only weakness" of the NA "is that it remains a classroom method, and for some students this prohibits the communication of interesting and relevant topics" (Krashen, 1982, p. 140). He implies that the interactional activities of the NA are not designed to be inherently interesting and practically relevant to the learner—something that can hardly be considered ideational in content.

If the NA, which emphasizes affective-humanistic activities, finds it difficult to promote interaction as an ideational activity in class, the CTP, which deemphasizes such activities, cannot obviously be expected to fare any better. However, one commentator actually finds that learning and teaching in the CTP "is achieved through making ideational meaning" (Berns, 1990, p. 164). Berns bases her argument on three points. First, she asserts, "emphasis on problem-solving tasks is emphasis on ideational meaning. For learners, this implies engaging in 'reasoning-gap activities'" (p. 157). But even Prabhu has defined problem-solving, reasoning-gap activity in terms of mind engagement rather than emotional involvement. It therefore seems to me that a problem-solving task that entails "deciding upon the best course of action for a given purpose and within given constraints" is not, as Berns (1990) claims, a "means of engaging learners in the expression of ideational meaning" (p. 158) but rather a means of engaging them in the exercise of cognitive effort.

Berns' (1990) second argument is that the difference between focus on meaning and focus on form is the difference between focus on lexis and focus on structure. She points out,

> in a series of questions based on information given in a train schedule learners would not distinguish between "when does the train reach Katpadi?, "When does the train leave Katpadi?" How long does the train stay at Katpadi." Instead, they would treat each question as being the same except for lexical changes . . . (p. 164)

Based on this observation, Berns concludes that the CTP is focusing on learning how to mean in the Hallidayan sense and is, therefore, concerned with ideational meaning. One wonders whether learning how to mean with all its social semiotic dimensions (cf: chap. 1, this volume) can be reduced to learning how to solve problems, which is almost entirely a cognitive activity.

Furthermore, Berns (1990) said rather emphatically that the purpose of the CTP "is, in fact, the development of communicative competence" (p. 166). She maintains that the Indian school-age learners develop communicative competence because, they "are developing the ability to express, interpret, and negotiate meaning in the classroom setting in which they use English" (p. 166). As we discussed earlier, what the CTP class offers in plenty is interaction as a textual activity where the learner's attempt to express, interpret, and negotiate is confined to developing linguistic knowledge/ability and not pragmatic knowledge/ability. It is unfair to expect the CTP pedagogists to deliver something that they say is not their business. Prabhu (1987, p. 1) makes it very clear that the focus of the CTP was not on "communicative competence" in the sense of achieving social or situational appropriacy, but rather on "grammatical competence" itself. In fact, one of the reasons why he rejects the suitability of learner-centered pedagogies with its emphasis on sociocultural elements of L2 to the Indian context is that Indian students do not generally need the English language for everyday communicative purposes. The CTP is fundamentally based on the philosophy that communication in the classroom could be "a good means of developing grammatical competence in learners, quite independently of the issue of developing functional or social appropriacy in language use" (Prabhu, 1987, pp. 15–16).

To sum up, as far as classroom procedures are concerned, learning-centered pedagogy is exclusively and narrowly concerned with meaning-based input modifications to the exclusion of explicit form-based, and form-and meaning-based input modifications. In terms of interactional activities, it is primarily concerned with interaction as a textual activity and narrowly with interaction as an interpersonal activity, and negligibly with interaction as an ideational activity.

7.3. A CRITICAL ASSESSMENT

Learning-centered methods represent, at least in theory, a radical departure from language- and learner-centered pedagogies. The idea of teaching an L2 through meaning-based activities using materials that are not preselected and presequenced had been suggested before. However, it was learning-centered pedagogists who, through well-articulated concepts of learning and teaching supported, at least partially, by research in L2 development, tried to seriously and systematically formulate theoretical principles and classroom procedures needed to translate an abstract idea into a workable proposition. Their prime contribution lies in attempting fundamental methodological changes rather than superficial curricular modifications, in shaping a pedagogic dialogue that directed our attention to the process of learning rather than the product of teaching, and in raising new questions that effectively challenged traditional ways of constructing an L2 pedagogy. This is a remarkable achievement, indeed.

Learning-centered pedagogists' rejection of linearity and systematicity geared to mastering a unitary target language system, and the acceptance of a cyclical, holistic process consisting of several transitional systems makes eminent sense in terms of intuitive appeal. However, the maximization of incidental learning and teacher input, and the marginalization of intentional learning and learner output render learning-centered methods empirically unfounded and pedagogically unsound. Because of its preoccupation with reasonably challenging comprehensible input, the learning-centered pedagogy pays scant attention, if at all, to several intake factors that have been found to play a crucial role in L2 development (see chap. 2, this volume).

Furthermore, all available classroom interactional analyses (see, e.g., a review of the literature presented in Gass, 1997) show that the instructional intervention and the control of language exercised by learning-centered teachers are at variance with the conceptual considerations that sought to provide "natural" linguistic input that is different from "contrived" linguistic input associated with earlier pedagogies. The input modifications advocated by learning-centered pedagogies create only limited interactional opportunities in the classroom because they largely promote interaction as a textual activity, neglecting interaction as interpersonal and ideational activities.

In the final analysis, learning-centered pedagogists have left many crucial questions unanswered. They include:

- How to determine the cognitive difficulty and the communicative difficulty of a task, and, more importantly, the difference between the two;
- how to formulate reasonably acceptable criteria for developing, grading, sequencing, and evaluating tasks;

- how to design relevant summative and formative evaluation measures that could reflect the learning-centered pedagogy, not only in terms of the content of teaching but also in terms of the process of learning;
- how to determine the kind of demand the new pedagogy makes on teachers in order to design appropriate teacher education measures.

Until some of these problems are satisfactorily addressed, any learning-centered method will remain "largely a matter of coping with the unknown . . ." (Prabhu, 1985, p. 173).

7.4. CONCLUSION

In this chapter, I attempted to define and describe the theoretical principles and classroom procedures associated with learning-centered pedagogy with particular reference to the Natural Approach and the Communicational Teaching Project. The discussion has shown how some of the methodological aspects of learning-centered pedagogy are innovative and how certain aspects of its classroom implementation bore close resemblance to the pedagogic orientation that it seeks to replace. Finally, the chapter has highlighted several issues that learning-centered pedagogists leave unanswered.

This chapter concludes Part Two, in which I have correlated some of the fundamental features of language, language learning, and teaching identified in Part One. As we journeyed through the historical developmental phases of language-teaching methods, it has become apparent that each of the methods tried to address some of the perceived shortcomings of the previous one. It is worthwhile to recall, once again, Mackey's distinction between method analysis and teaching analysis. What Part Two has focused on is method analysis. What practicing teachers actually do in class may not correspond to the analysis and description presented in Part Two.

It is common knowledge that practicing teachers, faced with unpredictable learning/teaching needs, wants, and situations, have always taken liberty with the pedagogic formulations prescribed by theorists of language-teaching methods. In committing such "transgressions," they have always attempted, using their robust common sense and rough-weather experience, to draw insights from several sources and put together highly personalized teaching strategies that go well beyond the concept of method as conceived and constructed by theorists. In the final part of this book, I discuss the limitations of the concept of method, and highlight some of the attempts that have been made so far to transcend those limitations.

Part Three

POSTMETHOD PERSPECTIVES

Chapter 8

Postmethod Condition

8. INTRODUCTION

With clearly identifiable sets of theoretical principles and classroom procedures associated with language-, learner- and learning-centered categories
of method, the language-teaching profession appears to have exhausted
the kind of psychological, linguistic, and pedagogic underpinnings it has
depended on for constructing alternative methods. In all probability, the
invention of a truly novel method that is fundamentally different from the
ones discussed in Part Two is very slim, at least in the foreseeable future.
Within the confines of the concept of method, what perhaps remain for further manipulation and management are different permutations and combinations of the familiar principles and procedures. This does not mean
that the profession has a reached a dead end; rather, it means that the profession has completed yet another phase in its long, cyclical history of methods, and has just set sail in uncharted waters. The new millennium has
brought new challenges as well as new opportunities for the profession to
venture beyond methods.

In recent times, the profession has witnessed a steady stream of critical
thoughts on the nature and scope of method. Scholars such as Allwright
(1991), Pennycook (1989), Prabhu (1990), and Stern (1983, 1985, 1992)
have not only cautioned language-teaching practitioners against the uncritical acceptance of untested methods but they have also counseled them
against the very concept of method itself. The uneasiness about the concept
of method expressed by them is hardly new. We find well-articulated arguments about the limitations of method even in the 1960s, as in Kelly (1969),

and Mackey (1965), just to mention two. However, this time around, the professional response has been significantly different. Having witnessed how methods go through endless cycles of life, death, and rebirth, the language teaching profession seems to have reached a state of heightened awareness—an awareness that as long as it is caught up in the web of method, it will continue to get entangled in an unending search for an unavailable solution, an awareness that such a search drives it to continually recycle and repackage the same old ideas, and an awareness that nothing short of breaking the cycle can salvage the situation. This renewed awareness coupled with a resolve to respond has created what I have called the *postmethod condition* (Kumaravadivelu, 1994b). What is meant by postmethod condition? How is it different from the earlier state of affairs? I address these and other related questions in terms of the limits of method, and the logic of postmethod.

8.1. THE LIMITS OF METHOD

The concept of method has severe limitations that have long been overlooked by many. They relate mainly to its ambiguous usage and application, to the exaggerated claims made by its proponents, and, consequently, to the gradual erosion of its utilitarian value. Let me briefly consider each under the headings: the meaning of method, the myth of method, and the death of method.

8.1.1. The Meaning of Method

"The question of method," declares the *Routledge Encyclopedia of Language Teaching and Learning* (2000), "is one of the central issues of instruction" (p. 616). Citing the original Greek word, *methodos*, which "includes the idea of a series of steps leading towards a conceived goal" (p. 617), the *Encyclopedia* defines method simply as "a planned way of doing something" (p. 617). Turning to the specific context of language teaching, it states, rather awkwardly: "A method implies an orderly way of going about something, a certain degree of advance planning and of control, then; also, a process rather than a product" (p. 617). As the quote indicates, the meaning of method, as used in second/foreign language teaching, is shrouded in a veil of vagueness, despite its central importance.

Recall our discussion in chapter 4 where a distinction between *method* and *methodology* was made. Method is a construct; methodology is a conduct. Method is an expert's notion derived from an understanding of the theories of language, of language learning, and of language teaching. It is also reflected in syllabus design, textbook production, and, above all, in recommended classroom procedures. Methodology, on the other hand, is what the teacher does in the classroom in order to maximize learning opportunities for the learner. Recall also that the distinction was made based on Mackey's (1965) perceptive observation that method analysis is different from teaching analysis: "method analysis determines how teaching is done by the book; teaching analysis shows how much is done by the teacher" (p. 139). There is, thus, a crucial distinction between method and methodology, a distinction that is seldom understood or maintained. Method, to continue with the thoughts expressed by Mackey, "has become a matter of opinion rather than of fact. It is not surprising that feelings run high in these matters, and that the very word 'method' means so little and so much" (p. 139).

Even the authors of popular textbooks on methods are not sure of the number of methods that are out there. A book published in the mid 1960s, for instance, has listed 15 "most common" types of methods "still in use in one form or another in various parts of the world" (Mackey, 1965 p. 151). Two books published in the mid-1980s (Larsen-Freeman, 1986; and Richards & Rodgers, 1986) provided, between them, a list of 11 methods. The same two books, in their revised, second editions published in 2000 and 2001 respectively, contain between them nearly twenty methods, such as (in alphabetical order): Audiolingual Method, Communicative Language Teaching, Community Language Learning, Competency-Based Language Teaching, Direct Method, Grammar-Translation Method, Natural Approach, Oral and Situational Language Teaching, Lexical Approach, Silent Way, Suggestopedia (or, Desuggestopedia), Task-Based Language Teaching, Total Physical Response, and more.

Each established method is supposed to have a specified set of theoretical principles and a specified set of classroom practices. One might, therefore, think that the methods listed above provide different pathways to language learning and teaching. That is not so. In fact, there is considerable overlap in their theory and practice. Sometimes, as Rivers (1991) rightly pointed out, what appears to be a radically new method is more often than not a variant of existing methods presented with "the fresh paint of a new terminology that camouflages their fundamental similarity" (p. 283). What is not a variant, however, is the myth surrounding the concept of method.

8.1.2. The Myth of Method

The established methods listed are motivated and maintained by multiple myths that have long been accepted as professional articles of faith. These myths have created an inflated image of the concept of method. Here are some of the myths:

Myth #1: There is a best method out there ready and waiting to be discovered. For a very long time, our profession has been preoccupied with, or as Stern

(1985) would say, obsessed with, a search for the best method—very much like Monty Python searching for the Holy Grail. We went on expedition after expedition searching for the best method. But still, the Holy Grail was not in sight, partly because, as Mackey (1965) observed, "while sciences have advanced by approximations in which each new stage results from an improvement, not rejection, of what has gone before, language-teaching methods have followed the pendulum of fashion from one extreme to the other" (p. 138). Besides, the history of methods "suggests a problematic progressivism, whereby whatever is happening now is presumed to be superior to what happened before" (*Routledge Encyclopedia of Language Teaching and Learning*, 2000, p. 278).

We thought we should be able to find that one magical method through objective analysis. Instead, we found out to our dismay that the formation and implementation of a method have to take into account many variables (such as language policy and planning, learning needs, wants and situations, learner variations, teacher profiles, etc.) most of which cannot be controlled for a systematic study. We also found out that we cannot even compare known methods to see which one works best. The last time a systematic and large-scale comparison of methods was carried out was in the late 1960s. Called the Pennsylvania Project, the experiment investigated the effectiveness of methods based on audiolingual and cognitive theories of language learning and teaching. The project revealed that, apart from the fact that method comparison was not a viable research activity, the type of methods did not really matter very much at all, even when the competing methods had been derived from competing, and mutually incompatible, theories of language learning. The result was so embarrassing, prompting the project leader to say: "these results were personally traumatic to the Project staff" (Smith, 1970, p. 271). Now we know that "objective evaluation is so difficult to implement that all attempts in the past have resulted in a wider agreement on the difficulties of doing an evaluation than on the resulting judgment on methods" (Prabhu, 1990, p. 168). But, the difficulties in analyzing and assessing a method have not prevented us from using it as a base for various aspects of language teaching, which leads us to the next myth.

Myth #2: Method constitutes the organizing principle for language teaching. We have all along believed, rather simplistically, that the concept of method can constitute the core of the entire language learning and teaching operations. We have treated method as an all-pervasive, all-powerful entity. It has guided the form and function of every conceivable component of language teaching including curriculum design, syllabus specifications, materials preparation, instructional strategies, and testing techniques. Take for instance, communicative language teaching. When it became fashionable, we started getting a steady stream of books on *communicative* curriculum, *com-*

municative syllabus, *communicative* tasks, *communicative* methods, *communicative* materials, *communicative* testing, and so on.

The use of method as organizing principles for language learning and teaching is unfortunate because method is too inadequate and too limited to satisfactorily explain the complexity of language learning and teaching. By concentrating excessively on method, we have ignored several other factors that govern classroom processes and practices—factors such as teacher cognition, learner perception, societal needs, cultural contexts, political exigencies, economic imperatives, and institutional constraints, all of which are inextricably linked together. Each of these factors shapes and reshapes the content and character of language learning and teaching; each having a huge impact on the success or failure of any language teaching enterprise.

The uncritical acceptance of the concept of method as the organizing principle has also (mis)led us to believe that method has the capacity to cater to various learning and teaching needs, wants and situations, thus, creating yet another myth.

Myth #3: Method has a universal and ahistorical value. Our quest for the best method has always directed us toward finding a universal, ahistorical method that can be used anywhere and everywhere. There are several drawbacks that are inherent in this outlook. First of all, established methods are founded on idealized concepts geared toward idealized contexts. And, as such, they are far removed from classroom reality. Because learning and teaching needs, wants, and situations are unpredictably numerous, no idealized method can visualize all the variables in advance in order to provide context-specific solutions that practicing teachers badly need in order to tackle the challenges they confront every day of their professional lives.

Secondly, our search for a universally applicable method has been predominantly and inevitably a top–down exercise. That is, the conception and construction of methods have been largely guided by a one-size-fits-all, cookie-cutter approach that assumes a common clientele with common goals. But, learners across the world do not learn a second or a foreign language for the same reason; they have different purposes, and follow different paths. Without acknowledging such a phenomenon, methods have been preoccupied with their potential global reach; and, hence, they have lacked an essential local touch.

Thirdly, and as a consequence of the conditions listed, we have completely ignored local knowledge. We forget that people have been learning and teaching foreign languages long before modern methods arrived on the scene. Teachers and teacher educators in periphery communities such as in South Asia, Southeast Asia, South America, and elsewhere have a tremendous amount of local knowledge sedimented through years and years of practical experience. But still, all the established methods are based on the theoretical insights derived almost exclusively from a Western knowledge base. The concept of method is bereft of any synthesis of external knowledge from center-based communities and local knowledge from periphery communities. Our misplaced faith in a universally applicable method and its top–down orientation has created and sustained another myth.

Myth #4: Theorists conceive knowledge, and teachers consume knowledge. In the field of language teaching, there is a clearly perceptible dichotomy between theory and practice, resulting in an unfortunate division of labor between the theorist and the teacher. The relationship between the theorist and the teacher that exists today is not unlike the relationship between the producer and the consumer of a marketable commodity. Such a commercialized relationship has inevitably resulted in the creation of a privileged class of theorists and an underprivileged class of practitioners. Unfortunately, the hierarchical relationship between the theorist and the teacher has not only minimized any meaningful dialogue between them, but has also contributed to some degree of mutual disrespect.

The artificial dichotomy between theory and practice has also led us to believe that teachers would gladly follow the principles and practices of established methods. They rarely do. They seem to know better. They know that none of the established methods can be realized in their purest form in the actual classroom primarily because they are not derived from their classroom but are artificially transplanted into it. They reveal their dissatisfaction with method through their actions in the classroom. Classroom-oriented research carried out in the last two decades (e.g., Kumaravadivelu, 1993a; Nunan, 1987; Swaffer, Arens, & Morgan, 1982) have revealed four interrelated facts:

- Teachers who claim to follow a particular method do not conform to its theoretical principles and classroom procedures at all;
- teachers who claim to follow different methods often use the same classroom procedures;
- teachers who claim to follow the same method often use different procedures, and
- teachers develop and follow in their classroom a carefully crafted sequence of activities not necessarily associated with any particular method.

In other words, teachers seem to be convinced that no single theory of learning and no single method of teaching will help them confront the challenges of everyday teaching. They use their own intuitive ability and experiential knowledge to decide what works and what does not work. There is thus a significant variance between what theorists advocate and what teachers do in their classroom.

Myth #5: Method is neutral, and has no ideological motivation. In chapter 1, we discussed the connection between ideology and language in general. The ideological nature of English language teaching has also been well-examined (e.g., Canagarajah, 1999; Pennycook, 1998; Phillipson, 1992; Ricento, 2000). In an incisive analysis of the concept of method in particular, Pennycook (1989) demonstrated how "the concept reflects a particular view of the world and is articulated in the interests of unequal power relationships" (pp. 589–590). Arguing that method represents what he calls *interested knowledge,* he showed how it "has diminished rather than enhanced our understanding of language teaching" (p. 597). Discussing the forms of resistance to such center-based interested knowledge imposed on the language classroom in periphery countries, Canagarajah (1999) called for a pedagogy in which members of the periphery communities will "have the agency to think critically and work out ideological alternatives that favor their own environment" (p. 2).

Furthermore, as I have observed elsewhere (Kumaravadivelu (2003b), the concept of method is indeed a construct of marginality. One aspect of this marginality has taken the form of gendered division in the English Language Teaching (ELT) workforce. As Pennycook (1989) suggested, the method concept "has played a major role in maintaining the gendered division of the workforce, a hierarchically organized division between male conceptualizers and female practitioners" (pp. 610–611). Another aspect has taken a broader form of native/nonnative division in the global ELT workforce, where nonnative professionals are marginalized.

Expanding on the last point, I have argued that that method as a means of marginality has four interrelated dimensions—scholastic, linguistic, cultural, and economic (Kumaravadivelu, 2003b):

- The scholastic dimension relates to the ways in which Western scholars have treated local knowledge, as discussed in Myth #3.

- The linguistic dimension relates to the ways in which methods prevent nonnative learners and teachers of English from putting to use their excellent L1 linguistic resource to serve the cause of their L2 education. It is a move that automatically privileges teachers who are native speakers of English, most of whom do not share the language of their learners. Phillipson (1992) has called it the *monolingual tenet of L2 pedagogy.*

- The cultural dimension treats second-language teaching as second culture teaching directed at helping L2 learner "gain an understanding of the native speaker's perspective" (Stern, 1992, p. 216). The overall aim is to help them develop sociocultural ability for the purpose of culturally empathizing, if not culturally assimilating, with native speakers of English.

- The economic dimension relates to the ways in which the monolingual tenet and the emphasis on culture teaching create and sustain global em-

ployment opportunities for native speakers of English, sometimes at the ex-
pense of qualified local candidates.

These four dimensions of method as a means of marginality tend to extend
and expand the agenda for sustaining "an ideological dependence" (Phillipson, 1992, p. 199).
    The matters raised so far, and particularly the ambiguous use of the
term, method, and the multiple myths that are associated with it, have contributed to a gradual erosion of its usability as a construct in language learning and teaching, prompting some to say that the concept of method is
dead.

8.1.3. The Death of Method

In 1991, the British applied linguist, Dick Allwright gave a plenary talk in a
conference at Carleton University in Ottawa, Canada and the talk (as well as
the published version) was titled, "The Death of the Method." In choosing
what he called a "deliberately contentious title," he was emphasizing "the
relative unhelpfulness of the existence of 'methods'" (Allwright, 1991, p.
1). Following his lead, the American scholar, Brown, has used the imagery
of death again and again (e.g., 2002). He has sought to "lay to rest" (p. 11)
the concept of method, and to write a "requiem" (p. 17) for "recently in-
terred methods" (p. 14). By opting for these colorful expressions, the two
reputed scholars from across the Atlantic are not being polemical; rather,
they wish to draw attention to the fact that the concept of method has lost
its significance. It should no longer be considered a valuable or a viable
construct in language learning and teaching. In fact, as indicated earlier,
several scholars (e.g., Mackey, 1965; Stern, 1985) have made similar observations before, using less vivid phrases.
    Allwright explains the "relative unhelpfulness" of the method concept by
listing six reasons. To quote:

- It is built on seeing differences where similarities may be more important, since methods that are different in abstract principle seem to be
  far less so in classroom practice;
- it simplifies unhelpfully a highly complex set of issues, for example seeing similarities among learners when differences may be more important . . . ;
- it diverts energies from potentially more productive concerns, since
  time spent learning how to implement a particular method is time not
  available for such alternative activities as classroom task design;
- it breeds a brand loyalty which is unlikely to be helpful to the profession, since it fosters pointless rivalries on essentially irrelevant issues;

- it breeds complacency, if, as it surely must, it conveys the impression that answers have indeed been found to all the major methodological questions in our profession;
- it offers a "cheap" externally derived sense of coherence for language teachers, which may itself inhibit the development of a personally "expensive," but ultimately far more valuable, internally derived sense of coherence . . . (Allwright, 1991, pp. 7–8)

Interestingly, most of these reasons are teacher related, and can be easily linked to some of the myths of the method discussed in the above section.

Allwright's observation that the concept of method may inhibit the development of a "valuable, internally-derived sense of coherence" on the part of the classroom teacher is an important one. It has been addressed in detail by Clarke (2003), who posited "coherence" as "the ideal to strive for" but laments that the concept of method shifts the focus to something else: "it is not uncommon for the focus to shift from improving learning to improving method, not unlike the gardener who spends an inordinate amount of time building the ideal hothouse and forgets to tend to the tomatoes" (p. 128).

Teachers find it difficult to develop a "valuable, internally-derived sense of coherence" about language teaching, in part, because the transmission model of teacher education they may have undergone does little more than passing on to them a ready-made package of methods and methods-related body of knowledge. They find such a methods-based teacher education woefully inadequate to meet the challenges of the practice of everyday teaching. Therefore, in an earnest attempt "to tend to the tomatoes," they try to develop a sense of what works in the classroom and what doesn't, based on their intuitive ability and experiential knowledge. In a clear repudiation of established methods and their estranged myths, teachers try to derive a "method" of their own and call it *eclectic method.*

Constructing a principled eclectic method is not easy. As Widdowson (1990) observed, "if by eclecticism is meant the random and expedient use of whatever technique comes most readily to hand, then it has no merit whatever" (p. 50). The difficulties faced by teachers in developing an enlightened eclectic method are not hard to find. Stern (1992) pointed out some of them:

the weakness of the eclectic position is that it offers no criteria according to which we can determine which is the best theory, nor does it provide any principles by which to include or exclude features which form part of existing theories or practices. The choice is left to the individual's intuitive judgment and is, therefore, too broad and too vague to be satisfactory as a theory in its own right. (p. 11)

As can be expected, methods-based, teacher-education programs do not make any sustained and systematic effort to develop in prospective teachers the knowledge and skill necessary to be responsibly eclectic.

The net result is that practicing teachers end up with some form of eclectic method that is, as Long writes in the *Routledge Encyclopedia of Language Teaching and Learning* (2000):

> usually little more than an amalgam of their inventors' prejudices. The same relative ignorance about SLA affects everyone, and makes the eclecticist's claim to be able to select the alleged "best parts" of several theories absurd. Worse, given that different theories by definition reflect different understandings, the resulting methodological mish-mash is guaranteed to be wrong, whereas an approach to language teaching based, in part, on one theory can at least be coherent, and, subject to the previously discussed caveats, has a chance of being right. (p. 4)

Consequently, teachers find themselves in an unenviable position where they have to straddle two pedagogic worlds: a method-based one that is imposed on them, and a methodological one that is improvised by them.

What the aforementioned discussion shows is that the concept of method has little theoretical validity and even less practical utility. Its meaning is ambiguous, and its claim dubious. Given such a checkered history, it has come to be looked on as "a label without substance" (Clarke, 1983, p. 109) that has only "diminished rather than enhanced our understanding of language teaching" (Pennycook, 1989, p. 597), resulting in the feeling that "language teaching might be better understood and better executed if the concept of method were not to exist at all" (Jarvis, 1991, p. 295). It is therefore no wonder that there is a strong sentiment to call it dead, sing a requiem, and assign it "to the dustbin" (Nunan, 1989, p. 2) of history.

For reasons discussed above, the deep discontent with the concept of method accumulating for a considerable length of time has finally resulted in the emergence of the postmethod condition. Synthesizing and expanding some of my earlier work (Kumaravadivelu, 1994b, 2001, 2002, 2003a), I briefly present the logic of *postmethod*.

8.2. THE LOGIC OF POSTMETHOD

The *postmethod condition* is a sustainable state of affairs that compels us to fundamentally restructure our view of language teaching and teacher education. It urges us to review the character and content of classroom teaching in all its pedagogical and ideological perspectives. It drives us to streamline our teacher education by refiguring the reified relationship between theory and practice. In short, it demands that we seriously contemplate the essentials of a coherent postmethod pedagogy. I present below the essentials of postmethod pedagogy in terms of pedagogic parameters and pedagogic indicators. How these parameters and indictors can shape the construction of a postmethod pedagogy will be the subject of chapter 9.

8.2.1. Pedagogic Parameters

Postmethod pedagogy can be visualized as a three-dimensional system consisting of three pedagogic parameters: particularity, practicality, and possibility. As will become clear, each parameter shapes and is shaped by the others. They interweave and interact with each other in a synergic relationship where the whole is much more than the sum of its parts. Let us consider each of them.

8.2.1.1. The Parameter of Particularity. The most important aspect of postmethod pedagogy is its *particularity*. That is to say, any postmethod pedagogy "must be sensitive to a particular group of teachers teaching a particular group of learners pursuing a particular set of goals within a particular institutional context embedded in a particular sociocultural mileu" (Kumaravadivelu, 2001, p. 538). The parameter of particularity then rejects the very idea method-based pedagogies are founded upon, namely, there can be one set of teaching aims and objectives realizable through one set of teaching principles and procedures. At its core, the idea of pedagogic particularity is consistent with the hermeneutic perspective of *situational understanding*, which claims that a meaningful pedagogy cannot be constructed without a holistic interpretation of particular situations, and that it cannot be improved without a general improvement of those particular situations (Elliott, 1993).

The parameter of particularity emphasizes local exigencies and lived experiences. Pedagogies that ignore them will ultimately prove to be "so disturbing for those affected by them—so threatening to their belief systems—that hostility is aroused and learning becomes impossible" (Coleman, 1996, p. 11). For instance, communicative language teaching with its focus on sociocultural negotiation, expression, and interpretation (see chap. 6, this volume, for details) has created a deep sense of disillusionment in certain parts of the world. Consider the following:

- From South Africa, Chick (1996) wondered whether "our choice of communicative language teaching as a goal was possibly a sort of naive ethnocentrism prompted by the thought that what is good for Europe or the USA had to be good for KwaZulu" (p. 22).
- From Pakistan, Shamim (1996) reported that her attempt to introduce communicative language teaching into her classroom met with a great

deal of resistance from her learners, making her "terribly exhausted," leading her to realize that, by introducing this methodology, she was actually "creating psychological barriers to learning . . ." (p. 109).

- From Singapore, Pakir (1999) suggested that communicative language teaching with its professional practices based on "Anglo-Saxon assumptions" (p. 112) has to be modified taking into account what she calls "glocal" linguistic and cultural considerations.
- From India, Tickoo (1996) narrated how even locally initiated, pedagogic innovations have failed because they merely tinkered with the method-based framework inherited from abroad.

All these research reports present a classic case of a centrally produced pedagogy that is out of sync with local linguistic, sociocultural, and political particularities. In fact, dealing with a similar situation within the United States, scholars such as Delpit (1995) and Smitherman (2000) stressed the need for a language education that is sensitive to the linguistic particularities of "nonstandard" speakers of English.

A context-sensitive language education can emerge only from the practice of particularity. It involves a critical awareness of local conditions of learning and teaching that policymakers and program administrators have to seriously consider in putting together an effective teaching agenda. More importantly, it involves practicing teachers, either individually or collectively, observing their teaching acts, evaluating their outcomes, identifying problems, finding solutions, and trying them out to see once again what works and what doesn't. In that sense, the particular is so deeply embedded in the practical, and cannot be achieved or understood without it. The parameter of particularity, therefore, merges into the parameter of *practicality*.

8.2.1.2. The Parameter of Practicality. The parameter of practicality relates broadly to the relationship between theory and practice, and narrowly to the teacher's skill in monitoring his or her own teaching effectiveness. As we discussed earlier, there is a harmful dichotomy between theory and practice, between the theorist's role and the teacher's role in education. One of the ways by which general educationists have addressed the dichotomy is by positing a distinction between professional theories and personal theories. According to O'Hanlon (1993), *professional theories* are those that are generated by experts, and are generally transmitted from centers of higher learning. *Personal theories*, on the other hand, are those that are developed by teachers by interpreting and applying professional theories in practical situations while they are on the job.

It is this distinction between theorists' theory and teachers' theory that has, in part, influenced the emphasis on action research. "The fundamental aim of action research," as Elliott (1991) makes it crystal clear, "is to improve practice rather than to produce knowledge" (p. 49). The teacher is advised to do action research in the classroom by testing, interpreting, and judging the usefulness of professional theories proposed by experts. Such an interpretation of teacher research is very narrow because it leaves very little room for self-conceptualization and self-construction of pedagogic knowledge on the part of the teacher.

The parameter of practicality goes beyond such deficiencies inherent in the theory versus practice and theorists' theory versus teachers' theory dichotomies. As I have argued elsewhere (Kumaravadivelu, 1999b), if context-sensitive pedagogic knowledge has to emerge from teachers and their practice of everyday teaching, then they ought to be enabled to theorize from their practice and practice what they theorize. Edge (2001) made similar observations when he stated that "the thinking teacher is no longer perceived as someone who applies theories, but someone who theorizes practice" (p. 6). This objective, however, cannot be achieved simply by asking them to put into practice professional theories proposed by others. It can be achieved only by helping them develop the knowledge and skill, attitude, and autonomy necessary to construct their own context-sensitive theory of practice.

A *theory of practice* is conceived when, to paraphrase van Manen (1991), there is a union of action and thought, or more precisely, when there is action in thought and thought in action. It is the result of what he has called "pedagogical thoughtfulness." In the context of deriving a theory of practice, pedagogical thoughtfulness simultaneously feeds and is fed by reflective thinking on the part of teachers. Freeman (1998) called such a reflective thinking *inquiry-oriented teacher research*, which he defines as "a state of being engaged in what is going on in the classroom that drives one to better understand what is happening—and can happen—there" (p. 14). He sees *inquiry* as something that "includes both the attitude that spawns this engagement and the energy and activity that put it into action" (p. 34). It enables them to understand and identify problems, analyze and assess information, consider and evaluate alternatives, and then choose the best available alternative that is then subjected to further critical evaluation.

The parameter of practicality, then, focuses on teachers' reflection and action, which are also based on their insights and intuition. Through prior and ongoing experience with learning and teaching, teachers gather an unexplained and sometimes unexplainable awareness of what constitutes good teaching. Prabhu (1990) called it teachers' *sense of plausibility*. It is their "personal conceptualization of how their teaching leads to desired learning, with a notion of causation that has a measure of credibility for them" (p. 172). In a similar vein, Hargreaves (1994) called it *the ethic of practicality*—a phrase he used to refer to the teacher's powerful sense of what works and what doesn't; of which changes will go and which will not—not in the abstract, or even as a general rule, but for *this* teacher in *this* context. In this simple yet deeply influential sense of practicality among teachers is the distillation of complex and potent combinations of purpose, person, politics and workplace constraints. (p. 12, emphasis in original)

More than a quarter century ago, van Manen (1977) called this awareness, simply, *sense-making.*

Teachers' sense-making matures over time as they learn to cope with competing pulls and pressures representing the content and character of professional preparation, personal beliefs, institutional constraints, learner expectations, assessment instruments, and other factors. This seemingly instinctive and idiosyncratic nature of the teacher's sense-making disguises the fact that it is formed and re-formed by the pedagogic factors governing the microcosm of the classroom as well as by the larger sociopolitical forces emanating from outside. In this sense, the parameter of practicality metamorphoses into the parameter of *possibility.*

8.2.1.3. The Parameter of Possibility.   The parameter of possibility owes much of its origin to the educational philosophy of the Brazilian intellectual, Paulo Freire. He and his followers (e.g., Giroux, 1988; Simon, 1988) took the position that pedagogy, any pedagogy, is closely linked to power and dominance, and is aimed at creating and sustaining social inequalities. They stress the importance of acknowledging and highlighting students' and teachers' individual identity, and they encourage them to question the status quo that keeps them subjugated. They also stress the "the need to develop theories, forms of knowledge, and social practices that *work with* the experiences that people bring to the pedagogical setting" (Giroux, 1988, p. 134, emphasis in original).

The experiences participants bring to the pedagogical setting are shaped, not just by what they experience in the classroom, but also by a broader social, economic, and political environment in which they grow up. These experiences have the potential to alter classroom aims and activities in ways unintended and unexpected by policy planners or curriculum designers or textbook producers. For instance, Canagarajah (1999) reported how Tamil students of English in the civil war-torn Sri Lanka offered resistance to Western representations of English language and culture and how they, motivated by their own cultural and historical backgrounds, appropriated the language and used it in their own terms according to their own aspirations, needs, and values. He reported how the students, through marginal comments and graphics, actually reframed, reinterpreted and rewrote the content of their ESL textbooks written and produced by Anglo-

American authors. The students' resistance, Canagarajah concluded, suggests "the strategic ways by which discourses may be negotiated, intimating the resilient ability of human subjects to creatively fashion a voice for themselves from amidst the deafening channels of domination" (p. 197).

The parameter of possibility is also concerned with language ideology and learner identity. As we saw in chapter 1, more than any other educational enterprise, language education provides its participants with challenges and opportunities for a continual quest for subjectivity and self-identity; for, as Weeden (1987) pointed out "language is the place where actual and possible forms of social organization and their likely social and political consequences are defined and contested. Yet it is also the place where our sense of ourselves, our subjectivity, is constructed" (p. 21). This is even more applicable to L2 education, which brings languages and cultures in contact. That this contact results in identity conflicts has been convincingly brought out by Norton's study of immigrant women in Canada. "The historically and socially constructed identity of learners," Norton (2000) wrote, "influences the subject position they take up in the language classroom and the relationship they establish with the language teacher" (p. 142).

Applying such a critical stance to teach English to speakers of other languages, Auerbach (1995), Benesch (2001), Morgan (1998) and others have suggested new ways of broadening the nature and scope of classroom aims and activities. More specifically, Auerbach has showed us how participatory pedagogy can bring together learners, teachers, and community activists in mutually beneficial, collaborative projects. Morgan has demonstrated how even in teaching units of language as system, such as phonological and grammatical features, the values of critical practice and community development can be profitably used. Similarly, Benesch has suggested ways and means of linking the linguistic text and sociopolitical context as well as the academic content and the larger community for the purpose of turning classroom input and interaction into effective instruments of transformation.

What follows from the aforementioned discussion is that language teachers can ill afford to ignore the sociocultural reality that influences identity formation in the classroom nor can they afford to separate the linguistic needs of learners from their social needs. They will be able to reconcile these seemingly competing forces if they "achieve a deepening awareness both of the sociocultural reality that shapes their lives and of their capacity to transform that reality" (van Manen, 1977, p. 222). Such a deepening awareness has a built-in quality to transform the life of the teachers themselves. Studies by Clandinin and her colleagues attest to this self-transforming phenomenon: "As we worked together we talked about ways of seeing new possibility in our practices as teachers, as teacher educators, and with children in our classroom. As we saw possibilities in our professional lives we also came to see new possibilities in our personal lives" (Clandinin, Davis, Hogan, & Kennard, 1993, p. 209).

In sum, the three pedagogic parameters of particularity, practicality, and possibility constitute the conceptual foundation for a postmethod pedagogy. They have the potential to function as operating principles, guiding various aspects of L2 learning and teaching. These operating principles manifest themselves in what may be called pedagogic indicators.

8.2.2. Pedagogic Indicators

Pedagogic indicators refer to those functions and features that are considered to reflect the role played by key participants in the L2 learning and teaching operations governing postmethod pedagogy. They are conceptually consistent with the three parameters already discussed. They indicate the degree to which shared decision making is incorporated into the planning and implementation of classroom aims and activities, especially the decision-making process shared by postmethod learners, teachers, and teacher educators.

8.2.2.1. The Postmethod Learner. Postmethod pedagogy seeks to make the most use of learner investment and learner interest by giving them, to the extent feasible, a meaningful role in pedagogic decision making. As Breen and Littlejohn (2000) observed, "a pedagogy that does not directly call upon students' capacities to make decisions conveys to them that either they are not allowed to or that they are incapable of doing so; or it may convey that the more overt struggle to interpret and plan is not part of 'proper' learning" (p. 21). Postmethod pedagogy allows learners a role in pedagogic decision making by treating them as active and autonomous players.

Postmethod pedagogy takes into account two views of learner autonomy, a narrow view and a broad view (Kumaravadivelu, 2003a). The narrow view seeks to develop in the learner a capacity to learn to learn whereas the broad view goes beyond that to include a capacity to learn to liberate as well. Helping learners learn to learn involves developing in them the ability to "take charge of one's own learning," (Holec, 1981, p. 3). Taking charge, according to Holec, means to (a) have and to hold the responsibility for determining learning objectives, (b) for defining contents and progressions, (c) for selecting methods and techniques to be used, (d) for monitoring the procedure of acquisition, and finally, (e) for evaluating what has been acquired.

Generally, *learning to learn* means learning to use appropriate strategies to realize desired learning objectives. In the L2 literature, one can find useful taxonomies of learning strategies (e.g., O'Malley & Chamot, 1990; Oxford, 1990) as well as user-friendly manuals (e.g., Chamot, et. al., 1999;

Scharle & Szabo, 2000), which offer learners insights into what they need to know and can do to plan and regulate their learning. These sources tell us that learners use several metacognitive, cognitive, social, and affective strategies to achieve their learning objectives. They also tell us that there are many individual ways of learning a language successfully, and that different learners will approach language learning differently. We further learn that more successful learners use a greater variety of strategies and use them in ways appropriate to the language learning task, and that less successful learners not only have fewer strategy types in their repertoire, but also frequently use strategies that are inappropriate to the task.

By using appropriate learning strategies, learners can monitor their learning process and maximize their learning potential. As I have stated elsewhere (Kumaravadivelu, 2003a, pp. 139–140), learners can exploit some of these opportunities by:

- Identifying their learning strategies and styles in order to know their strengths and weaknesses as language learners;
- stretching their strategies and styles by incorporating some of those employed by successful language learners;
- reaching out for opportunities for additional language reception or production beyond what they get in the classroom, for example, through library resources, learning centers and electronic media such as the Internet;
- collaborating with other learners to pool information on a specific project they are working on; and
- taking advantage of opportunities to communicate with competent speakers of the language.

Collectively, these activities help learners gain a sense of responsibility for aiding their own learning.

While the narrow view of learner autonomy treats learning to learn a language as an end in itself, the broad view treats learning to learn a language as a means to an end, the end being learning to liberate. In other words, the former stands for academic autonomy and the latter, for liberatory autonomy. If *academic autonomy* enables learners to be effective learners, *liberatory autonomy* empowers them to be critical thinkers. Thus, liberatory autonomy goes much further by actively seeking to help learners recognize sociopolitical impediments that prevent them from realizing their full human potential, and by providing them with the intellectual and cognitive tools necessary to overcome them.

More than any other educational enterprise, language teaching, where almost any and all topics can potentially constitute the content of classroom

activity, offers ample opportunities for teachers to experiment with liberatory autonomy. Meaningful liberatory autonomy can be promoted in the
language classroom by, among other things:

- Encouraging learners to assume, with the help of their teachers, the
  role of mini-ethnographers so that they can investigate and understand how, for instance, language as ideology serves vested interests;
- asking them to reflect on their developing identities by writing diaries
  or journal entries about issues that engage their sense of who they are
  and how they relate to the social world;
- helping them in the formation of learning communities where they
  develop into unified, socially cohesive, mutually supportive groups
  seeking self-awareness and self-improvement; and
- providing opportunities for them to explore the unlimited possibilities
  offered by online services on the World Wide Web, and bringing back
  to the class their own topics and materials for discussion, and their own
  perspectives on those topics.

Taken together, what the two types of autonomy promise is the development of overall academic ability, intellectual competence, social consciousness, and mental attitude necessary for learners to avail opportunities, and
overcome challenges both in and outside the classroom. Clearly, such a far-
reaching goal cannot be attained by learners working alone; they need the
willing cooperation of all others who directly or indirectly shape their educational agenda, particularly that of their teachers.

8.2.2.2. The Postmethod Teacher.   The postmethod teacher is considered to be an autonomous teacher. Teacher autonomy is so central that it
can be seen as defining the heart of postmethod pedagogy. Method-based
pedagogy "overlooks the fund of experience and tacit knowledge about
teaching which the teachers already have by virtue of their lives as students"
(Freeman, 1991, p. 35). Postmethod pedagogy, on the other hand, recognizes the teachers' prior knowledge as well as their potential to know not
only how to teach but also know how to act autonomously within the academic and administrative constraints imposed by institutions, curricula,
and textbooks. It also promotes the ability of teachers to know how to develop a reflective approach to their own teaching, how to analyze and evaluate their own teaching acts, how to initiate change in their classroom, and
how to monitor the effects of such changes (Wallace, 1991). Such an ability
can evolve only if teachers have a desire and a determination to acquire and
assert a fair degree of autonomy in pedagogic decision making.

In the field of L2 education, most teachers enter into the realm of professional knowledge, with very few exceptions, through a "methods" pack-

age. That is, they learn that the supposedly objective knowledge of language learning and teaching has been closely linked to a particular method which, in turn, is closely linked to a particular school of thought in psychology, linguistics, and other related disciplines. When they begin to teach, however, they quickly recognize the limitations of such a knowledge base, and try to break away from such a constraining concept of method. In the process, they attempt, as we saw earlier, to develop their own eclectic method. In order to do that, they have to increasingly rely on their prior and evolving personal knowledge of learning and teaching.

Personal knowledge "does not simply entail behavioral knowledge of how to do particular things in the classroom; it involves a cognitive dimension that links thought with activity, centering on the context-embedded, interpretive process of knowing what to do" (Freeman, 1996, p. 99). Personal knowledge does not develop instantly before one's peering eyes, as film develops in an instant camera. It evolves over time, through determined effort. Under these circumstances, it is evident that teachers can become autonomous only to the extent they are willing and able to embark on a continual process of self-development.

Facilitating teacher self-development, to a large extent, depends on what we know about teacher cognition which is a fairly new, but a rapidly growing, professional topic in L2 teacher education. Teacher cognition, as Borg (2003) said, refers to "what teachers know, believe, and think" (p. 81). According to his recent state-of-the-art review, teacher cognition has been the focus of 47 research studies since 1996. Some of these studies have shed useful light on how teachers interpret and evaluate the events, activities, and interactions that occur in the teaching process, and how these interpretations and evaluations can help them enrich their knowledge, and eventually enable them to become self-directed individuals. These and other studies on teacher cognition reveal "greater understanding of the contextual factors—e.g., institutional, social, instructional, physical—which shape what language teachers do are central to deeper insights into relationships between cognition and practice" (Borg, 2003, p. 106).

A study conducted in Australia by Breen and his colleagues (Breen, Hird, Milton, Oliver, & Thwaite, 2001) clearly brings out the possible relationship between teacher beliefs, guiding principles, and classroom actions, and their unfailing impact on immediate, ongoing thinking and decision making. Consider Fig. 8.1.

Studying a group of 18 Australian teachers of English as a second language (ESL) whose teaching experience varied from 5 to 33 years, Breen et al. (2001) found that teachers' beliefs comprise a set of guiding principles that, in turn, "appeared to derive from underlying beliefs or personal theories the teachers held regarding the nature of the broader educational process, the nature of language, how it is learned, and how it may be best

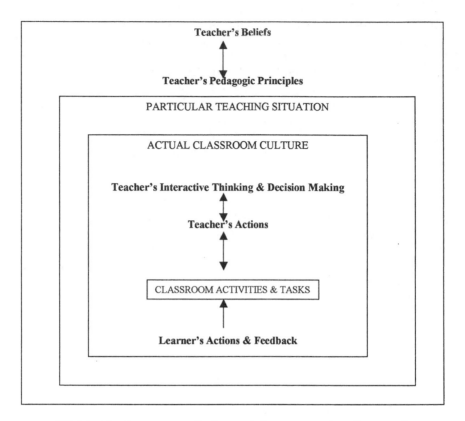

FIG 8.1. Teacher conceptualizations and classroom practices (Breen et al., 2001, p. 473).

taught" (pp. 472–473). According to them, the pedagogic principles mediate between the experientially informed teacher beliefs and the teacher's ongoing decision making and actions with a particular class of learners in a particular teaching situation. These principles are "reflexive in both shaping what the teacher does whilst being responsive to what the teacher observes about the learners' behavior and their achievements in class" (p. 473). Over time, teachers evolve a coherent pedagogic framework consisting of core principles that are applied across teaching situations. What postmethod pedagogy assumes is that this kind personal knowledge teachers develop over time will eventually lead them to construct their own theory of practice.

While the above-mentioned authors provide teachers' articulated encounters with certain aspects of particularity and practicality, scholars such as Clarke (2003), Edge (2002), and Johnston (2003) showed more recently how teachers can enlarge their vision by embracing aspects of possibility as well. Their contributions demonstrate once again that "language teachers cannot hope to fully satisfy their pedagogic obligations without at the same time satisfying their social obligations" (Kumaravadivelu, 2001, p. 544). In other words, teachers cannot afford to remain sociopolitically naive.

Sociopolitical naiveté commonly occurs, as Hargreaves (1994) wisely warned us,

> when teachers are encouraged to reflect on their personal biographies without also connecting them to broader histories of which they are a part; or when they are asked to reflect on their personal images of teaching and learning without also theorizing the conditions which gave rise to those images and the consequences which follow from them. (p. 74)

He argued, quite rightly, that when divorced from its surrounding social and political contexts, teachers' personal knowledge can quickly turn into "parochial knowledge."

In pursuing their professional self-development, postmethod teachers perform teacher research involving the triple parameters of particularity, practicality, and possibility. Teacher research is initiated and implemented by them, and is motivated mainly by their own desire to self-explore and self-improve. Contrary to common misconception, doing teacher research does not necessarily involve highly sophisticated, statistically laden, variable-controlled experimental studies for which practicing teachers have neither the time nor the energy. Rather, it involves keeping one's eyes, ears, and minds open in the classroom to see what works and what doesn't, with what group(s) of learners, for what reason, and assessing what changes are necessary to make instruction achieve its desired goals. Teachers can conduct teacher research by developing and using investigative capabilities derived from the practices of exploratory research (Allwright, 1993), teacher-research cycle (Freeman, 1998), and critical classroom discourse analysis (Kumaravadivelu, 1999a, 1999b).

The goal of teacher research is achieved when teachers exploit and extend their intuitively held pedagogic beliefs based on their educational histories and personal biographies by conducting a more structured and more goal-oriented teacher research based on the parameters of particularity, practicality, and possibility. Most part of such teacher research is doable if, as far as possible, it is not separated from and is fully integrated with day-to-day teaching and learning. As Allwright (1993) argued, language teachers and learners are in a privileged position to use class time for investigative purposes as long as the activities are done through the medium of the target language being taught and learned. To successfully carry out investigative as well as instructional responsibilities thrust on them by the postmethod condition, teachers, no doubt, need the services of committed teacher educators.

8.2.2.3. The Postmethod Teacher Educator. "Mainstream approaches to teacher education in TESOL," as Pennycook (2004) pointed out, "have frequently lacked a social or political dimension that helps locate English and English language teaching within the complex social, cultural, economic, and political environments in which it occurs" (p. 335). That is because most models of teacher education are designed to transmit a set of preselected and presequenced body of knowledge from the teacher educator to the prospective teacher. This is essentially a top–down approach in which teacher educators perceive their role to be one of engineering the classroom teaching of student teachers, offering them suggestions on the best way to teach, modeling appropriate teaching behaviors for them, and evaluating their mastery of discrete pedagogic behaviors through a capstone course called *practicum* or *practice teaching.* Such a transmission model of teacher education is hopelessly inadequate to produce self-directing and self-determining teachers who constitute the backbone of any postmethod pedagogy.

The task of the postmethod teacher educator is to create conditions for prospective teachers to acquire necessary authority and autonomy that will enable them to reflect on and shape their own pedagogic experiences, and in certain cases transform such experiences. In other words, it becomes necessary to have teacher education that does not merely pass on a body of knowledge, but rather one that is dialogically constructed by participants who think and act critically. In other words, the interaction between the teacher educator and the prospective teacher should become dialogic in the Bakhtinian sense (Kumaravadivelu, 1999b). According to Bakhtin (1981), interaction is "dialogic" when all the participants to an interactional exchange have the authority and the autonomy to express their voice and exhibit their identity. A dialogue, controlled by one individual, is "monologic" even if two or more individuals take part in it. Dialogic discourse, then, facilitates an interaction between meanings, between belief systems; an interaction that produces what Bakhtin calls, "a responsive understanding." In such a dialogic enterprise, the primary responsibility of the teacher educator is not to provide the teacher with a borrowed voice, however enlightened it may be, but to provide opportunities for the dialogic construction of meaning out of which an identity or voice may emerge.

From a postmethod perspective, teacher education is treated not as the experience and interpretation of a predetermined, prescribed pedagogic practice, but rather as an ongoing, dialogically constructed entity involving critically reflective participants. When teacher education is dialogic, a series of actions ensue: through purposeful interactions, channels of communication between student-teachers and teacher-educators open-up. Student teachers actively and freely use the linguistic, cultural and pedagogic capital they bring with them. Teacher educators show a willingness to use the student teacher's values, beliefs, and knowledge as an integral part of the learning process. When all this happens, the entire process of teacher education becomes reflective and rewarding.

In practical terms, what this discussion means is that the role of the postmethod teacher educator becomes one of:

- Recognizing and helping student teachers recognize the inequalities built into the current teacher education programs, which treat teacher educators as producers of knowledge, and practicing teachers as consumers of knowledge;
- enabling prospective teachers to articulate their thoughts and experience, and share with other student teachers in class their evolving personal beliefs, assumptions, and knowledge about language learning and teaching at the beginning, during, and at the end of their teacher education program;
- encouraging prospective teachers to think critically so that they may relate their personal knowledge with the professional knowledge they are being exposed to, monitor how each shapes and is shaped by the other, assess how the generic professional knowledge could be used to derive their own personal theory of practice;
- creating conditions for student teachers to acquire basic, classroom-discourse analytical skills that will help them understand the nature of classroom input and interaction;
- rechannelizing part of their own research agenda to do what Cameron, Frazer, Harvey, Rampton, and Richardson (1992) called "empowering research," that is, research *with* rather than *on* their student teachers; and
- exposing student teachers to a pedagogy of possibility by helping them critically engage authors who have raised our consciousness about power and politics, ideas and ideologies that inform L2 education.

These are, no doubt, challenging tasks. Unfortunately, most of the current teacher education programs are unable to meet these challenges. The programs require a fundamental restructuring that transforms an information-oriented teacher education into an inquiry-oriented one.

8.3. CONCLUSION

The purpose of this chapter has been threefold: first, to deconstruct the existing concept of method; second, to describe the antimethod sentiments; and third, to delineate the emerging postmethod condition. I have pointed out that the concept of method is beset with ambiguous meanings and multiple myths, and, as a result, has lost much of its significance. I have also stressed that a greater awareness of its limitations among a growing section of the professional community has caused the emergence of what has been called the postmethod condition.

I have argued that any postmethod pedagogy must take into account the pedagogic parameters of particularity, practicality, and possibility. The first relates to the advancement of a context-sensitive pedagogy based on a true understanding of local linguistic, sociocultural, and political particularities. The second seeks to enable and encourage teachers to theorize from their practice and practice what they theorize. And the third emphasizes the importance of larger social, political, educational, and institutional forces that shape identity formation and social transformation. The boundaries of the particular, the practical, and the possible are blurred as they shape and are shaped by the others.

I have also suggested that the three parameters have the potential to provide the organizing principles for the construction of a context-sensitive pedagogic framework. This potential opens up unlimited opportunities for the emergence of various types of postmethod pedagogies that are sensitive to various learning and teaching needs, wants, and situations. In chapter 9, I describe three recent attempts at formulating the basics of postmethod pedagogy that transcend the limitations of the concept of method in different ways.

Postmethod Pedagogy

9. INTRODUCTION

In this chapter, I focus on some of the attempts that have recently been made to lay the foundation for the construction of pedagogies that can be considered postmethod in their orientation. In order to do that, I consider only those proposals that (a) make a clear and consequential break with the concept of method, (b) provide a coherent and comprehensive framework to the extent allowed by the current state of knowledge, and (c) offer a well-defined and well-explained set of ideas that may guide important aspects of L2 classroom activity. I recognize that these requirements lack precise definitions, and that any choice based on them will remain subjective.

With those conditions and caveats in mind, I choose to highlight three postmethod frameworks: (a) Stern's three-dimensional framework, (b) Allwright's Exploratory Practice framework, and (c) Kumaravadivelu's macrostrategic framework. In choosing these three, I am not suggesting that they exemplify all, or even most, of the parameters and indicators of postmethod pedagogy discussed in chapter 8. In fact, it should be noted that the parameters and indicators are my personal views of what should constitute the fundamentals of a postmethod pedagogy. Neither Stern's nor Allwright's framework takes them as points of departure, although the essence of some of the parameters and indicators are implicit in their work. However, as the following discussion will, hopefully, show, all the three frameworks share certain basic characteristics in common. They, of course, vary in the treatment of those characteristics. Let me describe each of them.

In order to retain the authors' voice and vision, I present their frameworks in their own words, as much as possible.

9.1. THE THREE-DIMENSIONAL FRAMEWORK

The three-dimensional framework for language teaching may be considered the first attempt to come out with a coherent and wide-ranging plan for constructing a postmethod pedagogy. It was proposed by Stern who was founder and former head of the Modern Language Centre at the Ontario Institute for Studies in Education, Canada, from 1968 to 1981 and was Professor Emeritus at the same Institute from 1981 to 1987. One of Canada's distinguished educators, Stern is considered to be a prominent authority on second-language education. After retirement, he planned to write two books aimed at providing a critical survey of the field. His first, the highly acclaimed, *Fundamental Concepts of Language Teaching,* was published in 1983, and as the title suggests, gives a comprehensive account of the theoretical foundations of language teaching. His second volume with practical implications for language curriculum was at various stages of completion at the time of his death. It was edited by his colleagues, Allen and Harley, and was published, posthumously, in 1992 with the title, *Issues and Options in Language Teaching.* In the Preface to the book, the editors assure the readers that the Introduction as well as all the 12 chapters "closely follow the author's rough draft, and that they convey his intentions with reasonable accuracy" (p. ix). They wrote only the conclusion, to show how the various components of the multidimensional framework might be combined into an integrated whole.

Although it is in the second book that Stern provides the details of his multidimensional framework, he has mentioned it briefly in the last chapter (chap. 22) of his first book, thus indicating that he was in the process of developing it for a long time. His own motivation for designing the framework can be found in chapter 21, which is titled, significantly enough, "The Break with the Method Concept." He was concerned about "two major weaknesses" of all the language teaching methods that he surveyed: "One is that they represent a relatively fixed combination of language teaching beliefs, and another is that they are characterized by the over-emphasis of single aspects as the central issue of language teaching and learning" (1983, p. 473). He was also convinced that an eclectic approach would not be of any help either, because "eclecticism is still based on the notion of a conceptual distinctiveness of the different methods. However, it is the distinctiveness of the methods as complete entities that can be called into question" (1983, p. 482).

Abandoning the method concept, Stern opts for what he calls a "strategy concept." His framework consists of strategies and techniques. He uses the term *strategy* to refer to broad "intentional action" and the term *technique* to refer to specific "practical action" (Stern, 1992, p. 277). Strategies operate at the policy level, and techniques at the procedural level. He emphasizes that strategies "are not simply another term for what used to be called methods" (p. 277). They "operate with flexible sets of concepts which embody any useful lessons we can draw from the history of language teaching but which do not perpetuate the rigidities and dogmatic narrowness of the earlier methods concept" (p. 277).

Stern's strategy concept comprises teaching strategies and learning strategies that are based on three dimensions: (a) the L1–L2 connection, concerning the use or nonuse of the first language in learning the second; (b) the code-communication dilemma, concerning the structure–message relationship; and (c) the explicit–implicit option, concerning the basic approach to language learning. Thus, each dimension consists of two strategies plotted at two ends of a continuum. Let us briefly consider each of them. All the citations in the following three subsections, unless otherwise stated, are taken from Stern's 1992 book, and I shall note only the page numbers.

9.1.1. The Intralingual–Crosslingual Dimension

The terms *intralingual* and *intracultural* refer to those techniques that remain within the target language (L2) and target culture (C2) as the frame of reference for teaching. *Crosslingual* and *crosscultural* pertain to techniques that use features of the native language (L1) and native culture (C1) for comparison purposes. The intralingual strategy adheres to the policy of coordinate bilingualism, where the two language systems are kept completely separate from one another, whereas the crosslingual strategy believes in compound bilingualism, where the L2 is acquired and known through the use of L1. As the following box shows, the presence or the absence of translation as a technique marks the criterial feature of interlingual and crosslingual strategies.

Intralingual	Crosslingual
←--→	
Intracultural	Crosscultural
L2 used as a reference system	L1 used as a reference system
Immersion in L2/C2	Comparison between L1/L2, C1/C2
Keeping L2 apart from L1	
No translation from and into L2	Practice through translation from & into L2
Direct method	Grammar translation method
Co-ordinate bilingualism	Compound bilingualism

Intralingual and crosslingual teaching strategies (p. 279)

This dimension is a response to an everlasting controversy about the role of L1 in L2 teaching. Historically, when grammar-translation or earlier methods were popular, crosslingual techniques (particularly, translation-based ones) were widely employed. But, later methods, including the current communicative language teaching, have prohibited the use of L1 in the L2 class, emphasizing the importance of teaching a foreign language only through the medium of the foreign language. But in reality, practicing teachers everywhere have rarely stuck rigidly to intralingual techniques.

Arguing that "the L1-L2 connection is an indisputable fact of life" (p. 282), Stern offers three reasons why L1 should be allowed to be used in the L2 classroom. First, when we learn a new language, we always set out from a language we already know. Second, our first language offers a frame of reference system for L2. "It is in the nature of linguistic and communicative competence that we behave as if the L1 (or a second language previously learnt) is the yardstick and guide to our new L2" (pp. 282–283). Third, our native language and our native culture "are deeply bound up with our personal lives. A new language and culture demand a personal adjustment" (p. 283). We have to think of ways in which to deal with that adjustment in a gradual manner. The widely accepted phenomena of language transfer (see chap. 2, this volume), and the recently proposed concept of multicompetence (see chap. 1, this volume), both of which are based on psycholinguistic research, add strength to Stern's arguments against any exclusive intralingual strategy.

Stern treats the intralingual–crosslingual strategy as a continuum (see the box above) saying that a good case can be made "for either a mainly crosslingual or a mainly intralingual policy" (p. 284). He suggests that it may be useful, at the initial stages of language learning, to fall back on comparisons between L1 and L2 and explanations of L2 in L1 terms. Toward the more intermediate and advanced stages, it is important to opt for intralingual techniques. His conclusion is that "the emphasis on an intralingual or a crosslingual strategy should be decided in relation to the goals of the learners, their previous experience in the L2, the context in which the programme takes place, and the ability of the teacher to function intralingually or crosslingually" (p. 286).

Taking from popular ESL textbooks, Stern offers, for illustrative purposes, several useful intralingual as well as crosslingual classroom techniques for different stages of language learning. These activities, Stern points out, range from repetition of sounds, words, phrases, and sentences, to verbal utterances, based on real objects or pictorial representations, to drills and exercise, to dictation, to games, to communicative activities, to residence in an L2 environment. These techniques help to create or stimulate an L2 environment in varying degrees. As for crosslinguistic techniques, Stern favors techniques involving the comparison of "the two phonological, lexical, and grammatical systems and help learners to build up the new L2 reference system by making a gradual and deliberate transition from L1 to L2" (p. 284). He also recommends translation and interpretive activities. The former may involve L2–L1 translation, and use of an L2-to-L1 dictionary, and the latter may include introducing and summarizing an L2 text in L1, explaining the context of a text in L1; discussing in L1 the significance of an L2 text, and so on.

Stern makes it clear that at certain stages during the teaching and learning process, both intralingual and crosslingual strategies will be productive. His recommendation to teachers who follow a predominantly intralingual strategy is that, "it is advisable to allow certain well-defined periods in which the use of the L1 is allowed so that questions can be asked, meanings can be verified, uncertainties can be removed, and explanations given which would not be accessible to the learner in L2" (p. 298). Although unequivocally in favor of using L1 in the L2 classroom, he calls for a judicious balance so that the learner does not "rely too heavily on L1 support instead of taking the plunge and developing a new independent network of L2 verbal connections" (p. 292).

9.1.2. The Analytic-Experiential Dimension

The second strategic continuum relates to yet another perennial debate about the role of form and message, or what Stern calls, code and communication, in language teaching. The analytic strategy involves explicit focus on the formal properties of language, that is, grammar, vocabulary, and notions and functions whereas the experiential strategy involves message-oriented, interaction in communicative contexts. Consider the following contrastive terms collected by Stern (only a partial list is given here):

Analytic	Experiential
←--→	
focus on code	focus on communication
medium centered	message centered
observation	participation
usage	use
focus on language	focus on topic/purpose
decontextualized	contextualized
language practice	language use
predictability of response	information gap
emphasis on accuracy	emphasis on fluency
linguistic interaction	interpersonal interaction

Analytic and experiential teaching strategies (p. 302).

As the list of terms associated with analysis and experience shows, the experiential strategy "invites the learner to use the language for a purpose, and to focus on the message rather than any specific aspect of the code" (p. 301). The analytic strategy, on the other hand, "is based on techniques of study and practice. . . . The language learner is placed in the role of an observer who looks at the language and culture from outside and pays attention to formal or functional feature which are deliberately abstracted at least to some degree from the living context" (p. 301). Recall from the chapters in Part Two that language- and learner-centered pedagogies fall under the analytic end, and learning-centered pedagogies move toward the experiential end.

As can be expected, Stern advocates a mixture of experiential and analytic strategies and techniques because he finds positive aspects in both. The analytic strategy "abstracts, decontextualizes, and isolates language phenomena or skill aspects for scrutiny, diagnosis, and practice" (p. 310), all of which are essential for language education. And analytic techniques enable learners to focus on the code by helping them to "identify, explain, compare, illustrate, and practise a language feature or an aspect of language use" (p. 307). He does not dismiss the criticisms leveled against the analytic strategy (see chap. 5, this volume, for details) but considers that they "merely draw attention to limitations of studying a language by analytic methods alone, and suggest that an experiential strategy should complement the analytic approach because it deals with the language more globally" (p. 311).

In terms of classroom activities, Stern recommends the familiar analytic techniques that operate through study and practice of the language with full and explicit focus on linguistic features, and equally familiar experiential activities such as projects, inquiries, games, or problem-solving tasks. He favors the creation of "the conditions for real communication" by introducing information-gap activities that have "an element of unpredictability" (p. 316). He agrees with Prabhu (cf. chap. 7, this volume, on learning-centered pedagogy) that "it may be useful to introduce a reasoning gap, implying true inference, and an opinion gap, in which case the interlocutors do not know in advance what comment is likely to be made" (p. 316). With regard to listening, speaking, reading, and writing skills, he sees merit in both separation and integration:

> each skill can be treated abstractly as something to be developed, so to speak, for its own sake. This is typical of an analytical approach. On the other hand, the skills can form a natural part of a purposeful set of activities: giving a talk, listening to a recoding, participating in a group discussion, writing a report or a letter. (p. 320)

Summing up his arguments about the analytic–experiential dimension, he states that there is "no reason to assume that one strategy alone offers the royal road to proficiency. Therefore, some kind of combination of these two approaches appears to be the best policy to adopt pending more convincing evidence of the greater effectiveness of either one or the other" (p. 321).

9.1.3. The Explicit–Implicit Dimension

The third and final strategic dimension concerns the key issue of whether learning an L2 is a conscious intellectual exercise or an unconscious intuitive one. Stern uses familiar words, *explicit* and *implicit*, to refer to the two strategies. Here too, he has collected some contrastive terms from the literature (only a partial list is given here):

Explicit	Implicit
← - →	
rational/formal/intellectual	intuitive
conscious learning	subconscious acquisition
deliberate	incidental
analysis	global understanding
cognitivism	behaviorism
inferencing	mimicry and memory
rationalist approach	empiricist approach
systematic study	exposure to language in use

The explicit-implicit dimension (p. 327).

According to Stern, the other four strategies in the first two dimensions—intralingual/crosslingual, and analytic/experiential—can each be either explicit or implicit, and hence the mixed bag of concepts and terms.

In reaching a determination about this dimension, Stern seems to have been influenced by an early model of language learning proposed by Bialystok (1978), which she has since revised and expanded. Bialystok's early model consisted of three knowledge sources, and she had called them *explicit knowledge, implicit knowledge,* and *other knowledge.* This model, as Stern points out, claims that it is possible to know some things about a language explicitly, and others only implicitly, and that there is an interaction between explicit and implicit knowledge. In this respect, Bialystok's model is substantially different from Krashen's (e.g., 1981) Monitor Model, which keeps the explicit–implicit mechanisms separate, rejecting any movement from explicit to implicit, or vice versa. Stern finds Bialystok's interpretation more appealing than Krashen's.

Stern acknowledges the merits of both explicit and implicit strategies. An explicit strategy helps learners focus on the characteristics of the language and acquire a conscious and conceptual knowledge of it. They can use that knowledge to "know how the language functions, how it hangs together, what words mean, how meaning is conveyed, and so on" (p. 334). An implicit strategy rightly takes into account the fact that language "is much too complex to be fully described," and "even if the entire system could be described, it would be impossible to keep all the rules in mind and to rely on a consciously formulated system for effective learning" (p. 339).

Therefore, he concludes, for the purpose of developing an instructional policy, "we want to bear both strategies in mind and treat the explicit and implicit options as opposite ends of a continuum. In practice, we expect the two strategies to be combined, but the mix will be varied according to the language topic, the course objectives, the characteristics of the students, and the needs of the teaching situation" (p. 345). Besides, learners also may differ on their preference for explicit or implicit language learning, depending on their age, maturity, and previous educational experience.

In order to help with the implementation of his three-dimensional framework for language teaching, Stern has devised four types of syllabus with a wide range of objectives and options: the *language syllabus*, the *communicative activities syllabus*, the *cultural syllabus*, and the *general language education syllabus*. In a nutshell, the language syllabus deals with all aspects of language as system (see chap. 1, this volume, for details) and includes the phonological, syntactic, and semantic features of the target language, and also some aspects of language as discourse but mostly limited to textual features of cohesion and coherence. The communicative activities syllabus deals with language as discourse in its interactional orientation, thus focusing on social norms governing language communication. The cultural syllabus pertains to the relationship between language and culture, and language and society, thus focusing on cultural knowledge necessary for contact with the target-language community. The general language education syllabus serves to broaden the scope of the L2 curriculum and aims at helping learners generalize from their second-language learning experience to the learning of other languages as well as to education in general.

Based on the available notes and his earlier writings, the editors of the Stern volume, Allen and Harley, give an idea of how Stern would have integrated the four types of syllabus to meet the objectives of the multidimensional framework for language teaching. According to them (pp. 357–360), he would have advised teachers, syllabus designers and teacher educators (a) to recognize that the four syllabuses complement one another and that they are not separated by hard and fast boundaries; (b) to build bridges from syllabus to syllabus by seeking out common ground and making cross-references wherever possible; (c) to develop and use teaching materials that cut across the syllabus divisions; (d) to start from one syllabus (e.g., the language syllabus) and work toward the others; and finally (e) to establish a longitudinal, proportional pattern of content so that any individual teaching unit could be derived from one or more types of syllabus.

The editors point out that "Stern clearly considered integration of the multidimensional curriculum to be a matter of deliberate policy, for the most part carefully preplanned prior to implementation of the curriculum in the L2 class" (p. 360). They reiterate that out of the five items (a–e listed above), only the first one "suggests that integration can also occur spontaneously during classroom interaction at the implementation stage" (p. 360). The other four, according to them,

> imply that an integration policy is established either during or after the process of syllabus development, which is assumed to take place outside the classroom itself. How an integration policy is in fact translated into classroom practice in any particular context remains, of course, an issue to be investigated at the practical action level of Stern's analytic framework. (p. 360)

If I understand Stern's observations and the editors' commentaries correctly, it appears that the multidimensional framework is heavily weighted toward an integrated curricular agenda. I think it is fair to say that curricular objectives seem to drive classroom procedures. What is not fully clear is the role of the practicing teacher in the pedagogic decision-making process. The editors inform us that Stern had planned further chapters on social strategies, timing strategies, resources, and student evaluation as well as a chapter on vocabulary. It is highly probable that, given his disappointment with the top–down concept of method, Stern had planned to delve more deeply into the role of the teacher vis à vis his multidimensional framework. It is, indeed, a great loss to the profession that he could not complete his planned mission.

It is, however, abundantly clear that Stern's framework is theory neutral and method neutral. That is, he directly deals with major contentious dichotomous issues that marked the pendulum swing in language teaching, and in his own characteristic way, selects the middle path that balances the fundamental features of the intralingual and crosslingual, the analytic and experiential, and the explicit and implicit. His framework certainly rejects the rigidities associated with the concept of method, and looks beyond. Yet another framework that attempts to do that from an entirely different perspective is the Exploratory Practice framework.

9.2. THE EXPLORATORY PRACTICE FRAMEWORK

The *Exploratory Practice* framework has been evolving for nearly a decade now. Its principal author is Allwright, who retired as a Professor in the Department of Linguistics and Modern English Language at the University of Lancaster in Britain in the year 2003, after having served there for many years. An internationally reputed scholar, he is well-known for his pioneering work on classroom observation and teacher exploration. He has also played a leading role in the professional activities of the U.S.-based, international TESOL organization, and has served as its President.

Having been disillusioned with the concept of method and having declared it "dead" (see chap. 8, this volume, for details), Allwright has been exploring alternatives to method. His answer: Exploratory Practice (EP). Although the EP framework has had, as he puts it, an "academic" origin, it has gradually become a practitioner project shaped largely by teachers and learners. He traces the origin of the framework to a brief Epilogue in *Focus on the Language Classroom,* a 1991 book he coauthored with Bailey. The Epilogue forms part of the final chapter, titled "Towards Exploratory Teaching." In it, he explains the term *exploratory teaching* as "teaching that not only tries out new ideas" but also one that further explores tried and trusted ideas in order "to learn as much as possible from doing so" (p. 196). In other words, exploratory teaching "is a mater of trying to find out what makes the tried and trusted ideas successful. Because in the long run it is not enough to know that ideas do work; we need also to know why and how they work" (p. 196).

As he wrote in a subsequent paper published in 1993, an important aspect of exploratory teaching is teacher research that, if carried out properly, will not only enhance the teacher's understanding of classroom teaching but also contribute to progress in pedagogic research in general. Accordingly, he presented a set of appropriate criteria and practical possibilities for integrating research and pedagogy. "The central concern," he remarked, "is a wish to offer a practical way of bringing the research perspective properly into the classroom, without adding significantly and unacceptably to teachers' workloads, so as to contribute both professional development and to theory-building within and across the profession" (Allwright, 1993, p. 131). One could conclude that, at this initial phase of the framework, Allwright has been chiefly concerned about finding principled ways to connect the professional theory of the expert with the personal theory of the teacher, surely, for the benefit of both.

Allwright's theoretical views on his still-developing exploratory teaching took a decidedly "practical" turn when he was invited to teach classroom research skills to teachers at the Cultura Inglesa in Rio de Janeiro, a major nonprofit language teaching establishment in Brazil "with hundreds of teachers teaching thousands of students." He soon realized that both the nature and the scope of traditional classroom research would make impossible demands on the teachers, and more importantly, that he was getting practical ideas from classroom investigations from the very teachers he was supposed to be helping. To cut a long story short, his experience in Rio showed him how some of the ideas he sketched in the 1991 Epilogue might actually work out in practice. It marked the beginning of a still-ongoing collaboration between Allwright and the Cultura Inglesa. The collaboration has resulted in firming up the framework that is now called Exploratory Practice framework.

Information about the framework is disseminated to teachers mostly through workshops and newsletters. There have been very few reports in professional journals (see Allwright & Lenzuen, 1997, for one). Recently, in June of 2003, *Language Teaching Research* journal devoted an entire issue on EP, with reports from Allwright and others. There is also an Exploratory Practice Centre established at the University of Lancaster to facilitate networking around the globe. The Centre's Newsletter, and other reports are available at its Web site, http://www.ling.lancs.ac.uk/groups/crile/EPcentre/epcentre/htm. What follows is an outline of EP's principles and practices. A caution is in order: the terms, *principles* and *practices,* are used here very differently; the former does not refer to the theoretical principles of language, learning and teaching, nor does the latter refer to classroom teaching procedures or techniques associated with methods-based pedagogy (cf. Part Two of this volume).

9.2.1. The Principle of Exploratory Practice

Exploratory Practice is premised upon a philosophy that is stated in three fundamental tenets: (a) the *quality of life* in the language classroom is much more important than instructional efficiency; (b) ensuring our *understanding* of the quality of classroom life is far more essential than developing ever "improved" teaching techniques; and (c) understanding such a quality of life is a *social,* not an *asocial* matter, that is, all practitioners can expect to gain from this mutual process of working for understanding. Consistent with these philosophical tenets, Allwright presents the following "principles description" of EP in what he calls "one convoluted sentence":

Exploratory Practice involves

1. practitioners (e.g.: preferably teachers *and* learners together) working to understand:
   (a) what *they* want to understand, following their own agendas;
   (b) not necessarily *in order to* bring about change;
   (c) not primarily *by* changing;
   (d) but by *using* normal pedagogic practices as investigative tools, so that working for understanding is *part of* the teaching and learning, not extra to it;
   (e) in a way that does not lead to "burn-out," but that is *indefinitely sustainable;*
2. in order to contribute to:
   (f) *teaching and learning themselves;*
   (g) *professional development, both individual and collective.*
      (Allwright, 2003a, pp. 127–128, all italics in original)

From this one overarching sentence, seven general principles have been derived. They are:

Principle 1:   Put "quality of life" first.
Principle 2:   Work primarily to understand language classroom life.
Principle 3:   Involve everybody.
Principle 4:   Work to bring people together.
Principle 5:   Work also for mutual development.
Principle 6:   Integrate the work for understanding into classroom prac-
tice.
            Corollary to Principle 6: Let the need to integrate guide
            the conduct of the work for understanding.
Principle 7:   Make the work a continuous enterprise.
            Corollary to Principle 7: Avoid time-limited funding.

These seven principles have emerged from nearly a decade of collective action and thought by practitioners in a variety of groups. People and the roles they play are considered to be "at the heart" of the principles of EP; therefore, collegiality becomes crucial to the pedagogic enterprise. Allwright (2003a, pp. 131–135) lists six aspects of collegiality, particularly in relation to Principles 3, 4, and 5:

Collegiality between teachers and learners.
Collegiality among teachers in the same institution.
Collegiality and the hierarchy within an employing institution.
Collegiality between teachers and training and development people.
Collegiality between teachers and academic researchers.
Collegiality in a teacher association.

The collegiality of EP practitioners is emphasized partly because of the mutual benefit and the mutual dependence that any form of EP practice demands.

9.2.2. The Practice of Exploratory Practice

The principles of EP discussed above are expected to guide specific practices that are, again, ever-evolving. These practices are aimed at helping teachers (and potentially learners too) to investigate the areas of learning and teaching they wish to explore by using familiar classroom activities as the investigative tools. The use of classroom activities themselves as investigative tools is what differentiates, in a significant way, the practice of EP from the notion of Action Research, which uses standard academic research techniques aimed at solving practical classroom problems.

According to Allwright and Lenzuen (1997) and Allwright (2000), the EP practice involves a series of basic steps. I draw from them to present the following steps:

- *Step 1: Identifying a puzzle.* It involves finding something puzzling in a teaching and learning situation. The word *puzzle* is preferred to *problem* because of the negative connotation associated with the latter. A problem can be treated as a puzzle by turning it from a *how* question into a *why* one. For example, if there is a problem of unmotivated learners, it would be better to start, not by inventing "clever ways" of motivating them, but by asking why they are not motivated in the first place.
- *Step 2: Reflecting upon the puzzle.* It involves thinking about the puzzle in order understand it without actually taking any direct action. For example, if there is a problem of large classes, it may be beneficial to treat diversity as resource rather than think of eliminating it by taking any direct action.
- *Step 3: Monitoring.* It involves paying special attention, if necessary, to the phenomenon that is puzzling the teacher, in order to understand it better. For instance, keeping notes while learners are engaged upon group work, instead of spending time circulating to directly oversee their work, would be one way of monitoring.
- *Step 4: Taking direct action to generate data.* It involves generating additional data, if needed, by using classroom activities such as group work, not standard academic data-collection techniques.
- *Step 5: Considering the outcomes reached so far, and deciding what to do next.* It involves determining whether there is sufficient justification to move on, or whether a further period of reflection and more data are needed.
- *Step 6: Moving on.* It involves, provided adequate understanding has already been reached, deciding to choose from several options, such as discussing with students, or adjusting expectations, or protesting about the state of affairs, or actually doing something to alleviate the situation, or taking a critical pedagogic stance and moving toward transforming the educational system, and
- *Step 7: Going public.* It involves, if adequate understanding of the puzzle is reached, and if found an improved "quality of classroom life" to go public and share the benefit with others, or to get feedback from others. This may be done in the form of workshops, conference presentations, or publications.

These seven practical steps are, of course, flexible and are subject to change with experience.

9.2.3. The Global and the Local

An important concern Allwright seems to be wrestling with is the exact connection between the principles and the practices of EP. He sees the need for global principles for general guidance, but their implications need to be worked out for local everyday practice. He sees a cyclical connection between the two, as represented in what he calls a "crude loop diagram":

> Think globally, act locally, think locally.

He also believes "the thinking we do to find principled ways of acting in our local situation generates more thinking about our principles" (Allwright, 2003a, p. 115). Local action and local thinking produce practices potentially adaptable to any context, thereby developing our thinking about global principles. He asserts that some of the local practices he encountered in Rio actually served as the source for his statements of principle. That is why he states in his brief guide to EP (Allwright, 2003b) "at the Exploratory Practice Centre at Lancaster we feel we have largely *discovered* Exploratory Practice *in* teachers' current practices, rather than *invented* it 'out of the blue' *for* teachers" (p. 110, italics in original).

Given the contributions made by practicing teachers in firming up the EP framework, and the admirable personal and practical knowledge they have already demonstrated, Allwright (2000) was at one time puzzled as to why they still wanted to be trained as exploratory teachers. In other words, practicing teachers are always looking for certain underlying principles that they can use in their classroom to guide their practice of everyday teaching, although Allwright has been insisting on teachers themselves deriving the global principles. Stating that "we eventually surrendered" (Allwright, 2003a, p. 122), he narrates how the teachers' practices were summarized and given back to them for their consumption, with additional distinctive features of principles drawn from the practices.

In light of his experience, Allwright (2000) wonders:

> Is it likely to be better for us to try to carry our *principles* with us from context to context, than to carry our *practices* around? . . . But if our "global" principles are in fact themselves to a large and unknowable extent the product of context, we perhaps risk a great deal if we carry them around as if they were genuinely global.

In a moment of intense self-reflection, he talks about his "intellectual baggage," and observes (Allwright, 2000): "All I can add here is that, nearing retirement, I have inevitably accumulated a wide range of experiences in a wide variety of contexts. But that of course might mean only that my 'global' thinking is simply multiple context-bound, rather then in any strong sense 'context-free'." He thus creates a greater awareness of the complex issue of the deeply dialectical relationship between the principle and the practice, between the global and the local, between generalities and particularities—an issue that has prominently figured in yet another postmethod framework—the macrostrategic framework.

9.3. THE MACROSTRATEGIC FRAMEWORK

As I begin to discuss my *macrostrategic framework*, I think it is not out of place to strike a personal note of professional development, in order to provide some background information. The first opportunity to have a public discussion of some of the ideas I had been harboring about a macrostrategic framework for language teaching came in 1988 when I presented a paper titled "Creation and Utilization of Learning Opportunities" at the 22nd annual TESOL Convention held in Chicago during March 8–13 of that year. In the same year, I presented "Macrostrategies for ESL Teacher Education" at the Southeast Regional TESOL conference held in Orlando, Florida during October 29–November 1. The first print version of my thoughts appeared in 1992 when *The Modern Language Journal* published my paper, "Macrostrategies for the Second/Foreign Language Teacher."

Initially, I was only looking for effective ways of using the traditional classroom interaction analysis to see how teacher education can be made more sensitive to classroom events and activities. Like so many other colleagues, I have been, for a long time, skeptical of existing teacher education programs, which merely transfer a body of professional knowledge to prospective teachers, knowledge that may not even be relevant to their local needs. My 1992 paper, therefore, was

> based on the hypothesis that since second/foreign language (L2) learning/ teaching needs, wants and situations are unpredictably numerous, we cannot prepare teachers to tackle so many unpredictable needs, wants and situations; we can only help them develop a capacity to generate varied and situation-specific ideas within a general framework that makes sense in terms of current pedagogical and theoretical knowledge. (Kumaravadivelu, 1992, p. 41)

Accordingly, I proposed a framework in that paper consisting of five macrostrategies (see text to come for definition) supported by authentic classroom data. With subsequent work, I increased the number to 10.

In the meantime, I was growing more and more disillusioned with the constraining concept of method which, in my opinion, was also constraining the development of more useful models of teacher education. Even more broadly, I was getting impatient with my chosen field of TESOL that I thought, was marked by a poverty of intellectual stimulus. I felt that the field was going round and round within a narrow perimeter, jealously guarding its own safe zone, and without opening itself up to novel and challenging ideas from the outside world. For too long, I thought, we pretended (and some of us still pretend) that language teaching operates in a nonexistent ahistorical, asocial, and apolitical space. Disillusioned with the field itself, I turned elsewhere for intellectual sustenance.

I turned to cultural studies. I started reading, among other things, about poststructuralism, postmodernism, and postcolonialism. Cultural studies led me to the exciting but challenging world of European master thinkers such as Pierre Bourdieu, Michel de Certeau, and Michel Foucault, and of immigrant intellectuals such as Homi Bhabha, Edward Said, and Gayatri Spivak. I learned from them that the borders between the personal, the professional, and the political are indeed porous, and that we are all constantly crossing the boundaries whether we know it or not, whether we acknowledge it or not. Incidentally, it is gratifying to note that with some gentle nudging from scholars such as Elsa Auerbach, Sarah Benesch, Suresh Canagarajah, Ryuko Kubota, Angel Lin, Alastair Pennycook, Robert Phillipson, and a growing number of others, the field is ever so cautiously opening up to "alien" thoughts.

My forays into cultural studies opened up a treasure house of knowledge for me. Because of my own limitations, I think I have not been able to make full use of the knowledge or the tools of exploration the field offers, but it certainly has given me a broader perspective and a better vocabulary to express it. Equipped with a new-found enthusiasm, I "returned" to my parent field and to my still developing thoughts on the macrostrategic framework. The immediate result was my 1994 *TESOL Quarterly* paper on "The Postmethod Condition: (E)merging strategies for Second/Foreign Language teaching" (Kumaravadivelu, 1994b). Notice that the new term I used, *the postmethod condition,* is a clear echo of the title of Lyotard's (1989) seminal book, *The Postmodern Condition: A Report on Knowledge,* although, unlike Lyotard, I have tried to go beyond the constraints of postmodernism by bringing in postcolonial perspectives as well.

Further thoughts led me to my 2001 *TESOL Quarterly* paper titled "Towards a Postmethod Pedagogy" (Kumaravadivelu, 2001) in which I attempted to conceptualize the characteristics of postmethod pedagogy (see chap. 8, this volume, for details). In between, in 1999, I applied postmodern and postcolonial thoughts to critique the traditional ways of classroom interaction analysis, and presented, again in the *TESOL Quarterly,* a paper called "Critical Classroom Discourse Analysis" (Kumaravadivelu, 1999a). A more developed macrostrategic framework with illustrative samples, reflective tasks, and classroom-oriented projects appeared in my 2003 book, *Beyond Methods: Macrostrategies for Language Teaching* (Kumaravadi-velu, 2003a) published by Yale University Press.

Drawing from the just-mentioned works, I outline below my postmethod framework in terms of macrostrategies and microstrategies.

9.3.1. Macrostrategies

Macrostrategies are general plans derived from currently available theoreti-cal, empirical, and pedagogical knowledge related to L2 learning and teaching. A macrostrategy is a broad guideline based on which teachers can generate their own location-specific, need-based microstrategies or class-room procedures. In other words, macrostrategies are made operational in the classroom through microstrategies. Macrostrategies are considered the-ory-neutral, because they are not confined to underlying assumptions of any one specific theory of language, learning, and teaching, discussed in Part One. They are also considered method-neutral because they are not conditioned by a single set of principles or procedures associated with lan-guage teaching methods discussed in Part Two.

The strategic framework comprises 10 macrostrategies that are couched in operational terms. The choice of action verbs over static nouns is purely for the sake of convenience, and is not meant to convey any prescriptive character. The macrostrategies are

1. Maximize learning opportunities;
2. facilitate negotiated interaction;
3. minimize perceptual mismatches;
4. activate intuitive heuristics;
5. foster language awareness;
6. contextualize linguistic input;
7. integrate language skills;
8. promote learner autonomy;
9. ensure social relevance; and
10. raise cultural consciousness.

In what follows, I briefly explain each of these macrostrategies (see Kuma-ravadivelu, 2003a for details).

Macrostrategy 1: Maximize learning opportunities. The first macrostrategy envisages teaching as a process of creating and utilizing learning opportu-nities. Teachers are seen both as creators of learning opportunities for their learners and utilizers of learning opportunities created by learners. As cre-ators of learning opportunities teachers need to strike a balance between their role as planners of teaching acts and their role as mediators of learning acts. The former involves an a priori judgment based on, among other things, learners' current level of knowledge/ability, and their learning objectives, whereas the latter involves an ongoing assessment of how well learners handle classroom input and interaction.

Maximizing learning opportunities also entails a willingness on the part of teachers to modify their lesson plans continuously on the basis of ongoing feedback. This can be done only if they treat the predetermined syllabus as a presyllabus that is to be reconstructed to meet specific learner needs, wants, and situations, and treat the prescribed textbook as a pretext that is to be used only as a springboard for launching appropriate classroom activities.

Learners create learning opportunities for themselves and for other learners by seeking clarification, raising doubts, making suggestions, and so forth. If teachers wish to utilize learning opportunities created by learners, then, they can no longer see "teachers simply as teachers, and learners simply as learners, because both are, for good or ill, managers of learning" (Allwright, 1984, p.156). Because the production of classroom talk is a cooperative venture, teachers cannot afford to ignore any contribution from other partners jointly engaged in the process of creating and utilizing learning opportunities. In a class of learners with near-homogenous language ability, every time a learner indicates any difficulty in understanding a linguistic or propositional content of the lesson, we can assume that there may be other learners who experience a similar difficulty. Therefore, not bringing a particular learner's problem to the attention of the class indicates a failure on the part of the teacher to utilize the learning opportunity created by the learner.

Macrostrategy 2: Facilitate negotiated interaction. This macrostrategy refers to meaningful learner–learner, learner–teacher interaction in class where the learners have the freedom and flexibility to initiate and navigate talk, not just react and respond to it. Negotiated interaction means that the learner should be actively involved, as discussed in chapter 3, in interaction as a textual activity, interaction as an interpersonal activity and interaction as an ideational activity. During these interactional activities, teachers should facilitate the learner's understanding and use of language as system, language as discourse, and language as ideology (see chap. 1, this volume, for details).

As discussed in chapter 2 and chapter 3, there is overwhelming evidence to suggest that L2 learners need to be provided with opportunities for negotiated interaction in order to accelerate their comprehension and production. Studies on interactional modifications demonstrate that what enables learners to move beyond their current receptive and expressive capacities are opportunities to modify and restructure their interaction with their interlocutors until mutual comprehension is reached. Production, as opposed to comprehension, may very well be the trigger that forces learners to pay attention to form, to the relationship between form and meaning, and to the overall means of communication.

Macrostrategy 3: Minimize perceptual mismatches. Communication in general has been defined as a gradual reduction of uncertainty. In other words, every piece of human communication has the potential to contain ambiguities; more so, L2 classroom communication. Therefore, any L2 class, however well-planned and well-executed, will result in some kind of mismatch between teacher intention and learner interpretation. What impact classroom activities will have on the learning process depends as much on learner perception as on teacher preparation, as much on learner interpretation as on teacher intention. It is therefore essential to sensitize ourselves to the potential sources of mismatch between teacher intention and learner interpretation.

There are at least ten potential sources of perceptual mismatch that we should be aware of (Kumaravadivelu, 1991):

1. *Cognitive*: a source that refers to the knowledge of the world and mental processes through which learners obtain conceptual understanding of physical and natural phenomena;

2. *Communicative*: a source that refers to skills through which learners exchange messages, including the use of communication strategies;

3. *Linguistic*: a source that refers to linguistic repertoire—syntactic, semantic, and pragmatic knowledge of the target language—that is minimally required to participate in classroom activities;

4. *Pedagogic*: a source that refers to teacher/learner recognition of stated or unstated, short- and/or long-term objective(s) of classroom activities;

5. *Strategic*: a source that refers to learning strategies, that is, operations, steps, plans, and routines used by the learner to facilitate the obtaining, storage, retrieval, and use of information;

6. *Cultural*: a source that refers to prior knowledge of the target cultural norms minimally required for the learner to understand classroom activities;

7. *Evaluative*: a source that refers to articulated or unarticulated types and modes of ongoing self-evaluation measures used by learners to monitor their classroom performance;

8. *Procedural*: a source that refers to stated or unstated paths chosen by the learner to achieve an immediate goal. Procedural source pertains to locally specified, currently identified bottom–up tactics, which seek a quick resolution to a specific problem on hand, whereas strategic source, mentioned earlier, pertains to broad-based, higher-level, top–down strategy, which seeks an overall solution to a general language-learning situation;

9. *Instructional*: a source that refers to instructional directions given by the teacher and/or indicated by the textbook writer to help learners achieve their goal(s); and

10. *Attitudinal*: a source that refers to participants' attitude toward the nature of L2 learning and teaching, the nature of classroom culture, and the nature of participant role relationships.

An awareness of these mismatches can help us effectively intervene whenever we notice or whenever learners indicate problems in carrying out a specified classroom activity.

Macrostrategy 4: Activate intuitive heuristics.   In chapter 3, we discussed input modifications in terms of form and meaning. Doubts have been raised as to whether an L2 system can be neatly analyzed and explicitly explained to learners with the view to aiding grammar construction. The feasibility as well as the desirability of such an exercise has been repeatedly questioned. Such a concern echoes the Chomskyan premise that one cannot learn the entire gamut of the grammatical structure of a language through explanation and instruction beyond the rudimentary level, for the simple reason that no one has enough explicit knowledge about the structure to provide adequate explanation and instruction. It seems that teachers can assist their learners' grammar construction best by designing classroom activities "in such a way as to give free play to those creative principles that humans bring to the process of language learning . . . [and] create a rich linguistic environment for the intuitive heuristics that the normal human being automatically possesses" (Chomsky 1970, p.108). Although the discussion in chapters 3 calls into question the adequacy of an L2 teaching operation based entirely on such an assumption, one can hardly overstate the need to activate the intuitive heuristics of the learner as part of an overall teaching strategy.

One way of activating the intuitive heuristics of the learner is to provide enough textual data so that the learner can infer certain underlying rules of form and function. A good deal of linguistic and discoursal information can be conveyed, not directly through rules, but indirectly through examples. Learners may be encouraged to find the rule-governing pattern in the examples provided. They should encounter the linguistic structure several times so that "the design of the language may be observed, and its meaning (structural, lexical, and socio-cultural) inductively absorbed from its use in such varying situations" (Rivers, 1964, p. 152). Empirical studies discussed in chapter 3 show that self-discovery plays a crucial role in learner comprehension and retention regardless of the learners' language ability.

Macrostrategy 5: Foster language awareness.   Recall from chapter 1 that in the specific context of L2 learning and teaching, language awareness refers to the deliberate attempt to draw learners' attention to the formal properties of their L2 in order to increase the degree of explicitness required to promote L2 learning. Language awareness is based on strategies that emphasize understanding, general principles, and operational experience. Strategies based on language awareness have intellectual appeal and instructional applicability needed to speed up the rate of learning. They also help learners sensitize themselves to aspects of the L2 that would otherwise pass unnoticed, and unlearn initial incorrect analyses by supplying negative evidence.

We also learned in chapter 1 that learners need to develop critical language awareness so that they can identify ideological practices that deceptively use language in order to maintain a social and political power structure.

Macrostrategy 6: Contextualize linguistic input.   The features of language as discourse call for contextualization of linguistic input so that learners can benefit from the interactive effects of systemic as well as discoursal components of language. Introducing isolated, discrete items will result in pragmatic dissonance, depriving the learner of necessary pragmatic cues and rendering the process of meaning-making harder. The responsibility for contextualizing linguistic input lies more with the classroom teacher than with the syllabus designer or the textbook writer. This is because, regardless of what textbooks profess, it is the teacher who can succeed or fail in creating contexts that encourage meaning-making in the classroom.

Sentence comprehension and production involve rapid and simultaneous integration of syntactic, semantic, pragmatic, and discourse phenomena. Studies in L2 development show that the acquisition of syntax is constrained in part by pragmatics, that the phonological forms L2 learners produce depended crucially on the content of discourse, and that syntactic, semantic, and pragmatic features cannot be understood as isolated linguistic components with a unidirectional information flow (Gass, 1997). It is thus essential to bring to the learner's attention the integrated nature of language.

Macrostrategy 7: Integrate language skills.   During the days of language-centered methods, language skills that are traditionally identified as listening, speaking, reading, and writing were taught separately, a move that has very little empirical or theoretical justification (see chap. 5, this volume). We now know that the nature of L2 learning involves not merely an integration of linguistic components of language, but also an integration of language skills. It is true that the four language skills are still widely used in isolation as the fundamental organizing principle for curricular and materials design. It is done, however, more for logistical than for logical reasons. Our discomfort with the practice has surfaced from time to time in our attempt to group the skills in terms of active (speaking and writing) and passive (listening and reading) skills, and later as productive and receptive skills. As

Savignon (1990) pointed out, "lost in this encode/decode, message-sending representation is the collaborative nature of meaning-making" (p. 207).

Language skills are essentially interrelated and mutually reinforcing. Fragmenting them into manageable, atomistic items runs counter to the parallel and interactive nature of language and language behavior. Besides, the learning and use of any one skill can trigger cognitive and communicative associations with the others. Reading exposure alone, for instance, may be "the primary means of developing reading comprehension, writing style, and more sophisticated vocabulary and grammar" (Krashen 1989, p. 90). Similarly, listening activities help to make the broader connection between an integrated sociolinguistic concept of form and function and psycholinguistic processes of interpretation and expression. Furthermore, as we learn from the whole-language movement, language knowledge and language ability are best developed when language is learned and used holistically.

Learners rarely focus on one skill at a time in predictable and invariant ways. An empirical look at the integration and separation of language skills in the L2 classroom (Selinker & Tomlin, 1986) showed that even if the teacher follows textbooks that seek to promote serial integration where learners are supposed to move gradually from one language skill to another, what actually happens in the classroom is parallel integration, where learners use language skills in different combinations. Classroom activity seems to be much more complicated in terms of skill integration than envisioned by either the textbook writer or the teacher. All available empirical, theoretical, and pedagogical information points to the need to integrate language skills for effective language teaching.

Macrostrategy 8: Promote learner autonomy. The postmethod learner, as we saw in the previous chapter, is an autonomous learner. Because language learning is largely an autonomous activity, promoting learner autonomy is vitally important. It involves helping learners learn how to learn, equipping them with the metacognitive, cognitive, social, and affective strategies necessary to self-direct their own learning, raising the consciousness of good language learners about the learning strategies they seem to possess intuitively, and making the strategies explicit and systematic so that they are available to improve the language-learning abilities of other learners as well. It also involves helping learners learn how to liberate. Liberatory autonomy, as we discussed earlier, can provide the learner with the tools necessary to realize the potential for social transformation.

Owing to past experience, adult L2 learners tend to bring with them preconceived notions about what constitutes learning, what constitutes teaching, and prior expectations about what constraints learner- and teacher-role relationships in the classroom. A primary task of the teacher wishing to promote learner autonomy is to help learners take responsibility for their learning, and bring about necessary attitudinal changes in them. This psychological preparation should be combined with strategic training that helps learners understand what the learning strategies are, how to use them for accomplishing various problem-posing and problem-solving tasks, how to monitor their performance, and how to assess the outcome of their learning.

Macrostrategy 9: Ensure social relevance. Social relevance refers to the need for teachers to be sensitive to the societal, political, economic, and educational environment in which L2 education takes place. As discussed in the section on language as ideology in chapter 1, and the section on environmental factors in chapter 2, any serious attempt to understand L2 education necessarily entails an understanding of social and political contexts as important intake variables. L2 education is not a discrete activity; it is deeply embedded in the larger social context that has a profound effect on it. The social context shapes various learning and teaching issues such as (a) the motivation for L2 learning, (b) the goal of L2 learning, (c) the functions L2 is expected to perform at home and in the community, (d) the availability of input to the learner, (e) the variation in the input, (f) and the norms of proficiency acceptable to that particular speech community. It is impossible to insulate classroom life from the dynamics of social institutions. Teaching therefore makes little sense if it is not informed by social relevance.

Learning purpose and language use are perhaps most crucial in determining the social relevance of an L2 program. Different social contexts contribute to the emergence of various functions in an L2 speech community thereby influencing L2 learning and use in significantly different ways. In these contexts, learners are seldom exposed to the full range of their L2 in all its complexity that one would expect in a context where it is used as the primary vehicle of communication. In the use of an L2, "the learner is not becoming an imitation native speaker, but a person who can stand between the two languages, using both when appropriate" (Cook 1992, p. 583). Such an observation should inform the teacher's decision making in terms of appropriate instructional materials, evaluation measures, and target knowledge/ability.

Macrostrategy 10: Raise cultural consciousness. Culture teaching has always been an integral part of L2 teaching. Traditionally, it is aimed at creating in the L2 learner an awareness of and empathy toward the culture of the L2 community. According to a review by Stern (1992), culture teaching has included a cognitive component in terms of geographical knowledge, knowledge about the contributions of the target culture to world civilization, knowledge about differences in the way of life as well as an understanding of values and attitudes in the L2 community; an affective component in terms of interest, curiosity and empathy; and a behavioral component in terms of learners' ability to interpret culturally relevant behavior, and to conduct themselves in culturally appropriate ways. Thus, as Stern reiterates, one of the goals of culture teaching has been to help the learner gain an understanding of native speakers and their perspectives. In such a scenario, cultural diversity is seldom explored and explained.

Such a traditional view of culture teaching may be adequate for helping learners develop sociocultural knowledge/ability, but it may not serve the cause of language teaching in these days of cultural globalization. What is required now is global cultural consciousness. For that purpose, instead of privileging the teacher as the sole cultural informant, we need to treat the learner as a cultural informant as well. By treating learners as cultural informants, we can encourage them to engage in a process of participation that puts a premium on their power/knowledge. We can do so by identifying the cultural knowledge learners bring to the classroom and by using it to help them share their own individual perspectives with the teacher as well as other learners whose lives, and hence perspectives, differ from theirs. Such a multicultural approach can also dispel stereotypes that create and sustain cross-cultural misunderstandings and miscommunications (Kumaravadivelu, 2003c).

In sum, macrostrategies are guiding principles derived from current theoretical, empirical and experiential knowledge of L2 learning and teaching. They may change as our knowledge base grows or changes. Along with the pedagogic parameters of particularity, practicality, and possibility discussed in the previous chapter, they have the potential to constitute the operating principles for constructing a situation-specific postmethod pedagogy. The parameters and the macrostrategies are interconnected and are mutually reinforcing as shown in Fig. 9.1:

> the parameters of particularity, practicality and possibility function as the axle that connects and holds the center of the pedagogic wheel. The macrostrategies function as spokes that join the pedagogic wheel to its center thereby giving the wheel its stability and strength. The outer rim stands for language learning and language teaching. (Kumaravadivelu, 2003a, p. 41)

The macrostrategies provide only the general guiding principles for classroom teaching; they have to be implemented in the classroom through microstrategies.

9.3.2. Microstrategies

Microstrategies are classroom procedures that are designed to realize the objectives of a particular macrostrategy. Each macrostrategy can have any number of, and any type of, microstrategies, depending on the local learn-

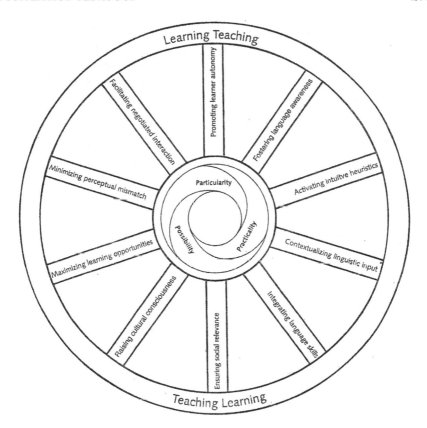

FIG. 9.1. The pedagoic wheel (from Kumaravadivelu, 2003a, p. 41).

ing and teaching situation; the possibilities are endless. However, micro-strategies are conditioned and constrained by the national, regional, or local language policy and planning, curricular objectives, institutional resources, and a host of other factors that shape the learning and teaching enterprise in a given context. Most of all, they have to be designed keeping in mind the learners' needs, wants, and lacks, as well as their current level of language knowledge/ability.

By way of illustration, I present below guidelines for designing a couple of microstrategies for *Macrostrategy 5: Foster language awareness.* Recall that *language awareness* refers to the deliberate attempt to draw learners' attention to the formal properties of their L2, and that there are two broad types of language awareness—the general one, dealing with language as system and discourse, and the critical one, dealing with language as ideology. The two microstrategies suggested below relate to the two types, and are adapted from Kumaravadivelu (2003a):

Sample microstrategy 1: Language use and levels of formality

1. The specific objective of this microstrategy is to create in the learner general language awareness about levels of formality involved in interpersonal communication. One simple example of formal–informal language use pertains to the way in which we address people at home, or in school, or at our workplace. Therefore, a useful microstrategy may be to ask L2 learners to explore how different cultural communities require different levels of formality in addressing people. Here's one way of doing it. The steps are written in procedural style for convenience, but they are obviously advisory, not prescriptive, in nature.

1.1. Write the following (or similar) forms of address on the board:

Madam President

Mr. Chairman

Your Honor

Sir

Hello Darling

Hey

Divide the class into small groups and ask each group to discuss in what context(s) and with whom would it be appropriate to use these forms of address. Also, ask them to discuss whether more than one of these forms can be used to address the same person in different contexts, and if so, in what contexts.

1.2. Have representatives from selected groups briefly share their discussion with the entire class. Let them also talk about any disagreements within their groups.

1.3. Have individual learners make a list of terms they use to address family members (grandfather, grandmother, father, mother, elder brother, younger brother, elder sister, younger sister, etc.,) in their cultural communities. Specifically, ask them to think about when and where they will use the address forms they listed, and when and where (and if) they will use actual names to address family members. Allow them to use their L1 script if they wish, but advise them to give English gloss as well. If they normally use any honorific terms, ask them to write them too.

1.4. Divide the class into small groups (or form pairs, depending on your convenience). Ask the learners to share their list with others and compare how forms of address work within a family in different linguistic or cultural communities.

1.5. Have them talk about how factors such as setting, age, and gender of participants affect forms of address, and in what contexts boundaries may be crossed.

1.6. Again in small groups, ask them to compare how forms of address are structured in their L1 (or in various L1s represented in class) and in L2. Depending on the proficiency level and cultural knowledge of your students, you may have to give them with different forms of address in L2.

1.7. Ask the students to share some of their salient points with the whole class. Lead a detailed discussion on any selected issues that came up in small groups.

1.8. Help them (if necessary, through leading questions) reflect on how different forms of address may actually reveal cultural values and beliefs, and how these are reflected in language use.

Sample microstrategy 2: Language use and doublespeak

2. The specific objective of this microstrategy is to foster critical language awareness in the learners by drawing their attention to doublespeak, that is, deceptive language that is widely used to mislead people—whether in a democratic society or in a totalitarian regime. For illustrative purposes, I am using the first paragraph from a book on doublespeak. It was written by Lutz in 1989 with a long title, *Doublespeak: From "Revenue Enhancement" to "Terminal Living." How Government, Business, Advertisers, and Others Use Language to Deceive you.* Here's a possible classroom activity:

2.1. Write the full title of Lutz's book on the board. Ask your students to focus on the key words in the title and give them some time to think about how (a) government, (b) business and (c) advertisers use language to deceive the general public. Let them share their thoughts and examples with the class.

2.2. Write the following paragraph on the board or if you have prepared a transparency, project it on the OHP screen. Ask your students to read it carefully.

There are no potholes in the streets of Tucson, Arizona, just "pavement deficiencies." The Reagon Administration didn't propose any new taxes, just "revenue enhancement" through new "user's fees." Those aren't bums on the street, just "non-goal oriented members of society." There was no robbery of an automatic teller machine, just an "unauthorized withdrawal." The patient didn't die of medical malpractice, it was just a "diagnostic misadventure of a high magnitude." The U.S. Army doesn't kill the enemy anymore, it just "services the target."

(Lutz, 1989, p. 1)

2.3. If there are any difficult vocabulary items, deal with them first, so that the students fully understand the text before proceeding further. If necessary, make a two-column table highlighting only the juxtaposed lexical items (potholes ↔ pavement deficiencies, etc.).

2.4. Form small groups and allot one or two sentences to each group for a detailed analysis. Ask them to think about critical questions such as: What is achieved by the use of such doublespeak? At what cost? At whose cost? Who benefits from such doublespeak and how?

2.5. Ask a representative from each group to present a brief report, followed by class discussion.

2.6. Help them (with leading questions, if necessary) to think why many people fail to notice doublespeak even though it is so common in public discourse and in private conversations.

2.7. Help them (again with leading questions, if necessary) to think of ways in which a critical awareness of doublespeak and its function can help them in their role as language learners, and in their role as educated citizens.

2.8. Give them a suitable take-home assignment. For instance, have them read a newspaper or a news magazine of their choice for 1 full week. Ask them to make a list of what they consider to be instances of doublespeak, and bring it to class on a specified day.

2.9. In class, form pairs and have them exchange their list with their partner. After a brief conversation between partners, ask them to share some of their interesting examples with the class.

2.10. Based on the class discussion, ask them to draft a letter to the editor of the newspaper or the news magazine drawing the editor's attention to doublespeak. Help them revise the draft, and encourage them to actually send the letter to the editor.

As the two suggested examples show, practicing teachers can make use of easily available content materials taken from newspapers, books, TV shows, or the Internet and design suitable microstrategies in order to achieve the instructional goals of a particular macrostrategy. Depending on the current communicative, linguistic, and conceptual knowledge/ability of their learners, teachers can vary the challenge level of the microstrategies. In fact, they can also involve their learners in the decision-making process, both in designing and in implementing them.

Clearly, the role of the teacher is crucial for the success of any post-method pedagogy. The macrostrategic framework seeks to transform classroom practitioners into strategic teachers and strategic researchers. As strategic teachers, they spend time and effort reflecting on the processes of learning and teaching; stretching their knowledge, skill and attitude to stay informed and involved; exploring and extending macrostrategies to meet the challenges of changing contexts of teaching; designing appropriate microstrategies to maximize learning potential in the classroom; and monitoring their ability to react to myriad situations in meaningful ways.

As strategic researchers, teachers can use the framework to develop investigative capabilities required for classroom exploration. By regularly audio/videotaping their own classroom performance and by using macrostrategies as interpretive strategies, they can analyze classroom input and interaction to assess how successful they have been in facilitating negotiated interaction, or in integrating language skills, or in contextualizing linguistic input, and so forth.

The macrostrategic framework, it seems to me, has the potential to empower teachers with the knowledge, skill, attitude, and autonomy necessary to devise for themselves a systematic, coherent, and relevant alternative to method that is informed by the pedagogic parameters of particularity, practicality, and possibility. They will be able to generate locally grounded, need-based microstrategies, ultimately developing the capacity to theorize from their practice and practice what they theorize. I firmly believe that practicing and prospective teachers will rise up to the challenge if given an appropriate framework that "strikes a balance between giving teachers the guidance they need and want, and the independence they deserve and desire" (Kumaravadivelu, 1994b, p.44).

9.4. CONCLUSION

I have described in this chapter Stern's three-dimensional framework, Allwright's Exploratory Practice framework, and Kumaravadivelu's macrostrategic framework. They are all variations of one and the same theme, namely, *postmethod*. They are all attempts to respond, in a principled way, to an imperative need to transcend the limitations of the concept of method. None of them may be seen as fully meeting the essentials of postmethod pedagogy featured in the previous chapter; nevertheless, each of them represents an earnest attempt to tackle the complex issue of finding alternatives to method.

It is important to keep in mind that the three pedagogic frameworks merely seek to lay the foundation for the construction of a postmethod pedagogy. Any actual postmethod pedagogy has to be constructed by the classroom teacher. The pedagogic frameworks offer certain options and certain operating principles. Based on them, and on their own attempt to theorize what they practice and to practice what they theorize, practicing teachers may be able to develop their own location-specific postmethod pedagogies.

The conceptual framing of a postmethod pedagogy, although still evolving, is a welcome step. At least, it sends the signal that the profession is ready and willing to explore alternatives to method rather than taking the failed path of finding alternative methods. But, it is only a first step on a steep road with full of stumbling blocks and sturdy detours. Some of them are the focus of chapter 10.

Postmethod Predicament

10. INTRODUCTION

The plans for postmethod pedagogies, proposed with different degrees of emphasis as outlined in chapter 9, are all based on a different way of looking at the problems and prospects of language teaching in the postmethod era. They call for substantial and sustained change in our perception of what constitutes language teaching and language teacher education. Educational change, like any other systemic change, involves both challenges and opportunities. Change of the kind postmethod pedagogy demands is beset with more than the normal share of difficulties because it involves not merely changing attitudes and beliefs, but also creating and maintaining favorable conditions for change. It also involves making hard choices. In such circumstances, there will always be a tendency to doubt the need for change, and to reject any proposal for change out of hand for any number of seemingly valid reasons.

A balanced response to change, however, would require that we make a serious attempt to take stock of the prevailing situation, explore the conditions that have created the need for change, and, if they are found plausible, then, try to make a sincere attempt to create the conditions necessary to effect desired change. A balanced approach would also seek to establish a dialogue "between the barriers that inhibit change and the factors that help overcome those barriers" (Kahaney, 1993, p. ix). In the context of the proposed transition from method-based pedagogies to postmethod pedagogies, there certainly are several challenging barriers as well as facilitating factors. Let us consider some of them.

215

10.1. CHALLENGING BARRIERS

The challenges facing the construction and implementation of postmethod pedagogy may be considered to constitute a postmethod predicament that puts key players in a quandary. The most stubborn aspect of the predicament is that the concept of method is a remarkably entrenched one. For all its inherent weaknesses and recurrent criticisms, it has survived for an incredible period of time. "It has had," as I have remarked elsewhere (Kumaravadivelu, 2001), "a magical hold on us" (p. 557). At one level of understanding, the reason seems to be simple—human nature. Pradl (1993) observed it in the context of general educational reforms; and, what he said about the field of education is true of our profession as well.

> Most of us would simply prefer things to remain the same—the *status quo* looks more appealing, especially when we think that somehow we are benefiting. Accordingly, incumbency with all its faults is generally more assuring than a future that risks being in doubt, risks placing us in some positions we are unsure of. (p. xii, emphasis in original)

Although that may make sense, looking at it from another level of sophistication, it is still puzzling why, in spite of the extended and extensive dissatisfaction with the concept of method, it has taken so long for the emergence of even rudimentary forms of a coherent framework necessary for constructing a postmethod pedagogy that we discussed in chapters 8 and 9. The puzzle, it seems to me, may be explained if we consider two powerful barriers. One is pedagogical and the other is ideological.

10.1.1. The Pedagogical Barrier

The pedagogical barrier relates to the content and character of L2 teacher education. It stands as a harmful hurdle blocking the effective construction and implementation of any postmethod pedagogy by practicing teachers. As is well known by now, most models of L2 teacher preparation that have been in place for a long time merely transfer a set of predetermined, preselected, and presequenced body of knowledge from the teacher educator to the prospective teacher. And, what does the body of knowledge usually consist of? A method-based package put together by researchers, containing a generous menu of theories of language, language learning, and language teaching—a package resembling the ingredients of any of the three categories of method we discussed in Part Two. The teacher educator, often playing the role of a conduit, serves the package on a platter, with easily digestible bits and pieces of discrete items of knowledge, leaving very little food for critical thought. This *is* the general scenario, while there are always a handful of institutions and individuals that try to go against the grain.

This kind of transmission model of L2 teacher education entails a master–pupil relationship in which student teachers are expected to learn some of their master teacher's pedagogic knowledge and skills, and to apply them in their classrooms. As Freeman has repeatedly emphasized (e.g., Freeman, 1991), transmission models of teacher education are very ineffective because they depend on received knowledge to influence teacher behavior and do not acknowledge, much less encourage, student teachers to construct their own versions of teaching. He has also pointed out that these models ignore the fact that student teachers may have already built up their own personal theories of learning and teaching based on their actual experience in the classroom, and on their exposure to the "doing" of teaching.

From the postmethod perspective, transmission models prove to be unproductive because they are also premised on a debilitating dichotomy between theory and practice, between the theorist and the teacher. This dichotomy has been institutionalized in our professional discourse community, that is, most teachers have been trained to accept it as something that naturally goes with the territory. Most prospective teachers believe, not without justification, that it is the cardinal duty of teacher educators to provide them with appropriate pedagogic knowledge and skills that are required for successfully carrying out classroom teaching. What the transmission model fails to do, with very few exceptions, is to develop in them classroom discourse analytical skills necessary for them to analyze and understand their own teaching acts in order to ultimately derive their own theory of practice (for details, see Kumaravadivelu, 1999b, and chap. 13 in Kumaravadivelu, 2003a).

Thus, current practices of teacher education pose a serious pedagogic barrier to any type of postmethod pedagogy. What is surely and sorely needed is what the Canadian educationist Diamond (e.g., 1993) called a *transformative* teacher education program. According to him, the central goal of transformative teacher education "is not the easy reproduction of any ready-made package or knowledge but, rather, the continued recreation of personal meaning" (p. 56). Personal meaning can be created and recreated only through personal pedagogic exploration. Diamond believes that teachers can easily "form and reform their own pedagogical theories and relationships" if teacher educators can help them "see themselves as capable of imagining and trying alternatives—and eventually as self-directing and self-determining" (p. 52). And, it is precisely this kind of transformative teacher education that can alter the role played by learners, teachers, and teacher educators that postmethod pedagogy seeks to accomplish (see the discussion on pedagogic indicators in chap. 8, this volume).

10.1.2. The Ideological Barrier

The harmful effect of the pedagogical barrier described above pales into insignificance when compared to the ideological barrier with which any postmethod pedagogy has to wrestle. The ideological barrier is much more daunting than the pedagogical one if only because it is managed and manipulated by much larger forces with a formidable political, economic, and cultural agenda. It pertains to the imperialistic (Phillipson, 1992) and colonial (Pennycook, 1998) character of English and English-language education. These and other authors have amply demonstrated that, in its march to its current global status, the English language was aided by imperialist and colonial projects. Pennycook (1998), for instance, has located English-language teaching and teacher education within the broader context of colonialism "to show how language policies and practices developed in different colonial contexts, and to demonstrate how the discourses of colonialism still adhere to English" (p. 2). The ideological barrier, with its colonial coloration, casts a long hegemonic shadow over the English-language teaching enterprise around the world, and manifests itself in the process of marginalization, and the practice of self-marginalization (Kumaravadivelu, 2003b).

To put it briefly, the process of *marginalization* refers to overt and covert mechanisms that are used to valorize everything associated with the colonial *Self*, and marginalize everything associated with the colonized *Other*. In the specific context of English language teaching and teacher education across the world, this colonial strategy of power, for instance, purposely projects the image of Western knowledge, and deliberately diminishes the value of local knowledge. In order to survive in a postcolonial world, it strives endlessly to keep interested Western knowledge dominant over subjugated local knowledge. This overwhelming dominance places any aspiring or accomplished pedagogic change agent in a peculiar predicament.

Here is a case in point. Consider the fact, and note the predicament, that the macrostrategic framework I have proposed is based, in part, on the theoretical insights derived from an already documented Western knowledge-base (see chap. 9, this volume, for details). Given the stated objectives of transcending center-based methods and of deriving a bottom–up pedagogy, it would, of course, be highly desirable if the theoretical support for it has come from the findings of empirical research conducted and documented in and by periphery communities where English is learned and taught as a second/foreign language. Although some can be retrieved with some effort, the range and amount of local knowledge-base required for citation purposes is nowhere to be seen adequately documented. Part of the (neo)colonial agenda is precisely to render local knowledge invisible and inaccessible, thereby ensuring the dependence on the center for a documented knowledge base.

The visible and invisible power of the "center" is a major impediment with which a pedagogic change agent has to deal. However, it is not the only source of postmethod predicament. What has aided the center in perpetuating its strategy of subtle power, and what continues to aid it, is the practice of self-marginalization on the part of the members of the periphery community. I firmly believe that the process of marginalization cannot survive without the practice of self-marginalization.

The practice of self-marginalization refers to how members of the dominated group, knowingly or unknowingly, legitimize the characteristics of inferiority attributed to them by the dominating group. In the context of global English language teaching (ELT), this practice is manifested, not only in the widespread acceptance of the superiority of Western methods over local practices, but also in the carefully cultivated belief that, when it comes to teaching English as a second/foreign language, somehow, native speakers are far superior to nonnative speakers, in spite of the latter's expertise and experience in learning and teaching the English language. It is common knowledge that many program administrators, teacher educators, and classroom teachers in certain periphery communities practice self-marginalization in many different ways. For instance, even today, private as well governmental agencies in several periphery communities openly state, when they post job announcements, that they "require" or at least "prefer" native speakers. At times, they even prefer to hire semiqualified native speakers over fully qualified nonnative speakers.

Following the example set by their academic administrators and policy-makers, many teachers and teacher educators also look up to native speakers for inspiration thinking that they have ready-made answers to all the recurrent problems of classroom teaching. By their uncritical acceptance of the native speaker dominance, nonnative professionals legitimize their own marginalization. Nayar (2002) investigated the ideological binarism represented in a popular electronic discussion group owned and operated by ELT professionals, TESL-L (tesl-l@cunyvm.cuny.edu), which attracts at least 20 postings a day from among thousands of members spread all over the world. Through a critical sociolinguistic analysis, Nayar has found that on this network, "the rubric of native speaker dominance and power is very strongly sustained and conveyed in a variety of overt and covert ways" thus, reinforcing the assumption that native speakers, "*ipso facto*, are also the ideal teachers or experts of pedagogy, with a clear implication that NNS English and language teaching expertise are suspect" (p. 465). Participating actively in the reinforcement of such assumptions are not just native speakers but also nonnative teachers who, according to Nayar (2002), "often seek expert advise from the NS openly and it is not uncommon to see advisory suggestions from NS 'experts' that are more noteworthy for their self-assuredness, sincerity and eagerness to help than their linguistic or pedagogic soundness" (p. 466).

From this discussion, it is rather apparent that there are many subtle and not so subtle ways in which the ideological and pedagogical barriers cause impediments for progress in postmethod pedagogy. There is no gainsaying the fact that it is only a transmission model of teacher education that can effectively maintain the authority of traditional knowledge producers and knowledge transmitters even though it fails to instill in the student teachers the much-needed capacity for autonomous decision making and the ability for systematic, reflective classroom observation. It is only a universally applicable concept of method that can, with its global reach, "make sure that the fountainhead of global employment opportunities for native speakers of English does not dry up any time soon" (Kumaravadivelu, 2003b, p. 543). It is only a method-based pedagogy, not any locally generated postmethod pedagogy, that can continue to promote a centrally produced, multimillion dollar textbook industry, which churns out ELT materials based on the concept of method to be used all over the world.

The pedagogic decision-making authority vested in the center should not be seen as impacting on English-language teaching in the periphery communities alone. British applied linguist, Skehan (1998), for instance, emphasizes its ill effects on teaching English as a second language inside English speaking countries. He points the accusing finger, not just at the publishing industry, which, after all, can be forgiven for being commercially motivated, but also at the whole crew of methods purveyors, syllabus designers, textbook writers, teacher educators, and their power relations. He comes down heavily on teacher educators in particular:

> [T]he teacher training profession acts to consolidate many of these implicit power relations, by generally concentrating on how entire classes can be organized; by teaching teachers how to implement official syllabuses and course books, and by testing in an approved manner. There is little emphasis, in most teacher training courses, on the development of techniques which serve to adapt material to the individual learner, or on ways of fostering individuality in learning. The teacher is usually equipped to be a pawn within a larger structure, rather than a mediator between materials, syllabuses, and the learners themselves. (Skehan, 1998, pp. 260–261)

In sum, the pedagogical and ideological barriers outlined constitute two major aspects of the postmethod predicament. We should, however, put the predicament in a broader perspective. The hegemonic power exercised by vested interests that spread "interested knowledge" for the purpose of its own political and economic gain is not a phenomenon unique to our profession. Hegemonic tendencies even in the supposedly objective field of science have been very well documented (see, e.g., Alvares, 1979/1991; Cohn,

1996). Furthermore, these tendencies are quite consistent with French sociologist Foucault's (1980) observation that citizens of modern democracies are controlled less by the naked power of autocrats than by grand pronouncements of professionals who organize knowledge in "regimes of truth"—sets of understandings that legitimate certain attitudes and practices, and delegitimate certain others. The regimes of truth easily become professional articles of faith that render academic discourse into a medium of communication that expresses and reproduces pedagogical power (Bourdieu, Passeron, & Martin, 1994).

The reproduction of pedagogical power, like any other power, is never absolute. The challenging barriers to the construction and implementation of postmethod pedagogy are not insurmountable. I chose the term *challenging barriers* advisedly. Notice that it does not merely indicate barriers that are indeed challenging, but it also implies that there are ways of challenging these barriers. Below, I highlight some of them in terms of facilitating factors, yet another term of double interpretation.

10.2. FACILITATING FACTORS

Facilitating factors refer to recent developments that may help cope with, and eventually overcome, the harmful effects of barriers to postmethod pedagogy. Perhaps the most important facilitating factor is the growing attempt to legitimize local knowledge (Canagarajah, 2004). There is now a greater awareness than ever before that simply because periphery communities have not adequately documented their knowledge base in second-language learning and teaching does not mean that they have no knowledge base at all. It only means that the knowledge base that really exists has not been well documented or widely disseminated.

For instance, commenting on the macrostrategic framework for language teaching discussed in chapter 9, Canagarajah (2002) correctly asserted:

> such strategies have been used by those in the periphery always. They simply haven't been documented in the professional literature. What is available in published form are pedagogical approaches from the communities that enjoy literate/publishing resources. Periphery teachers have shared their teaching strategies orally in their local contexts. (p. 148)

Also, recall from chapter 9 how, in recounting the principles of Exploratory Practice framework, Allwright has concluded that practicing teachers in Rio have already been doing the kind of exploratory practice that he has been advocating, and that they actually assisted him in firming up his framework. Local knowledge was waiting to be recognized by global players!

In fact, the ELT professional community, both in the center countries and in the periphery regions, has recently been exploring the nature and scope of local knowledge particularly in light of the emerging process of globalization. For instance, the *Journal of Language, Identity and Education* (2002) published a thematic issue focusing on local knowledge. A volume on *Globalization and Language Teaching*, edited by Block and Cameron (2002) explored the changing language teaching policies and practices around the world in light of the emerging process of globalization. In the same year, Singh, Kell, and Pandian (2002) published *Appropriating English: Innovation in the Global Business of English Language Teaching*, in which they discuss the challenges facing teachers and teacher educators in the transnational ELT market.

Likewise, the ELT communities in the periphery have been loudly expressing their local voices and local visions through books, journals, and the Internet. The publication of professional journals such as *Asian Journal of English Language Teaching* and *HKBU Papers in Applied Language Studies,* both from Hong Kong, *Indian Journal of Applied Linguistics* and *CIEFL Bulletin,* both from India, *RELC Journal* from Singapore, *SPELT Quarterly* from Pakistan, and *The ACELT Journal* from the Philippines is an indication of growing awareness of the importance of local knowledge, and of a desire to make it public. It is, however, a pity that these journals are little known outside their regions of origin.

A remarkable development following the recent events in the Middle East is the emergence of a group of ELT professionals there who have formed an organization called TESOL Islamia. The chief mission of this Abu Dhabi-based professional organization is to promote ELT in ways that best serve the sociopolitical, sociocultural, and socioeconomic interests of Arabs and Muslims. Interestingly, according to their Web site, www.tesolislamia.org, one of their goals is to assume "a critical stance towards 'mainstream' TESOL activity particularly in the area of language policy, curriculum design, materials development, language testing, teaching methodology, program evaluation, and second language research." Even a cursory reading of files in their "Discussion Forum" clearly reveals that they are all seized upon the global politics of English-language teaching and teacher education, and are exploring ways of bringing in an element of particularity to their professional enterprise.

Yet another facilitating factor is the rapid expansion, in recent times, of the research agenda of some of the TESOL professionals on both sides of the Atlantic. A cluster of books that appeared recently offer ideas, in different ways, to overcome some of the stumbling blocks mentioned earlier. For instance, Breen and Littlejohn (2000) bring together personal accounts from teachers who all have shared their pedagogic decision-making process with their students through a process of negotiation. Brumfit (2001) suggests how to maintain a high degree of individual freedom and teacher choice in language teaching by integrating theoretical and empirical work with individual and institutional needs. Johnson and Golombek (2002) have collected personal, contextualized stories of teachers assessing their own "ways of knowing," thus contributing to our understanding of teacher cognition and teacher knowledge. Edge (2002) provides an interactive framework showing how teachers can profitably combine observational research with more formal action research activities. Clarke (2003) uses systems approach to discuss coherence in teachers' activities and shows how they, as they are working for systemic change, are also changing themselves. Finally, Johnston (2003) exemplifies moralities and values in the language classroom through personal narratives that puts the teacher–student relationship, rather than the concept of method, at the core of language teaching.

While the aforementioned works may appear to be a disparate collection of books, there is a common thread that runs through all of them: They all go beyond the methods fetish to explore the professional life of language teachers and, in the process, help us understand teachers as individuals who are self-directing, self-determining, and self-motivating. They also provide compelling arguments for putting teachers, rather than anybody else, at the center of educational change.

10.3. CONCLUSION

This final chapter has looked at the postmethod predicament. The brief discussion has showed that the transitional path from the long established methods-based pedagogy to an emerging postmethod pedagogy is, no doubt, paved with challenging barriers. There are, however, encouraging signposts that point to useful directions that might help us negotiate the stumbling blocks. The short account of facilitating factors provides indications of a growing awareness to tap local resources to solve local problems using local expertise and experiences. Such awareness may also, in due course, move the conflict between central control and local initiative to a higher plane of thought and action. Clearly, there are concerted, but not in any sense coordinated, actions being carried out on several fronts, which, when they come to cumulative fruition, are likely to bring the idea of teacher-generated postmethod pedagogies closer to reality.

Postscript: The Pattern Which Comforts

The central goal of this book has been to explore the pattern which connects the higher order philosophical, pedagogical, and ideological tenets and norms of language teaching enterprise. We started the exploration by looking at the landscape of language, learning, and teaching, with all their systemic, discoursal, and ideological terrains. We then proceeded to survey, with a critical eye, the historical exigencies, the theoretical principles, and the classroom procedures associated with language-, learner-, and learning-centered methods. Finally, after recognizing the limitations of the concept of method, we moved beyond methods, entered the uncertain arena of postmethod condition, and took a peek into the still-evolving world of postmethod pedagogies. In all this, we tried to notice the pattern which connects.

In a sense, the book seeks to contribute to a true understanding of language teaching methods, in addition to being both a critique of, and a corrective to, method-based approaches to language teaching. By exposing the problems of method, and by expounding the potential of postmethod, it seeks to open up certain options that, hopefully, will lead to a re-view of the way we conceive pedagogic principles and procedures, and to a re-visioning of the way we conduct language teaching and teacher education.

The challenge, of course, is how to meet the demands the concept of postmethod makes in its effort to advance a context-sensitive, location-specific pedagogy that is based on a true understanding of local linguistic, sociocultural, and political particularities. And, how to help prospective and practicing teachers acquire and sharpen the knowledge, skill, attitude, and autonomy necessary to devise for themselves a systematic, coherent, and relevant theory of practice. In presenting three different frameworks on the foundations of a postmethod pedagogy, the book points to the ongoing process of change.

I work under the assumption that change is not only desirable and possible, but it is also inevitable. If we take a historical perspective to the process of change in language teaching, we see a pattern which comforts. We seem to go through the same cycle of action and reaction in which we first have absolute, and sometimes almost evangelical, faith in a method, only to develop serious doubts about its efficacy in due course. A new method wrapped in a new package comes along, faces initial resistance only to eventually become popular, and get entrenched in a short period of time.

When the audiolingual method was introduced, it was hailed as scientific, systematic, and teacher friendly, and soon it replaced the "discredited" grammar-translation method that held sway for a long time. The textbook industry gladly seized the commercial opportunities opened up by the new method, and produced instructional materials for the global market. Again, when the communicative language teaching came along, there was a hue and cry about how it demands too much from practicing teachers, how ill-prepared they are to embrace it, and how it is bound to fail, and so forth. Within a decade, almost everybody was swearing by it, and it has easily dethroned the "discredited" audiolingual method. The textbook industry, once again, gladly seized the commercial opportunities opened up by the new method, and produced instructional materials for the global market. The pattern we see is the pattern which comforts. Change, after all, does come about. Eventually.

History also shows that change produces anxiety, particularly if it involves a move from a comfortable climate of familiarity to an unpredictable arena of uncertainty. But, such a change can be less disorienting if it develops within a context in which the participants themselves play a role in making decisions and in implementing those decisions. In the context of educational change, this means making change part of the learning process itself. As Kahaney (1993) aptly puts it,

> . . . if change can be viewed as a component in an ongoing process called "learning," instead of as a product or a "thing," then it would be easier to have a different relationship to change itself. Instead of experiencing resistance to change as an obstacle, we as teachers could come to expect resistance to change as part of the learning process and thus plan for various kinds of and degrees of resistance. (p. 193)

We can also draw comfort from the fact that, as history shows, we have all along been engaged in the learning process, absorbed in a relentless pursuit of continuous improvement. Change is an integral part of that pursuit.

As educationist Pradl (1993) rightly observes, change "is not some material object or process over there waiting to be discovered. Instead, *change* remains what *we* make of it for our own purposes" (p. xii, emphasis in original). I believe that when we allow ourselves to be guided by bright distant stars, and not by dim street lights, and, when we resist the temptation to be lulled by what is easily manageable and what is easily measurable, and are willing to work with doubts and uncertainties, then, change becomes less onerous and more desirous.

I began the Preface to this book with a Batesonian observation. I would like to end the Postscript with another. In the Foreword to his book, *Steps to an Ecology of Mind,* in which he develops a new way of thinking about the nature of order in living systems, Gregory Bateson (1972) states,

> I have been impatient with colleagues who seemed unable to discern the difference between the trivial and the profound. But when students asked me to define that difference, I have been struck dumb. I have said vaguely, that any study which throws light upon the nature of "order" or "pattern" in the universe is surely nontrivial. (p. xvi)

This book represents my attempt to throw light upon the nature of the pattern which connects the higher order philosophical, theoretical, pedagogical, and ideological tenets and norms of language teaching, and, as such, I may be pardoned for believing that it is "surely nontrivial."

References

Allwright, R. L. (1984). Why don't learners learn what teachers teach?—The interaction hypothesis. In D. M. Singleton & D. G. Little (Eds.), *Language learning in formal and informal contexts* (pp. 3–18). Dublin: IRAAL.

Allwright, R. L. (1991). *The death of the method* (Working Paper #10). The Exploratory Practice Centre, The University of Lancaster, England.

Allwright, R. L. (1993). Integrating 'research' and 'pedagogy': Appropriate criteria and practical problems. In J. Edge & K. Richards (Eds.), *Teachers develop teachers research* (pp. 125–135). London: Heinemann.

Allwright, R. L. (2000). *Exploratory Practice: An 'appropriate methodology' for language teacher development?* Paper presented at the 8th IALS Symposium for Language Teacher Educators, Scotland.

Allwright, R. L. (2003a). Exploratory Practice: Rethinking practitioner research in language teaching. *Language Teaching Research, 7*, 113–141.

Allwright, R. L. (2003b). A brief guide to 'Exploratory Practice: Rethinking practitioner research in language teaching.' *Language Teaching Research, 7*, 109–110.

Allwright, R. L., & Bailey, K. M. (1991). *Focus on the language classroom.* Cambridge, England: Cambridge University Press.

Allwright, R. L., & Lenzuen, R. (1997). Exploratory Practice: Work at the Cultura Inglesa, Rio de Janeiro, Brazil. *Language Teaching Research, 1*, 73–79.

Alpert, R., & Haber, R. (1960). Anxiety in academic achievement situations. *Journal of Abnormal and Social Psychology, 61*, 207–215.

Alvares, C. (1991). *Decolonizing history: Technology and culture in India, China, and the West 1492 to the present day.* New York: The Apex Press. (Original work published 1979)

Anderson, J. R. (1983). *The architecture of cognition.* Cambridge, MA: Harvard University Press.

Antony, E. M. (1963). Approach, method, technique. *English Language Teaching, 17*, 63–67.

Ard, J., & Gass, S. M. (1987). Lexical constraints on syntactic acquisition. *Studies in Second Language Acquisition, 9*, 233–251.

Aston, G. (1986). Trouble-shooting in interaction with learners. The more the merrier? *Applied Linguistics, 7*, 128–143.

Au, S. Y. (1988). A critical appraisal of Gardner's social-psychological theory of second language (L2) learning. *Language Learning, 38*, 75–100.

Auerbach, E. R. (1995). The politics of the ESL classroom: Issues of power in pedagogical choices. In J. W. Tollefson (Ed.), *Power and inequality in language education* (pp. 9–33). Cambridge, England: Cambridge University Press.

Austin, J. L. (1962). *How to do things with words.* London: Oxford University Press.

Bachman, L. F. (1990). *Fundamental considerations in language testing.* Oxford: Oxford University Press.

Bachman, L. F., & Palmer, A. S. (1996). *Language testing in practice.* Oxford: Oxford University Press.

Bakhtin, M. M. (1981). *The dialogic imagination* (C. Emerson & M. Holquist, Trans.). Austin: University of Texas Press.

Bateson, G. (1972). *Steps to an ecology of mind.* New York: Ballantine Books.

Bateson, G. (1979). *Mind and nature: A necessary unity.* London: Fontana.

Becker, A. L. (1983). Toward a post-structuralist view of language learning: A short essay. *Language Learning, 33*, 217–220.

Becker, A. L. (1986). Language in particular: A lecture. In D. Tannen (Ed.), *Linguistics in context: Connecting observation and understanding.* Norwood, NJ: Ablex.

Beebe, L. M. (1985). Input: Choosing the right stuff. In S. M. Gass & C. Madden (Eds.), *Input in second language acquisition* (pp. 404–414). Rowley, MA: Newbury House.

Benesch, S. (2001). *Critical English for academic purposes: Theory, politics, and practice.* Mahwah, NJ: Lawrence Erlbaum Associates.

Benson, P. (2001). *Teaching and researching autonomy in language learning.* London: Longman.

Beretta, A. (1990). What can be learned from the Bangalore evaluation. In J. C. Alderson & A. Beretta (Eds.), *Evaluating second language education* (pp. 250–271). Cambridge, England: Cambridge University Press.

Beretta, A., & Davies, A. (1985). Evaluation of the Bangalore project. *ELT Journal, 29*, 121–127.

Berns, M. (1990). *Contexts of competence: Social and cultural considerations in communicative language teaching.* New York: Plenum.

Bialystok, E. (1978). A theoretical model of second language learning. *Language Learning, 28*, 69–83.

Bialystok, E. (1982). On the relationship between knowing and using linguistic forms. *Applied Linguistics, 3*, 181–206.

Bialystok, E. (1983). Inferencing: Testing the "hypothesis-testing" hypothesis. In H. W. Seliger & M. H. Long (Eds.), *Classroom oriented research in second language acquisition* (pp. 104–123). Rowley, MA: Newbury House.

Bialystok, E. (1988). Psycholinguistic dimensions of second language proficiency. In W. Rutherford & M. Sharwood-Smith (Eds.), *Grammar and second language teaching: A book of readings* (pp. 31–50). New York: Newbury House/Harper & Row.

Bialystok, E. (1990). *Communication strategies: A psychological analysis of second language use.* Oxford: Basil Blackwell.

Bialystok, E. (2002). Cognitive processes of L2 user. In V. J. Cook (Ed.), *Portaits of the L2 user* (pp. 145–165). Clevedon, England: Multilingual Matters.

Bialystok, E., & Kellerman, E. (1987). Language strategies in the classroom. In B. Das (Ed.), *Communication and learning in the classroom community* (pp. 160–175). Singapore: SEAMEO Regional Language Centre.

Bialystok, E., & Sharwood-Smith, M. (1985). Interlanguage is not a state of mind: An evaluation of the construct for second language acquisition. *Applied Linguistics, 6*, 101–107.

Block, D., & Cameron, D. (Eds.). (2002). *Globalization and language teaching.* London: Routledge.

Bloome, D., & Green, J. L. (1992). Educational contexts of literacy. *Annual Review of Applied Linguistics, 12*, 49–70.

Bloomfield, L. (1942). *Outline guide for the practical study of foreign languages.* Baltimore: Linguistic Society of America.

Borg, S. (2003). Teacher cognition in language teaching: A review of research on what language teachers think, know, believe, and do. *Language Teaching, 36,* 81–109.

Bourdieu, P. (1977). The economics of linguistic exchanges. *Social Sciences Information, 16,* 645–668.

Bourdieu, P. (1991). *Language and symbolic power* (G. Reymond & M. Adamson, Trans.). Cambridge, MA: Polity Press.

Bourdieu, P., Passeron, J.-C., & Martin, M. (1994). *Academic discourse: Linguistic misunderstanding and professional power.* Cambridge, MA: Polity Press.

Breen, M. P. (1985). The social context for language learning—a neglected situation? *Studies in Second Language Acquisition, 7,* 135–158.

Breen, M. P. (1987). Learner contributions to task design. In C. N. Candlin & D. F. Murphy (Eds.), *Language learning tasks* (pp. 23–46). London: Prentice Hall.

Breen, M. P. (2001). *Learner contributions to language learning.* New York: Pearson Education.

Breen, M. P., & Candlin, C. N. (1980). The essentials of a communicative curriculum for language teaching. *Applied Linguistics, 1,* 89–112.

Breen, M. P., Hird, B., Milton, M., Oliver, R., & Thwaite, A. (2001). Making sense of language teaching: Teachers' principles and classroom practices. *Applied Linguistics, 22,* 470–501.

Breen, M. P., & Littlejohn, A. (Eds.). (2000). *Classroom decision-making.* Cambridge, England: Cambridge University Press.

Brooks, N. (1964/1960). *Language and language learning: Theory and practice* (2nd ed.). New York: Harcourt, Brace & World.

Brown, D. (2002). English language teaching in the "Post-Method" era: Towards better diagnosis, treatment, and assessment. In J. C. Richards & W. A. Renandya (Eds.), *Methodology in language teaching* (pp. 9–18). Cambridge, England: Cambridge University Press.

Brown, G., Malmkjaer, K., & Williams, J. (Eds.). (1996). *Performance and competence in second language acquisition.* Cambridge, England: Cambridge University Press.

Brown, J. M., & Palmer, A. S. (1988). *The listening approach.* London: Longman.

Brown, R. (1973). *A first language.* Cambridge, MA: Harvard University Press.

Brumfit, C. J. (1984). *Communicative methodology in language teaching.* Cambridge, England: Cambridge University Press.

Brumfit, C. (2001). *Individual freedom in language teaching.* Oxford: Oxford University Press.

Brumfit, C. J., & Johnson, K. (1979). *The communicative approach to language teaching.* Oxford: Oxford University Press.

Bygate, M., Skehan, P., & Swain, M. (Eds.). (2001). *Researching pedagogic tasks: Second language learning, teaching and testing.* New York: Pearson Education.

Cameron, D., Frazer, E., Harvey, P., Rampton, M. B. H., & Richardson, K. (1992). *Researching language: Issues of power and method.* London: Routledge.

Canagarajah, A. S. (1999). *Resisting linguistic imperialism in English teaching.* Oxford: Oxford University Press.

Canagarajah, A. S. (2002). Globalization, methods, and practice in periphery classrooms. In D. Block & D. Cameron (Eds.), *Globalization and language teaching* (pp. 134–150). London: Routledge.

Canagarajah, A. S. (Ed.). (2004). *Reclaiming the local in language policy and practice.* Mahwah, NJ: Lawrence Erlbaum Associates.

Canale, M. (1983). On some dimension of language proficiency. In J. Oller (Ed.), *Issues in language testing research* (pp. 333–342). Rowley, MA: Newbury House.

Canale, M., & Swain, M. (1980). Theoretical bases of communicative approaches to second language teaching and testing. *Applied Linguistics, 1,* 1–47.

Candlin, C. N. (1987). Towards task-based language learning. In C. N. Candlin & D. F. Murphy (Eds.), *Language learning tasks* (pp. 1–22). London: Prentice-Hall.

Celce-Murcia, M., Dornyei, Z., & Thurrell, S. (1995). A pedagogical framework for communicative competence: A pedagogically motivated model with content specifications. *Issues in Applied Linguistics, 6,* 5–35.

Celce-Murcia, M., & Olshtain, E. (2000). *Discourse and context in language teaching: A guide for language teachers.* Cambridge, England: Cambridge University Press.

Chamot, A. U., Barnhardt, S., El-Dinary, P. B., & Robbins, J. (1999). *The learning strategies handbook.* London: Longman.

Chastain, K. (1971). *The development of modern language skills: Theory to practice.* Philadelphia: The Center for Curriculum Development.

Chaudron, C. (1983). Simplification of input: Topic reinstatements and their effects on L2 learners' recognition and recall. *TESOL Quarterly, 17,* 437–458.

Chaudron, C. (1985). Intake: On models and methods for discovering learners' processing of input. *Studies in Second Language Acquisition, 7,* 1–14.

Cheng, P. W. (1985). Restructuring versus automaticity: Alternative accounts of skill acquisition. *Psychological Review, 92,* 414–423.

Chick, K. J. (1995). The interactional accomplishment of discrimination in South Africa. *Language in Society, 14*(3), 229–326.

Chick, K. J. (1996). Safe-talk: Collusion in apartheid education. In H. Coleman (Ed.), *Society and the language classroom* (pp. 21–39). Cambridge, England: Cambridge University Press.

Chihara, T., & Oller, J. W. (1978). Attitudes and attained proficiency in EFL: A sociolinguistic study of adult Japanese speakers. *Language Learning, 28,* 55–68.

Chomsky, N. (1959). [Review of B. F. Skinner, *Verbal Behavior*]. *Language, 35,* 26–58.

Chomsky, N. (1965). *Aspects of the theory of syntax.* Cambridge, MA: MIT Press.

Chomsky, N. (1970). BBC interviews with Stuart Hampshire. Noam Chomsky's view of language. In M. Lester (Ed.), *Readings in applied transformational grammar* (pp. 96–113). New York: Holt & Rinehart.

Chomsky, N. (1980). *Rules and representations.* Oxford: Blackwell.

Clandinin, D. J., Davies, A., Hogan, P., & Kennard, B. (1993). *Learning to teach, teaching to learn.* New York: Teachers College Press, Columbia University.

Clarke, M. A. (1983). The scope of approach, the importance of method, and the nature of technique. In J. E. Alatis, H. Stern, & P. Strevens (Eds.), *Georgetown University Round Table on Languages and Linguistics 1983: Applied linguistics and the preparation of second language teachers* (pp. 106–115). Washington, DC: Georgetown University.

Clarke, M. A. (2003). *A place to stand.* Ann Arbor: The University of Michigan Press.

Cohn, B. S. (1996). *Colonialism and its forms of knowledge.* Princeton, NJ: Princeton University Press.

Coleman, H. (1996). Autonomy and ideology in the English language classroom. In H. Coleman (Ed.), *Society and the language classroom* (pp. 1–15). Cambridge, England: Cambridge University Press.

Cook, G. (1989). *Discourse.* Oxford: Oxford University Press.

Cook, G. (1994). *Discourse and literature.* Oxford: Oxford University Press.

Cook, V. J. (1991). *Second language learning and language teaching.* London: Edward Arnold.

Cook, V. J. (1992). Evidence for multicompetence. *Language Learning, 42,* 557–591.

Cook, V. J. (1996). Competence and multi-competence. In G. Brown, K. Malmkjaer, & J. Williams (Eds.), *Performance & competence in second language acquisition* (pp. 54–69). Cambridge, England: Cambridge University Press.

Cook, V. J. (Ed.). (2002). Language teaching methodology and the L2 user perspective. In V. Cook (Ed.), *Portraits of the L2 user* (pp. 325–343). Clevedon, England: Multilingual Matters.

Cooper, R. L., & Fishman, J. A. (1977). A study of language attitudes. In J. A. Fishman, R. L. Cooper, & A. W. Conrad (Eds.), *The spread of English* (pp. 239–276). Rowley, MA: Newbury House.

Corder, S. P. (1967). The significance of learners' errors. *International Review of Applied Linguistics, 5,* 161–170.

Corder, S. P. (1973). *Introducing applied linguistics.* Harmondsworth, Middlesex, England: Penguin Books.

Corder, S. P. (1978). Language learner language. In J. C. Richards (Ed.), *Understanding second and foreign language learning: Issues and approaches* (pp. 71–93). Rowley, MA: Newbury House.

Corder, S. P. (1983). A role for the mother tongue. In S. M. Gass & L. Selinker (Eds.), *Language transfer in language learning* (pp. 85–97). Rowley, MA: Newbury House.

Corder, S. P. (1984). [Review of Krashen's *Second language acquisition and second language learning,* and *Principles and practice in second language acquisition*]. *Applied Linguistics, 5,* 56–58.

Crookes, G., & Gass, S. (Eds.). (1993). *Tasks and language learning: Integrating theory and practice.* Clevedon, England: Multilingual Matters.

Crookes, G., & Schmidt, R. W. (1991). Motivation: Reopening the research agenda. *Language Learning, 41,* 469–512.

Csikszentmihalyi, M. (1975). *Beyond boredom and anxiety.* San Francisco: Jossey-Bass.

Deci, E. L. (1975). *Intrinsic motivation.* New York: Plenum.

Deci, E. L., & Ryan, R. M. (1985). *Intrinsic motivation and self-determination in human behavior.* New York: Plenum.

Delpit, L. (1995). *Other people's children: Cultural conflict in the classroom.* New York: Norton.

Diamond, C. T. P. (1993). In-service education as something more: A personal construct approach. In P. Kahaney, L. Perry, & J. Janangelo (Eds.), *Theoretical and critical perspectives on teacher change* (pp. 45–66). Norwood, NJ: Ablex.

Donato, R., & Adair-Hauck, B. (1992). Discourse perspectives on formal instruction. *Language Awareness, 1,* 74–89.

Dornyei, Z. (2000). Motivation. In M. Byram (Ed.), *Routledge encyclopedia of language teaching and learning* (pp. 425–432). New York: Routledge.

Dornyei, Z., & Scott, M. L. (1997). Communication strategies in a second language: Definitions and taxonomies. *Language Learning, 47,* 173–210.

Dornyei, Z., & Skehan, P. (2003). Individual differences in second language learning. In C. Doughty & M. H. Long (Eds.), *The handbook of second language acquisition* (pp. 589–630). Oxford: Blackwell.

Doughty, C. (1991). Second language acquisition does make a difference: Evidence from an empirical study on SL relativization. *Studies in Second Language Acquisition, 31,* 431–469.

Doughty, C. (2003). Instructed SLA: Constraints, compensation, and enhancement. In C. Doughty & M. H. Long (Eds.), *The handbook of second language acquisition* (pp. 256–310). Oxford: Blackwell.

Doughty, C., & Long, M. H. (Eds.). (2003). *The handbook of second language acquisition.* Oxford: Blackwell.

Doughty, C., & Williams, J. (Eds.). (1998). *Focus on form in classroom second language acquisition.* Cambridge, England: Cambridge University Press.

Dulay, H., & Burt, M. (1974). Natural sequences in child second language acquisition. *Language Learning, 24,* 37–53.

Edge, J. (Ed.). (2001). *Action research.* Washington, DC: TESOL.

Edge, J. (2002). *Continuing cooperative development.* Ann Arbor: The University of Michigan Press.

Eiser, J. R. (1987). *The expression of attitude.* New York: Springer-Verlag.

Elliott, J. (1991). *Action research for educational change.* Buckingham, England: Open University Press.

Elliott, J. (1993). *Reconstructing teacher education: Teacher development.* London: Falmer.

Ellis, G., & Sinclair, B. (1989). *Learning to learn English: A course in learner training.* Cambridge, England: Cambridge University Press.

Ellis, R. (1985). *Understanding second language acquisition*. Oxford: Oxford University Press.

Ellis, R. (1990). *Instructed second language acquisition*. Cambridge, England: Basil Blackwell.

Ellis, R. (1992). The classroom context: An acquisition-rich or an acquisition-poor environment? In C. Kramsch & S. McConnell-Ginet (Eds.), *Text and context: Cross-disciplinary perspectives on language study* (pp. 171–186). Toronto: D. C. Heath & Co.

Ellis, R. (1997). *SLA research and language teaching*. Oxford: Oxford University Press.

Ellis, R. (1999). *Learning a second language through interaction*. Philadelphia: John Benjamins.

Ellis, R. (2003). *Task-based language learning and teaching*. Oxford: Oxford University Press.

Faerch, C., & Kasper, G. (1980). Processes and strategies in foreign language learning and communication. *Interlanguage Studies Bulletin, 5*, 47–118.

Fairclough, N. (1995). *Critical discourse analysis: The critical study of language*. London: Longman.

Felix, S. (1981). The effect of formal instruction on second language acquisition. *Language Learning, 31*, 87–112.

Ferguson, C. A. (1975). Towards a characterization of English foreign talk. *Anthropological Linguistics, 17*, 1–14.

Finocchario, M., & Brumfit, C. (1983). *The notional-functional approach: From theory to practice*. Oxford: Oxford University Press.

Fotos, S. (1993). Consciousness-raising and noticing through focus on form: Grammar task performance vs. formal instruction. *Applied Linguistics, 14*, 385–407.

Fotos, S., & Ellis, R. (1991). Communicating about grammar: A task-based approach. *TESOL Quarterly, 25*, 605–628.

Foucault, M. (1970). *The order of things: An archeology of human sciences*. New York: Pantheon.

Foucault, M. (1972). *The archeology of knowledge*. New York: Tavistock.

Foucault, M. (1980). *Power/knowledge: Selected interviews and other writings, 1972–1977*. New York: Pantheon.

Fowler, R. (1996). On critical linguistics. In C. R. Coulthard & M. Coulthard (Eds.), *Texts and practices* (pp. 3–14). New York: Routledge.

Freeman, D. (1991). Mistaken constructs: Re-examining the nature and assumptions of language teacher education. In J. Alatis (Ed.), *Georgetown University Round Table on Languages and Linguistics 1991: Linguistics and language pedagogy: The state of the art* (pp. 25–39). Washington, DC: Georgetown University Press.

Freeman, D. (1996). Redefining the relationship between research and what teachers know. In K. Bailey & D. Nunan (Eds.), *Voices from the language classroom* (pp. 88–115). New York: Cambridge University Press.

Freeman, D. (1998). *Doing teacher research*. Boston, MA: Heinle & Heinle.

Freudenstein, R. (1986). The influence of Robert Lado on language teaching. In D. Tannen & J. E. Alatis (Eds.), *Georgetown University Round Table on Languages and Linguistics*. Washington, DC: Georgetown University Press.

Fries, C. C., & Fries, A. C. (1961). *Foundations of English teaching*. Tokyo: Kenkyusha.

Gaies, S. J. (1977). Linguistic input in formal second language learning: Linguistic and communicative strategies in ESL teachers' classroom language. In H. D. Brown, C. A. Yorio, & R. Crymes (Eds.), *Teaching and learning English as a second language: Trends in research and practice* (pp. 204–212). Washington, DC: TESOL.

Gardner, R. C. (1985). *Social psychological and second language learning: The role of attitudes and motivation*. London: Edward Arnold.

Gardner, R. C. (1988). The socio-educational model of second language learning: Assumptions, findings, and issues. *Language Learning, 38*, 101–126.

Gardner, R. C., Day, J. B., & MacIntyre, P. D. (1992). Integrative motivation, induced anxiety, and language learning in a controlled environment. *Studies in Second Language Acquisition, 14*, 197–214.

Gardner, R. C., & Lambert, W. E. (1972). *Attitude and motivation in second language learning.* Rowley, MA: Newbury House.

Gardner, R. C., & MacIntyre, P. D. (1991). An instrumental motivation in language study: Who says it isn't effective? *Studies in Second Language Acquisition, 13,* 57–72.

Gardner, D., & Miller, L. (1996). *Tasks for independent language learning.* Washington, DC: TESOL.

Gass, S. M. (1983). The development of L2 intuitions. *TESOL Quarterly, 17,* 273–291.

Gass, S. M. (1986). An interactionist approach to L2 sentence interpretation. *Studies in Second Language Acquisition, 8,* 19–37.

Gass, S. M. (1988). Integrating research areas: A framework for second language studies. *Applied Linguistics, 9,* 198–217.

Gass, S. M. (1997). *Input, interaction, and the second language learner.* Mahwah, NJ: Lawrence Erlbaum Associates.

Gass, S. M. (2003). Input and interaction. In C. Doughty & M. H. Long (Eds.), *The handbook of second language acquisition* (pp. 224–255). Oxford: Blackwell.

Gass, S. M., & Ard, J. (1984). Second language acquisition and the ontology of language universals. In W. Rutherford (Ed.), *Language universals and second language acquisition* (pp. 33–68). Amsterdam: John Benjamins.

Gass, S. M., & Selinker, L. (2001). *Second language acquisition: An introductory course* (2nd ed.). Mahwah, NJ: Lawrence Erlbaum Associates.

Giroux, H. A. (1988). *Teachers as intellectuals: Towards a critical pedagogy of learning.* South Hadley, MA: Bergin & Garvey.

Giroux, H. A., & Simon, R. (1988). *Popular culture, schooling and everyday life.* New York: Bergin & Garvey.

Green, P. S., & Hecht, K. (1992). Implicit and explicit grammar: An empirical study. *Applied Linguistics, 13,* 168–184.

Gregg, K. (2003). SLA theory: Construction and assessment. In C. Doughty & M. H. Long (Eds.), *The handbook of second language acquisition* (pp. 831–865). Oxford: Blackwell.

Gumperz, J. J. (1982). *Discourse strategies.* Cambridge, England: Cambridge University Press.

Hall, J. K. (2002). *Teaching and researching language and culture.* London: Pearson Education.

Halliday, M. A. K. (1973). *Explorations in the functions of language.* London: Arnold.

Halliday, M. A. K. (1978). *Language as a social semiotic.* London: Arnold.

Hamilton, J. (1996). *Inspiring innovations in language teaching.* Clevedon, England: Multilingual Matters.

Hargreaves, A. (1994). *Changing teachers; changing times.* New York: Teachers College Press.

Hatch, E. (1978). Discourse analysis and second language acquisition. In E. Hatch (Ed.), *Second language acquisition* (pp. 401–435). Rowley, MA: Newbury House.

Hatch, E. (1983). Simplified input and second language acquisition. In R. Andersen (Ed.), *Pidginization and creolization as language acquisition* (pp. 64–86). Rowley, MA: Newbury House.

Hatch, E. (1992). *Discourse and language education.* Cambridge, England: Cambridge University Press.

Heath, S. B. (1983). *Ways with words: Language and work in communities and classrooms.* Cambridge, England: Cambridge University Press.

Henzl, V. (1974). Linguistic register of foreign language instruction. *Language Learning, 23,* 207–222.

Hockett, C. F. (1959). *A course in modern linguistics.* New York: Macmillan.

Holec, H. (1988). *Autonomy and self-directed learning: Present fields of application.* Strasbourg, France: Council of Europe.

Hornby, A. S. (1954). *Guide to pattern and usage in English.* London: Oxford University Press.

Horwitz, E. K., Horwitz, M. B., & Cope, J. (1986). Foreign language classroom anxiety. *Modern Language Journal, 70,* 125–132.

Howatt, A. P. R. (1984). *A history of English language teaching.* Oxford: Oxford University Press.

Hulstjin, J. H. (2003). Incidental and intentional learning. In C. Doughty & M. H. Long (Eds.), *The handbook of second language acquisition* (pp. 349–381). Oxford: Blackwell.

Hyltenstam, K., & Abrhamsson, N. (2003). Maturational constraints in SLA. In C. Doughty & M. H. Long (Eds.), *The handbook of second language acquisition* (pp. 539–588). Oxford: Blackwell.

Hymes, D. (1972). On communicative competence. In J. Pride & J. Holmes (Eds.), *Sociolinguistics: Selected readings.* Harmondsworth, England: Penguin Books.

Jarvis, G. A. (1991). Research on teaching methodology: Its evolution and prospects. In B. Feed (Ed.), *Foreign language acquisition research and the classroom* (pp. 295–306). Lexington, MA: D. C. Heath & Co.

Johnson, K. (1982). *Communicative syllabus design and methodology.* Oxford: Pergamon.

Johnson, K. (2001). *An introduction to foreign language learning and teaching.* London: Longman.

Johnson, K. (2003). *Designing language teaching task.* London: Palgrave.

Johnson, K. E., & Golombek, P. R. (Eds.). (2002). *Teachers' narrative inquiry as professional development.* Cambridge, England: Cambridge University Press.

Johnston, B. (2003). *Values in English language teaching.* Mahwah, NJ: Lawrence Erlbaum Associates.

Joseph, J. E., Love, N., & Taylor, T. J. (2001). *Landmarks in linguistic thought II.* London: Routledge.

Kahaney, P. (1993). Afterword: Knowledge, learning and change. In P. Kahaney, L. Perry, & J. Janangelo (Eds.), *Theoretical and critical perspectives on teacher change* (pp. 191–200). Norwood, NJ: Ablex.

Kasper, G. (2001). Classroom research on interlanguage pragmatics. In K. R. Rose & G. Kasper (Eds.), *Pragmatics in language teaching* (pp. 33–60). Cambridge, England: Cambridge University Press.

Kelly, L. G. (1969). *25 centuries of language teaching.* Rowley, MA: Newbury House.

Kimball, M. C., & Palmer, A. S. (1978). The dialog game: A prototypical activity for providing proper intake in formal instruction. *TESOL Quarterly, 12,* 17–29.

Klein, W. (1990). A theory of language acquisition is not so easy. *Studies in Second Language Acquisition, 12,* 219–231.

Krashen, S. (1981). *Second language acquisition and second language learning.* New York: Pergamon Press.

Krashen, S. (1982). *Principles and practice in second language acquisition.* New York: Pergamon Press.

Krashen, S. (1983). Newmark's ignorance hypothesis and current second language acquisition theory. In S. M. Gass & L. Selinker (Eds.), *Language transfer in language learning* (pp. 135–153). Rowley, MA: Newbury House.

Krashen, S. (1984). *Writing: Research, theory, and applications.* New York: Pergamon.

Krashen, S. (1985). *The input hypothesis: Issues and implications.* Harlow: Longman.

Krashen, S. (1989). *Language acquisition and language education.* London: Prentice-Hall.

Krashen, S. (1998). Comprehensible output? *System, 26,* 175–182.

Krashen, S. D., & Terrell, T. D. (1983). *The natural approach: Language acquisition in the classroom.* Hayward, CA: The Alemany Press.

Kress, G., & Hodge, R. (1979). *Language as ideology.* London: Routledge & Kegan Paul.

Krishnaswamy, N., & Burde, A. S. (1998). *The politics of Indians' English: Linguistic colonialism and the expanding English empire.* Delhi: Oxford University Press.

Kristeva, J. (1989). *Language the unknown* (A. Menke, Trans.). New York: Columbia University Press.

Kroskrity, P. V. (2000). Regimenting languages: Language ideological perspectives. In P. V. Kiroskrity (Ed.), *Regimes of language* (pp. 1–34). Sante Fe, NM: School of American Research Press.

Kumaravadivelu, B. (1988). Communication strategies and psychological processes underlying lexical simplification. *International Review of Applied Linguistics, 25,* 309–319.

Kumaravadivelu, B. (1991). Language learning tasks: Teacher intention and learner interpretation. *ELT Journal, 45,* 98–107.

Kumaravadivelu, B. (1992). Macrostrategies for the second/foreign language teacher. *Modern Language Journal, 76*(1), 41–49.

Kumaravadivelu, B. (1993a). Maximizing learning potential in the communicative classroom. *ELT Journal, 47,* 12–21.

Kumaravadivelu, B. (1993b). The name of the task and the task of naming: Methodological aspects of task-based pedagogy. In G. Crookes & S. Gass (Eds.), *Tasks in a pedagogical context* (pp. 69–96). Clevedon, England: Multilingual Matters.

Kumaravadivelu, B. (1994a). Intake factors and intake processes in adult language learning. *Applied Language Learning, 5,* 33–71.

Kumaravadivelu, B. (1994b). The postmethod condition: (E)merging strategies for second/foreign language teaching. *TESOL Quarterly, 28,* 27–48.

Kumaravadivelu, B. (1995). The author responds. *TESOL Quarterly, 29,* 177–180.

Kumaravadivelu, B. (1999a). Critical classroom discourse analysis. *TESOL Quarterly, 33,* 453–484.

Kumaravadivelu, B. (1999b). Theorizing practice, practicing theory: The role of critical classroom observation. In H. Trappes-Lomax & I. McGrath (Eds.), *Theory in language teacher education* (pp. 33–45). London: Longman.

Kumaravadivelu, B. (2001). Toward a postmethod pedagogy. *TESOL Quarterly, 35,* 537–560.

Kumaravadivelu, B. (2002). Method, antimethod, postmethod. In A. Pulverness (Ed.), *IATEFL 2002 York Conference selections.* Kent, England: IATEFL.

Kumaravadivelu, B. (2003a). *Beyond methods: Macrostrategies for language teaching.* New Haven, CT: Yale University Press.

Kumaravadivelu, B. (2003b). A postmethod perspective on English language teaching. *World Englishes, 22,* 539–550.

Kumaravadivelu, B. (2003c). Problematizing cultural stereotypes in TESOL. *TESOL Quarterly, 37,* 709–719.

Lado, R. (1964). *Language teaching: A scientific approach.* New York: McGraw-Hill.

Lamendella, J. (1977). General principles of neurofunctional organization and their manifestation in primary and nonprimary language acquisition. *Language Learning, 27,* 155–196.

Lantoff, J. P. (Ed.). (2000). *Sociocultural theory and second language learning.* Oxford: Oxford University Press.

Larsen-Freeman, D. (1976). An explanation for the morpheme accuracy order of learners of English as a second language. *Language Learning, 26,* 125–135.

Larsen-Freeman, D. (1983). Second language acquisition: Getting the whole picture. In K. M. Bailey, M. Long, & S. Peck (Eds.), *Second language acquisition studies* (pp. 3–22). Rowley, MA: Newbury House.

Larsen-Freeman, D. (1986). *Techniques and principles in language teaching.* Oxford: Oxford University Press.

Larsen-Freeman, D. (2000). Grammar: Rules and reasons working together. *ESL Magazine, 3,* 10–12.

Larsen-Freeman, D. (2003). *Teaching language: From grammar to grammaring.* Boston: Heinle & Heinle.

Larsen-Freeman, D., & Long, M. (1991). *An introduction to second language acquisition research.* London: Longman.

Legutke, M., & Thomas, H. (1991). *Process and experience in the language classroom.* London: Longman.

Lenneberg, E. (1967). *Biological foundations of language.* New York: Wiley.

Lewis, M. (1993). *The lexical approach.* London: Language Teaching Publications.

Liceras, J. (1985). The role of intake in the determination of learners' competence. In S. M. Gass & C. Madden (Eds.), *Input in second language acquisition* (pp. 354–373). Rowley, MA: Newbury House.

Lightbown, P. M. (1985). Great expectations: Second language acquisition research and classroom teaching. *Applied Linguistics, 6,* 173–189.

Lightbown, P. (1991). What have we here? Some observations on the influence of instruction on L2 learning. In R. Phillipson, E. Kellerman, L. Selinker, M. Sharwood-Smith, & M. Swain (Eds.), *Foreign/second language pedagogy research* (pp. 197–233). Clevedon, England: Multilingual Matters.

Lightbown, P. (1992). Can they do it themselves? A comprehension-based ESL course for young children. In R. Courchene, J. Glidden, J. S. John, & C. Therien (Eds.), *Comprehension-based second language teaching* (pp. 353–370). Ottawa: University of Ottawa Press.

Lightbown, P., & Spada, N. (1990). Focus-on-form and corrective feedback in communicative language teaching: Effects on second language learning. *Studies in Second Language Acquisition, 12,* 429–448.

Lightbown, P., & Spada, N. (1993). *How languages are learned.* Oxford: Oxford University Press.

Littlewood, W. (1981). *Communicative language teaching: An introduction.* Cambridge, England: Cambridge University Press.

Long, M. H. (1981). Input, interaction and second language acquisition. In H. Winitz (Ed.), *Native language and foreign language acquisition* (pp. 259–278). New York: Annals of the New York Academy of Sciences.

Long, M. H. (1983). Does second language instruction make a difference? A review of the reseach. *TESOL Quarterly, 17,* 359–382.

Long, M. H. (1985). The role of instruction in second language acquisition: Task-based language teaching. In K. Hyltenstam & M. Pienemann (Eds.), *Modelling and assessing second language acquisition* (pp. 77–99). San Diego, CA: College-Hill Press.

Long, M. H. (1991). Focus on form: A design feature in language teaching methodology. In K. de Bot, R. Ginsberg, & C. Kramsch (Eds.), *Foreign language research in cross-cultural perspectives* (pp. 39–52). Amsterdam: John Benjamins.

Long, M. H. (1996). The role of the linguistic environment in second language acquisition. In W. Ritchie & T. Bhatia (Eds.), *Handbook of research on second language acquisition* (pp. 413–468). New York: Academic Press.

Long, M. H. (in press). *Task-based language teaching.* Oxford: Blackwell.

Long, M. H., & Robinson, P. (1998). Focus on form: Theory, research, and practice. In C. Doughty & J. Williams (Eds.), *Focus on form in classroom second language acquisition* (pp. 15–41). Cambridge, England: Cambridge University Press.

Lukmani, Y. (1972). Motivation to learn and language proficiency. *Language Learning, 22,* 261–273.

Lutz, W. (1989). *Doublespeak: From "revenue enhancement" to "terminal living." How government, business, advertisers, and others use language to deceive you.* New York: Harper & Row.

Lyons, J. (1996). On competence and performance and related notions. In G. Brown, K. Malmkjaer, & J. Williams (Eds.), *Performance and competence in second language acquisition* (pp. 11–32). Cambridge, England: Cambridge University Press.

Lyotard, J.-F. (1989). *The postmodern condition: A report on knowledge.* Minneapolis: University of Minnesota Press.

MacIntyre, P. D., & Gardner, R. C. (1989). Anxiety and second language learning: Toward a theoretical clarification. *Language Learning, 39,* 251–275.

MacIntyre, P. D., & Gardner, R. C. (1991). Methods and results in the study of anxiety and language learning: A review of the literature. *Language Learning, 41,* 125–159.

MacIntyre, P. D., & Gardner, R. C. (1994). The subtle effects of language anxiety on cognitive processing in the second language. *Language Learning, 44*(2), 283–305.

Mackey, W. F. (1965). *Language teaching analysis.* Bloomington: Indiana University Press.

MacWhinney, B. (1987). The competition model. In B. MacWhinney (Ed.), *Mechanisms of language acquisition* (pp. 249–308). Hillsdale, NJ: Lawrence Erlbaum Asscociates.

Madsen, H. S., Brown, B. L., & Jones, R. L. (1991). Evaluating student attitudes toward second-language tests. In E. K. Horwitz & D. J. Young (Eds.), *Language anxiety: From theory and research to classroom implications* (pp. 65–86). Englewood Cliffs, NJ: Prentice-Hall.

Malcolm, I. G. (1987). Continuities in communicative patterns in crosscultural classrooms. In B. K. Das (Ed.), *Communication and learning in the classroom community* (pp. 37–63). Singapore: Singapore University Press.

Masny, D., & d'Anglejan, A. (1985). Language, cognition and second language grammaticality judgments. *Journal of Psycholinguistic Research, 14,* 175–197.

McCarthy, M., & Carter, R. (1994). *Language as discourse: Perspectives for language teaching.* London: Longman.

McClelland, D. C., Atkinson, J. W., Clark, R. W., & Lowell, E. L. (1953). *The achievement motive.* New York: Appleton-Century-Crofts.

McClelland, J. L., Rumelhart, D. E., & The PDP Research Group. (Eds.). (1986). Parallel distributed processing. *Explorations in the microstructure of cognition: Vol. 2. Psychological and biological models.* Cambridge, MA: MIT Press.

McLaughlin, B. (1987). *Theories of second language learning.* London: Edward Arnold.

McLaughlin, B. (1990). Restructuring. *Applied Linguistics, 11,* 113–128.

McLeod, B., & McLaughlin, B. (1986). Restructuring or automatization? Reading in a second language. *Language Learning, 36,* 109–127.

Morgan, B. (1998). *The ESL classroom: Teaching, critical practice, and community.* Toronto: Toronto University Press.

Munby, J. (1978). *Communicative syllabus design.* Cambridge, England: Cambridge University Press.

Naiman, N., Frolich, M., Stern, H. H., & Todesco, A. (1978). *The good language learner.* (Research in education series #7). Toronto: Ontario Institute of Studies in Education.

Nayar, B. (2002). Ideological binarisms in the identities of native and non-native English speakers. In A. Duszac (Ed.), *Us and others: Social identities across languages, discourses and cultures* (pp. 463–480). Amsterdam: John Benjamins.

Newmark, L. (1963/1971). Grammatical theory and the teaching of English as a foreign language. In D. Harris (Ed.), *The 1963 conference papers of the English language section of the National Association for Foreign Affairs.* Also in M. Lester (Ed.), *Readings in applied transformational grammar* (pp. 201–218). New York: Holt, Rinehart & Winston.

Newmark, L. (1966/1970). How not to interfere with language learning. *International Journal of American Linguistics, 32,* 77–83. Also in M. Lester (Ed.), *Readings in applied transformational grammar* (pp. 219–227). New York: Holt, Rinehart & Winston.

Newmark, L., & Reibel, D. (1968). Necessity and sufficiency in language learning. *International Review of Applied Linguistics, 6,* 145–164.

Norris, J., & Ortega, L. (2000). Effectiveness of L2 instruction: A research synthesis and quantitative meta-analysis. *Language Learning, 50,* 417–528.

Norton, B. (2000). *Identity and language learning.* London: Longman.

Nunan, D. (1987). Communicative language teaching: Making it work. *ELT Journal, 41,* 136–145.

Nunan, D. (1989). *Designing tasks for the communicative classroom.* Cambridge, England: Cambridge University Press.

Nunan, D. (1991). *Language teaching methodology.* London: Prentice-Hall.

Nunan, D. (1996). Towards autonomous learning: Some theoretical, empirical and practical issues. In R. Pemberton, E. Li, W. Or, & H. Pierson (Eds.), *Taking control: Autonomy in language learning.* Hong Kong: Hong Kong University Press.

Nunan, D. (2004). *Task-based language teaching.* Cambridge, England: Cambridge University Press.

O'Hanlon, C. (1993). The importance of an articulated personal theory of professional development. In J. Elliott (Ed.), *Reconstructing teacher education: Teacher development* (pp. 243–255). London: The Falmer Press.

Oller, J., Baca, L., & Vigil, F. (1977). Attitude and attained proficiency in ESL: A sociolinguistic study of native speakers of Chinese in the United States. *Language Learning, 27,* 1–26.

Omaggio, A. C. (1986). *Teaching language in context.* Boston: Heinle & Heinle.

O'Malley, J. M., & Chamot, A. U. (1990). *Learning strategies in second language acquisition.* Cambridge, England: Cambridge University Press.

Oxford, R. (1990). *Language learning strategies: What every teacher should know.* New York: Newbury House/Harper & Row.

Pakir, A. (1999). Connecting with English in the context of internationalization. *TESOL Quarterly, 33,* 103–114.

Palmer, H. E. (1921). *The principles of language study.* London: Harrap.

Paribakht, T. (1985). Strategic competence and language proficiency. *Applied Linguistics, 6,* 132–146.

Parrott, M. (1993). *Tasks for language teachers.* Cambridge, England: Cambridge University Press.

Paulston, C. B., & Bruder, M. (1975). *From substitution to substance.* Rowley, MA: Newbury House.

Pavlenko, A. (2002). Poststructuralist approaches to the study of social factors in second language learning and use. In V. J. Cook (Ed.), *Portraits of the L2 user* (pp. 275–302). Clevedon, England: Multilingual Matters.

Pennycook, A. (1989). The concept of method, interested knowledge, and the politics of language teaching. *TESOL Quarterly, 23,* 589–618.

Pennycook, A. (1998). *English and the discourses of colonialism.* London: Routledge.

Pennycook, A. (2001). *Critical applied linguistics: A critical introduction.* Mahwah, NJ: Lawrence Erlbaum Associates.

Pennycook, A. (2004). Critical moments in a TESOL praxicum. In B. Norton & K. Toohey (Eds.), *Critical pedagogies and language learning* (pp. 327–345). Cambridge, England: Cambridge University Press.

Phillipson, R. (1992). *Linguistic imperialism.* Oxford: Oxford University Press.

Pica, T. (1987). Second language acquisition, social interaction, and the classroom. *Applied Linguistics, 8,* 3–21.

Pica, T. (1992). The textual outcomes of native speaker–non-native speaker negotiations: What do they reveal about second language learning? In C. Kramsch & S. McConnell-Ginet (Eds.), *Text and context: Cross-disciplinary perspectives on language study* (pp. 198–237). Lexington, MA: D. C. Heath & Co.

Pica, T., & Doughty, C. (1985). Non-native speaker interaction in the ESL classroom. In S. Gass & C. Madden (Eds.), *Input in second language acquisition* (pp. 115–132). Rowley, MA: Newbury House.

Pica, T., Holliday, L., Lewis, N., & Morgenthaler, L. (1989). Comprehensible output as an outcome of linguistic demands on the learner. *Studies in Second Language Acquisition, 11,* 63–90.

Pica, T., Young, R., & Doughty, C. (1987). The impact of interaction on comprehension. *TESOL Quarterly, 21,* 737–758.

Pienemann, M. (1984). Psychological constraints on the teachability of languages. *Studies in Second Language Acquisition, 6,* 186–214.

Pienemann, M. (1987). Determining the influence of instruction on L2 speech processing. *Australian Review of Applied Linguistics, 9,* 92–122.

Pienemann, M. (2003). Language processing capacity. In In C. Doughty & M. H. Long (Eds.), *The handbook of second language acquisition* (pp. 679–714). Oxford: Blackwell.

Pinker, S. (1994). *The language instinct.* New York: HarperCollins.

Prabhu, N. S. (1985). Coping with the unknown in language pedagogy. In R. Quirk & H. G. Widdowson (Eds.), *English in the world: Teaching and learning the language and literatures* (pp. 164–173). Cambridge, England: Cambridge University Press.

Prabhu, N. S. (1987). *Second language pedagogy.* Oxford: Oxford University Press.

Prabhu, N. S. (1990). There is no best method—why? *TESOL Quarterly, 24,* 161–176.

Pradl, G. M. (1993). Introduction. In P. Kahaney, L. Perry, & J. Janangelo (Eds.), *Theoretical and critical perspectives on teacher change* (pp. xi–xxii). Norwood, NJ: Ablex.

Ricento, T. (2000). Ideology, politics and language policies: Introduction. In T. Ricento (Ed.), *Ideology, politics and language policies: Focus on English.* Amsterdam: John Benjamins.

Richards, J., & Rodgers, T. (1982). Method: Approach, design, procedure. *TESOL Quarterly, 16,* 153–168.

Richards, J. C., & Rodgers, T. (1986). *Approaches and methods in language teaching.* Cambridge, England: Cambridge University Press.

Rivers, W. M. (1964). *The psychologist and the foreign language teacher.* Illinois: University of Chicago Press.

Rivers, W. M. (1972). *Speaking in many tongues: Essays in foreign language teaching.* Rowley, MA: Newbury House.

Rivers, W. M. (1991). Mental representations and language in action. *The Canadian Modern Language Review, 47,* 249–265.

Rose, K. R., & Kasper, G. (2001). *Pragmatics in language teaching.* Cambridge, England: Cambridge University Press.

Routledge Encyclopedia of Language Teaching and Learning. (2000). London: Routledge.

Rubin, J. (1975). What the good language learner can teach us. *TESOL Quarterly, 9,* 41–51.

Rubin, J. (1987). Learner strategies: Theoretical assumptions, research, history, and typology. In A. Wenden & J. Rubin (Eds.), *Learner strategies in language learning* (pp. 15–30). Englewood Cliffs, NJ: Prentice-Hall.

Rutherford, W. E. (1987). *Second language grammar: Learning and teaching.* London: Longman.

Said, E. (1978). *Orientalism.* New York: Pantheon.

Savignon, S. (1983). *Communicative competence: Theory and classroom practice.* Reading, MA: Addison-Wesley.

Savignon, S. (1990). Communicative language teaching: Definitions and directions. In J. E. Alatis (Ed.), *Georgetown University Round Table on Languages and Linguistics, 1990.* Washington, DC: Georgetown University Press.

Savignon, S. (2002). Communicative language teaching: Linguistic theory and classroom practice. In S. Savignon (Ed.), *Interpreting communicative language teaching.* New Haven, CT: Yale University Press.

Schachter, J. (1983). A new account of language transfer. In S. M. Gass & L. Selinker (Eds.), *Language transfer in language learning* (pp. 98–111). Rowley, MA: Newbury House.

Schank, R. C., & Abelson, R. (1977). *Scripts, plans, goals and understanding.* Hillsdale, NJ: Lawrence Erlbaum Associates.

Scharle, A., & Szabo, A. (2000). *Learner autonomy: A guide to developing learner responsibility.* Cambridge, England: Cambridge University Press.

Schmidt, R. (1990). The role of consciousness in second language learning. *Applied Linguistics, 11,* 129–158.

Schmidt, R. (1992). Psychological mechanisms underlying second language fluency. *Studies in Second Language Acquisition, 14,* 357–385.

Schmidt, R. (1993). Awareness and second language acquisition. *Annual Review of Applied Linguistics, 13,* 206–226.

Schmidt, R., & Frota, S. (1986). Developing basic conversational ability in a second language: A case study of an adult learner of Portuguese. In R. Day (Ed.), *Talking to learn: Conversation in second language acquisition* (pp. 237–326). Rowley, MA: Newbury House.

Schumann, F., & Schumann, J. (1977). Diary of a language learner: An introspective study of second language learning. In H. Brown, C. Yurio, & R. Crymes (Eds.), *On TESOL '77* (pp. 241–249). Washington, DC: TESOL.

Scovel, T. (1988). *A time to speak: A psycholinguistic inquiry into the critical period for human speech.* New York: Newbury House/Harper & Row.

Scovel, T. (2001). *Learning new languages.* Boston: Heinle & Heinle.

Seliger, H. W. (1983). Learner interaction in the classroom and its effects on language acquisition. In H. W. Seliger & M. H. Long (Eds.), *Classroom oriented research in second language acquisition* (pp.246–267). Rowley, MA: Newbury House.

Seliger, H. W. (1984). Processing universals in second language acquisition. In F. R. Eckman, L. H. Bell, & D. Nelson. (Eds.), *Universals of second language acquisition* (pp. 36–47). Rowley, MA:Newbury House.

Selinker, L. (1992). *Rediscovering interlanguage.* London: Longman.

Selinker, L., & Tomlin, R. S. (1986). An empirical look at the integration and separation of skills in ELT. *ELT Journal, 40,* 227–235.

Shamim, F. (1996). Learner resistance to innovation in classroom methodology. In H. Coleman (Ed.), *Society and the language classroom* (pp. 105–121). Cambridge, England: Cambridge University Press.

Sharwood-Smith, M. (1985). From input into intake: On argumentation in second language acquisition. In S. M. Gass & C. Madden (Eds.), *Input in second language acquisition* (pp. 394–404). Rowley, MA: Newbury House.

Sharwood-Smith, M. (1991). Speaking to many minds: On the relevance of different types of language information for the L2 learner. *Second Language Research, 7,* 118–132.

Shohamy, E. (1996). Competence and performance in language testing. In G. Brown, K. Malmkjaer, & J. Williams (Eds.), *Performance and competence in second language acquisition* (pp. 138–151). Cambridge, England: Cambridge University Press.

Shor, I. (1992). *Empowering education: Critical teaching for social change.* Illinois: The University of Chicago Press.

Siegel, J. (2003). Social context. In C. Doughty & M. H. Long (Eds.), *The handbook of second language acquisition* (pp. 178–223). Oxford: Blackwell.

Simon, R. I. (1987). Empowerment as a pedagogy of possibility. *Language Arts, 64,* 379–388.

Simon, R. I. (1988). For a pedagogy of possibility. In J. Smyth (Ed.), *The critical pedagogy networker, 1*(1–4). Victoria, Australia: Deakin University Press.

Singh, M., Kell, P., & Pandian, A. (2002). *Appropriating English: Innovation in the global business of English language teaching.* New York: Peter Lang.

Singleton, D. (1989). *Language acquisition: The age factor.* Clevedon, England: Multilingual Matters.

Skehan, P. (1998). *A cognitive approach to language learning.* Oxford: Oxford University Press.

Slimani, A. (1989). The role of topicalization in classroom language learning. *System, 17,* 223–234.

Smith, P. D. (1970). *A comparison of the cognitive and audiolingual approaches to foreign language instruction: The Pennsylvania Project.* Philadelphia: Center for Curriculum Development.

Smitherman, G. (2000). *Talkin that talk: Language, culture and education in African America.* London: Routledge.

Snow, C. (1972). Mothers' speech to children learning language. *Child Development, 43,* 49–65.

Snow, C. (1983). Age differences in second language acquisition: Research findings and folk psychology. In K. M. Bailey, M. Long, & S. Peck (Eds.), *Second language acquisition studies* (pp. 141–150). Rowley, MA: Newbury House.

Snow, C. (1987). Beyond conversation: Second language learners' acquisition of description and explanation. In J. Lantolf & A. Labarca (Eds.), *Research in second language learning: Focus on the classroom.* Norwood, NJ: Ablex.

Snow, C. E., & Ferguson, C. A. (1977). *Talking to children: Language input and acquisition.* Cambridge, England: Cambridge University Press.

Spada, N. (1986). The interaction between types of content and type of instruction: Some effects on the L2 proficiency of adult learners. *Studies in Second Language Acquisition, 8,* 181–199.

Spada, N. (1987). Relationships between instructional differences and learning outcomes: A process-product study of communicative language teaching. *Applied Linguistics, 8,* 137–155.

Spolsky, B. (1989). *Conditions for second language learning.* Oxford: Oxford University Press.

Sridhar, K. K., & Sridhar, N. (1986). Bridging the paradigm gap: Second language acquisition theory and indiginized varieties of English. *World Englishes, 5,* 3–14.

Stern, H. H. (1983). *Fundamental concepts of language teaching.* Oxford: Oxford University Press.

Stern, H. H. (1985). [Review of J. W. Oller and P. A. Richard-Amato's *Methods That Work*]. *Studies in Second Language Acquisition, 7,* 249–251.

Stern, H. H. (1992). *Issues and options in language teaching.* Oxford: Oxford University Press.

Swaffar, J., Arens, K., & Morgan, M. (1982). Teacher classroom practices: Redefining method as task hierarchy. *Modern Language Journal, 66,* 24–33.

Swain, M. (1985). Communicative competence: Some roles of comprehensible input and comprehensible output in its development. In S. M. Gass & C. Madden (Eds.), *Input in second language acquisition* (pp. 235–253). Rowley, MA: Newbury House.

Swain, M. (1991). Manipulating and complementing content teaching to maximize second language learning. In E. Kellerman, R. Phillipson, L. Selinker, M. Sharwood-Smith, & M. Swain (Eds.), *Foreign/second language pedagogical research* (pp. 234–250). Clevedon, England: Multilingual Matters.

Swain, M. (1995). Three functions of output in second language learning. In G. Cook & B. Seidlhofer (Eds.), *Principle and practice in applied linguistics* (pp. 125–144). Oxford: Oxford University Press.

Swain, M., & Lapkin, S. (1982). *Evaluating bilingual education: A Canadian case study.* Clevedon, England: Multilingual Matters.

Swan, M. (1985). A critical look at the communicative approach. *English Language Teaching Journal, 39,* 2–12.

Tannen, D. (1992). Rethinking power and solidarity in gender and dominance. In C. Kramsch & S. McConnell-Ginet (Eds.), *Text and context: Cross-disciplinary perspectives on language study* (pp. 135–147). Lexington, MA: D. C. Heath & Co.

Tanner, R., & Green, C. (1998). *Tasks for teacher education.* London: Longman.

Tarone, E. (1977). Conscious communication strategies in interlanguage. In D. H. Brown, C. Yorio, & R. Crymes (Eds.), *On TESOL '77* (pp. 194–203). Washington, DC: TESOL.

Taylor, D. (1988). The meaning and use of the term 'competence' in linguistics and applied linguistics. *Applied Linguistics, 9,* 148–168.

Thomas, J. (1983). Cross-cultural pragmatic failure. *Applied Linguistics, 4,* 91–112.

Thompson, J. B. (1990). *Ideology and modern culture.* Oxford, England: Polity Press.

Thornbury, S. (1996). Teachers research teacher talk. *English Language Teaching, 50,* 279–288.

Thornbury, S. (1997). *About language: Tasks for teachers of English.* Cambridge, England: Cambridge University Press.

Tickoo, M. L. (1996). Forward from Bangalore. In B. Kenny & W. Savage (Eds.), *Language and development: Teachers in a changing world.* London: Longman.

Tobias, S. (1986). Anxiety and cognitive processing of instruction. In R. Schwarzer (Ed.), *Self related cognition in anxiety and motivation* (pp. 35–54). Hillsdale, NJ: Lawrence Erlbaum Associates.

Tollefson, J. W. (Ed.). (1995). *Power and inequality in language education.* Cambridge: Cambridge University Press.

Tollefson, J. W. (2002). *Language policies in education.* Mahwah, NJ: Lawrence Erlbaum Associates.

Tucker, G., & Lambert, W. (1973). Sociocultural aspects of language study. In J. Oller & J. Richards (Eds.), *Focus on the learner.* Rowley, MA: Newbury House.

Van Dijk, T. (1977). The study of discourse. In T. van Dijk (Ed.), *Discourse as structure and process. Discourse studies* (Vol. 1, pp. 1–34). London: Sage.

Van Ek, J. (1975), *The threshold level.* Strasbourg, France: Council of Europe.

Van Lier, L. (1991). Inside the classroom: Learning processes and teaching procedures. *Applied Language Learning, 2,* 29–69.

Van Manen, M. (1977). Linking ways of knowing with ways of being practical. *Curriculum Inquiry, 6,* 205–228.

Van Manen, M. (1991). *The tact of teaching; The meaning of pedagogical thoughtfulness.* Albany: State University of New York Press.

Van Patten, B. (1990). Attending to content and form in the input: An experiment in consciousness. *Studies in Second Language Acquisition, 12,* 287–301.

Van Patten, B. (1996). *Input processing and grammar instruction.* Norwood, NJ: Ablex.

Van Patten, B., & Cadierno, T. (1993). Input processing and second language acquisition: A role for instruction. *Modern Language Journal, 77,* 45–57.

Wajnryb, R. (1992). *Classroom observation tasks.* Cambridge, England: Cambridge University Press.

Wallace, M. J. (1991). *Training foreign language teachers: A reflective approach.* Cambridge, England: Cambridge University Press.

Weedon, C. (1997). *Feminist practice and poststructuralist theory.* London: Blackwell.

Wenden, A. (1991). *Learner strategies for learner autonomy.* London: Prentice-Hall.

Wenden, A., & Rubin, J. (Eds.). (1987). *Learner strategies in language learning.* London: Prentice-Hall.

West, M. (Ed.). (1953). *A general service list of English words, with semantic frequencies and a supplementary word-list for the writing of popular science and technology.* London: Longmans, Green.

Widdowson, H. G. (1978). *Teaching language as communication.* Oxford: Oxford University Press.

Widdowson, H. G. (1979). *Explorations in applied linguistics.* Oxford: Oxford University Press.

Widdowson, H. G. (1983). *Learning purposes and language use.* Oxford: Oxford University Press.

Widdowson, H. G. (1989). Knowledge of language and ability for use. *Applied Linguistics, 10,* 128–137.

Widdowson, H. G. (1990). *Aspects of language teaching.* Oxford: Oxford University Press.

Widdowson, H. G. (1993). Innovation in teacher development. *Annual Review of Applied Linguistics, 13,* 260–275.

Widdowson, H. G. (2003). *Defining issues in English language teaching.* Oxford: Oxford University Press.

Wilkins, D. A. (1972). *The linguistic and situational content of the common core in a unit/credit system.* Strasbourg, France: Council of Europe.

Wilkins, D. A. (1976). *National syllabuses.* Oxford: Oxford University Press.

Williams, R. (1976). *Keywords: A vocabulary of culture and society.* New York: Oxford University Press.

Williams, R. (1977). *Marxism and literature.* Oxford: Oxford University Press.

Willis, D. (1990). *The lexical syllabus.* London: Collins Cobuild.

Willis, J. (1996). *A framework for task-based learning.* London: Longman.

Winitz, H. (Ed.). (1981). *The comprehension approach to foreign language instruction.* Rowley, MA: Newbury House.

Wode, H. (1976). Developmental sequences in naturalistic L2 acquisition. *Working Papers on Bilingualism, 11,* 1–13.

Wong-Fillmore, L. (1989). Language learning in social context: The view from research in second language learning. In R. Dietrich & C. F. Graumann (Eds.), *Language processing in social context* (pp. 277–302). Amsterdam: Elsevier.

Woods, D. (1996). *Teacher cognition in language teaching.* Cambridge, England: Cambridge University Press.

Yule, G., & Gregory, W. (1989). Using survey-interviews to foster interactive language learning. *English Language Teaching Journal, 43.*

Zeichner, K. (1996). Teachers as reflective practitioners and the democratization of school reform. In K. Zeichner, S. Melnick, & M. L. Gomez (Eds.), *Currents of reform in preservice teacher education* (pp. 199–214). New York: Teachers College Press.

Zobl, H. (1985). Grammar in search of input and intake. In S. M. Gass & C. Madden (Eds.), *Input in second language acquisition* (pp. 329–344). Rowley, MA: Newbury House.

Author Index

Subject Index